Crime, Prosecution and Social Relations

Crime, Prosecution and Social Relations

The Summary Courts of the City of London in the Late Eighteenth Century

Drew D. Gray

Senior Lecturer in History, University of Northampton

palgrave
macmillan

First published 2009 by
PALGRAVE MACMILLAN

Palgrave Macmillan in the UK is an imprint of Macmillan Publishers Limited,
registered in England, company number 785998, of Houndmills, Basingstoke,
Hampshire RG21 6XS.

Palgrave Macmillan in the US is a division of St Martin's Press LLC,
175 Fifth Avenue, New York, NY 10010.

Palgrave Macmillan is the global academic imprint of the above companies
and has companies and representatives throughout the world.

Palgrave® and Macmillan® are registered trademarks in the United States,
the United Kingdom, Europe and other countries.

ISBN-13: 978–0–230–20397–6 hardback

This book is printed on paper suitable for recycling and made from fully
managed and sustained forest sources. Logging, pulping and manufacturing
processes are expected to conform to the environmental regulations of the
country of origin.

A catalogue record for this book is available from the British Library.

A catalog record for this book is available from the Library of Congress.

10   9   8   7   6   5   4   3   2   1
18   17   16   15   14   13   12   11   10   09

Printed and bound in Great Britain by
CPI Antony Rowe, Chippenham and Eastbourne

In England, justice is open to all – like the Ritz Hotel.

James Mathew (1830–1908)

Contents

List of Tables

List of Figures

List of Abbreviations

LMA London Metropolitan Archives
OBO Old Bailey Proceedings Online
PP   Parliamentary Papers

Acknowledgements

First I would like to thank Peter King for his invaluable help and advice both in the writing of this book and for supervising my doctoral thesis. His guidance, faith and attention to detail leave me a debt I will find hard to discharge; a supervisor is truly for life, not just for Christmas! I have also received encouragement and advice from a great number of people over the years. My colleagues at the University of Northampton have all been very supportive, in particular Matthew McCormack, Cathy Smith and Sally Sokoloff. I am also grateful to John Beattie, Matthew Feldman, Paul Griffiths, Elizabeth Hurren, Joanna Innes, Ruth Paley, Greg Smith and John Stobart and others who have all given advice and support in the course of my research. The archivists and support staff at the London Metropolitan Archives have been immensely helpful as I have sought to understand the inner workings of the City's judicial system. I am also lucky to have had the practical, emotional and financial support of many others without which this project would never have been completed. In particular I would like to thank my mother, Diana Falkiner, who has always had belief in me and offered constructive criticism of my work and editorial advice as it has progressed.

This book is respectfully dedicated to the memory of Ed Falkiner, who would I think, have enjoyed it.

1
Introduction

On the 18 April 1786 a letter appeared in the *Morning Chronicle* condemning the treatment of three prisoners in the Poultry compter, one of London's many gaols. The letter – written by Josiah Dornford, a critic of the criminal justice system – was addressed to the lord mayor and aldermen of the City of London, within whose jurisdiction the Poultry was situated.[1] Dornford alleged that two prisoners had died through want of proper care and another had been treated unnecessarily harshly. Dornford's allegations were investigated by a committee set up by the Court of Aldermen, but were eventually dismissed as unproven. The individual cases of Robert May (a debtor), Elizabeth Gurney (a vagrant) and John Martin (a petty thief) can usefully afford us a window into the machinations of the late Hanoverian justice system and the lives of those caught up in it. This is a book about the administration of justice within the City of London. It is about the men who ruled this disproportionately wealthy conclave of Georgian England and about those who attempted to negotiate the potentially fatal pathways through the justice system that supported it. It is a book about the use of the law by ordinary people in their attempts to resolve the problems and disputes they encountered in their everyday lives.

Let us return to Dornford's allegations of neglect and abuse. Dornford had been informed that a debtor in the Poultry was seriously ill and deteriorating through lack of food and care. Robert May had been admitted to the compter in January 1785 when he had become finally unable to meet his creditors' demands. He was housed in the King's ward until his ill-health – brought on by a dependence on drink – caused him to be removed to the sick ward. In this time his marriage collapsed and his wife had taken up with another man (which he 'took to heart very much' according to one of his gaolers). Dornford found him in a

1

desperate state and paid the turnkey 7s to provide the poor man with some broth. May died on the 17 November; his death was attributed to 'sloth and indolence' and his addiction to peppermint liquor. When the turnkey discovered his body the shirt he wore 'swarmed with vermin'.

Elizabeth Gurney had been begging in a doorway in Cheapside, when James Davis, a City constable, found her in 'a deplorable, weak state'. Davis took her to the Poultry as it was nearer than the workhouse and his orders forbade him from being 'above half an hour from the watch house'. The Poultry was, however, ill-equipped to deal with dangerously sick paupers like Elizabeth. She was placed in the 'women felons room', which had no fire 'nor any allowance for one'. Although a turnkey and several prisoners tried to get Elizabeth to eat some bread and soup and weak beer, she could not keep anything down. Later that day another constable arrived to take her to the Guildhall to be examined as a vagrant. Here she might have hoped for some little charity and a pass out of the area that might enable her to get some limited support. But the Guildhall clerk was busy with 'some very extraordinary hearing' and Elizabeth was taken back to the compter. The next morning she was too sick to be taken before the clerk and on the following Monday she was found dead, wrapped in a rug supplied by one of the turnkeys.

John Martin, a 'poor sailor who had served his king and country [for] many years' had been arrested in July 1784 and sentenced to six months imprisonment in Newgate and a whipping for stealing a ten-penny pewter pot from a City tavern. In November 1785 he was indicted to appear at the Old Bailey for feloniously taking iron bars, but, as his prosecutor failed to turn up, 'he escaped justice'. Martin had, 'by a stroke of palsy', almost lost the use of one side and 'could only hobble about'; he turned to crime, he said, in order to 'preserve his life'. His decision led him back to court in January 1786 when the lord mayor committed him to Bridewell for another felony and ordered he be removed to his parish of last settlement. However, he never made it (or he returned) for in March he was once again accused of stealing metal and was sentenced to transportation.[2] Dornford did not contest the man's conviction but felt it was a 'species of Barbarism not becoming a polite nation' that Martin was shackled with leg irons while he was held in the compter. Without the money to pay for lighter irons Martin was, in the opinion of Dornford, treated unnecessarily cruelly by the prison staff.

The stories of May, Gurney and Martin illustrate the wretchedness of many plebeian lives in the late eighteenth century. Robert May's drinking and poor financial management landed him in gaol for debt, an all too common occurrence in the period. Once imprisoned, he was at the mercy of a prison system that mirrored the inequality of wealth of the society that existed outside of its gates. The Court of Aldermen chose to believe the witnesses produced by the keeper of the Poultry rather than those brought by Dornford, but any visitor to an eighteenth-century gaol would have been shocked by the sheer squalor that inmates were expected to inhabit.

Elizabeth Gurney was the unfortunate victim of poverty and the desire of the City to keep its streets free of beggars and other undesirables. Many of those brought low by ill-health, unemployment, accident or (as was frequently the case for plebeian women) abandonment, were arrested, prosecuted, imprisoned, beaten and forced out of the City by a governing clique that wanted to hold down parochial expenses. The institutions that had to lock up these individuals were not able to differentiate between the genuinely in need and the idle or criminal.

We might view John Martin as a serial offender, a petty criminal rather than a victim of circumstance. But Martin was a sailor, a 'tar' that had served on the *Vengeance*, the *Heart of Oak* and the *Endeavour* over a period of nearly 19 years. He was owed wages in 1784 but without them, and unable to work through ill-health, he had little option but to take his chances as a petty thief. Martin was, like the others, in the Poultry because he was poor and his treatment there reflected this.

With the exception of Robert May all of these individuals could have appeared before the magistrates of the City of London at either the Guildhall or the Mansion House justice rooms. Tens of thousands of Londoners passed through these courts as defendants, prosecutors and witnesses every year. Whilst we are now familiar with the images of the gallows at Tyburn, the dark horror of Newgate prison and the drama of the Old Bailey courtroom this was not how most Londoners experienced the law in the late Georgian period. Many more people would have come into the matted gallery at Guildhall to be summarily judged by one of the City's mercantile elite sitting as justices or would have brought their complaint before the lord mayor in his residence at Mansion House. Sometimes this was but the beginning of a longer journey through the criminal justice system but for most it was where justice was done and 'seen to be done'. This study is concerned with this process and how it served the City of London and its many inhabitants. Hearings at the Guildhall and Mansion House may lack the ultimate drama of life and death but the stories they contain reveal arguably more about the lives and social relations of City dwellers in a period of rising concerns about law and order in England.

Using the records of the City of London's summary courts in the late eighteenth century this study will examine who was able to use the summary process, which kinds of offences were prosecuted there and the style of hearings and the nature of the outcomes arrived at. Surviving records about those tried in the major courts and sentenced to hang at Tyburn and elsewhere have provided rich pickings for researchers, however they are limited in the extent to which they allow us to understand the workings of the criminal justice system in eighteenth-century society. Most individuals who experienced the law did so at summary level and only by a detailed study of these courts can we develop a full picture of attitudes towards, and the use of, the criminal justice system. It has been suggested that the Hanoverian criminal justice system was a tool of the ruling elite that they used to underpin their hegemony.[3] However, much of the research that has sought to explore this paradigm has been based upon the records of the higher courts of assize and quarter sessions and is largely provincial in focus.[4] The crucial question of who was able to use the law needs both a summary and an urban dimension and is therefore central to this book.

This study explores the nature of authority and court use in the half century after 1750. It will analyse the character of the summary process and question whether these were *criminal* courts or *civil* arenas of negotiation. What sorts of cases came before the magistrates and how did these courts fit into the wider criminal justice system? By looking at the style, nature and outcomes of hearings and at those who attended them this study aims both to answer these questions and to contribute useful insights into the use of discretion by magistrates, prosecutors and policing agents. As we shall see, large numbers of London's poor regularly appeared in the summary courts, and not always as defendants. Indeed many came to complain about those who assaulted, offended, robbed or defrauded them. This study can therefore usefully contribute to the history of London's labouring poor as well as to the nature of social relations in the City.

The neglect of summary proceedings

The summary process and the role of magistrates were often ignored in the early stages of the development of the history of crime. Most work has focused on the jury courts of assize and quarter session, on indictable property crime, and on offences that attracted the most punitive sentences of hanging and transportation.[5] There are some general works on justices of the peace, along with the publication of a number of individual justice's diaries with brief but interesting introductions.[6] Historians have also used the records of summary processes in rural England to explore the erosion of customary rights and the prosecution of poaching and workplace appropriation.[7] This has been followed more recently by extensive research on some of the work of the courts at the summary level, notably in relation to disputes between masters and servants and the prosecution of minor property crimes.[8] Recent research has produced a small number of articles that engage in a broader approach to the nature of summary proceedings and the role of the justice of the peace.[9] However, while the work of magistrates in Hackney and Middlesex has been touched upon in other works there has been no detailed analysis of summary proceedings in London in the second half of the eighteenth century.[10] This study will therefore add a specific metropolitan dimension to this approach and complement the work of previous researchers.[11]

Amongst the most valuable studies we have of London's poor and the labouring process is Peter Linebaugh's analysis of some of those prosecuted for property offending at the Old Bailey in the eighteenth century.[12] For Linebaugh it was the Tyburn gallows and its role in the protection of the wealth of the rich from theft by the poor that characterised the criminal law in the Hanoverian age. However, Linebaugh overlooked the summary courts. In equating capital punishment with capital accumulation Linebaugh missed the opportunity to explore how the labouring men and women of London utilised the courts of law available to them to resolve their everyday difficulties and interpersonal tensions. He also ignored an opportunity to study a legal arena in which the labouring poor were frequently prosecuted for pilfering activities which they often regarded as customary rights. More recently Tim Hitchcock has produced a study that makes use of a much wider range of sources to explore the lives and social relations of London's poor.[13] While Hitchcock touches upon the summary courts he does not undertake an examination of how they operated. This study will look at how poorer Londoners used the City summary courts for a variety of purposes.

The importance of the City of London and the nature of its magistracy

Britain was one of the most powerful nations in the eighteenth-century world. She had a burgeoning empire, with a navy that guaranteed its naval supremacy and ensured that many of the commodities of the rest of the world entered Europe through its ports. England's capital city reflected the diversity that this growing empire represented. The streets of London overflowed with migrants from all corners of the British Isles as well as Europe. As Daniel Defoe declared:

> London consumes all, circulates all, exports all, and at last pays for all, and this greatness and wealth of the City is the Soul of the Commerce to all the Nation.[14]

London's shops were filled to overflowing with all manner of exotic goods that offered a tempting display to shoppers and thieves alike.[15] Each day the docks that lined the Thames unloaded spices, foodstuffs, cloth and fuel in vast quantities, providing more opportunities for illegal appropriation. London was the largest city in Europe and was home to one-tenth of England's population. At the heart of the metropolis lay the City of London, an administrative centre that prided itself on its independence from national government. While recent works have begun to look at the City's police in the late eighteenth and early nineteenth centuries and its courts in the period before 1750 they have left large gaps in our understanding of how the population of the City used the criminal justice system.[16]

This study will also consider the pattern of summary business, and the extent to which the pattern in London was different to that elsewhere.[17] The nature of the magistracy in the City was certainly not the same as that found in many other parts of England. It is possible to outline a broad fourfold typology of justices of the peace, although there were many exceptions and variations. In provincial areas outside the boroughs justices of the peace were appointed from amongst the ranks of the landed gentry and by the second half of the century, because a 'growing proportion' of these individuals were refusing to serve, this increasingly began to include 'minor gentry, clergy, and professional men'.[18] These were essentially amateurs and had no legal obligation to carry out the duties of a local magistrate. As Peter King has pointed out, of those justices in Essex, Kent, Oxfordshire and Surrey that were eligible to undertake judicial business at summary level 'only a small handful were truly active'.[19] It was therefore possible to attain the office of justice of the peace without having to take on the onerous responsibilities of dispensing justice. Some were, certainly, 'committed, conscientious men' but many were 'at best casual in the carrying out of their duties'.[20]

The situation in Middlesex was slightly different. Here, a considerable proportion of magistrates were essentially entrepreneurial in character and were drawn from a lower social stratum. Justices earned a living from the law by extracting fees for a range of services. Given that there was a demand for the issuing of legal documents such as warrants, and considerable opportunities to levy money in fines, the so-called trading justices of Middlesex could administer justice profitably.[21] However, in the City of London the nature of the role of justice of the peace was different to both the provincial amateurs and the trading justices. By the middle of the eighteenth century, all City aldermen were sworn as justices. A rotation system, instigated in 1737, meant that every alderman had to take his turn in discharging his summary duties as a magistrate if he wanted to maintain his position in civic government.[22] Thus the City had a semi-compulsory system for the discharge of magisterial duties that was essentially different to most of the rest of England.[23] A fourth type of magistracy emerged after 1792 when the new stipendiary police offices were established across metropolitan Middlesex, each with three paid magistrates at the helm.

This difference between the nature and role of the magistracy in the City and elsewhere might have affected the sorts of offences and disputes that were brought before them. Studies of summary proceedings elsewhere have revealed that considerable amounts of poor law appeals, employment disputes and interpersonal violence prosecutions came before justices of the peace.[24] This study will consider whether there was a marked difference in the quantities or proportions of these types of hearing in the City courts. To what extent did the nature of the City's magistracy affect the pattern of summary business?

As Greg Smith has recently shown, London's residents had a number of prosecutorial options open to them.[25] The Londoner with a grievance could take his case before the lord mayor or the aldermen magistrates (if the offence occurred within the square mile), before the Bow Street office run by the Fieldings or to the quarter sessions, Old Bailey, or even the Court of King's Bench when they were sitting. All of these were in relatively easy reach.[26] The same cannot be said of the rural litigant who often had to travel considerable distances to bring a prosecution. The additional cost incurred in taking time off work, travelling and possible overnight lodgings for oneself and any witnesses all increased the already onerous costs of prosecuting one's case. It would therefore seem reasonable to expect that the rate of prosecutions in the City would be greater than in the provinces. Crime was also more of a problem in the metropolis. In the eighteenth century the rapidly growing London area held greater temptations and opportunities for crime, as well as being characterised by looser communal ties which possibly increased the levels of poverty and want.[27]

The character of summary proceedings in the City

What sort of justice were the summary courts in the eighteenth century dispensing? Were they primarily criminal or civil courts, or a delicate mixture of both? Previous work on the prosecution of assault has suggested that in the eighteenth century interpersonal violence was usually treated as a civil offence by the criminal justice system.[28] Recent studies have also shown that a considerable amount of non-violent offences were being negotiated at the summary level.[29] In Essex property appropriation was also frequently resolved at the summary level, and in London in the first half of the eighteenth century Beattie's brief overview has suggested that most petty theft that came before the City magistrates was dealt with without recourse to the jury courts.[30] The picture that is emerging suggests that the defining line between what was a civil and a criminal offence in this period was a mutable one. By looking at the operation of the summary courts in the City it is possible to gain a deeper sense of the differences between the civil and criminal processes.

The availability of discretion to a range of individuals characterised the criminal law at this time.[31] At the jury courts discretion extended to prosecutors, juries and witnesses, as well as judges. At the summary level discretion was less widely distributed but was still a vital element in the proceedings. Both Shoemaker and Landau have commented upon the actual application of discretion by magistrates in the hearings before them, notably in the use of recognisances to bring pressure to bear on both parties involved to achieve a settlement.[32] In these instances the Justice of the Peace (JP) was seen to be acting as arbiter between disputing parties. This study will analyse the use of discretion at the summary courts to contextualise the role of the summary courts in the administration of power and authority in the capital.

The accessibility of the City's summary courts has already been noted but it is also important to establish how public these arenas of negotiation were. Outside of London most justices held their examinations in their parlours.[33] These were essentially private rather than public spaces. While this situation began to change over the course of the century, as more petty sessions were convened in local inns and county halls, in the City the justice rooms were centrally located public venues throughout the same period. These were busy public courtrooms, and this may have had implications for the way in which they were used.

Gender

Within this study the issue of gender can also be addressed in a number of interesting ways. Gender was a key variable in the prosecution and punishment of offenders. Several historians have suggested that the jury courts frequently handed down more lenient sentences to female property criminals.[34] However, it is not clear that the same leniency prevailed in the lower courts. Recent work has suggested that females may have been subject to harsher treatment than males in some instances.[35] This study offers both an urban and a summary perspective on the treatment of women by the eighteenth-century criminal justice system. By looking at the outcomes of the prosecutions of women for property, violent and regulatory offences this study will be able to examine the extent to which the summary process in the City treated female offenders differently to males.

The summary courts may also have offered female victims of male violence a less intimidating environment than the male-dominated jury courts. While there has been some work on the use of the summary process by female victims of domestic violence there is much less work on female prosecutors of other forms of violence or crimes of property.[36] This study will therefore help to inform our understanding of how useful the summary courts were to female prosecutors.

Sources and methodology

This book is focused upon the surviving records of the City's two summary or petty sessions courts, namely the Guildhall and Mansion House justice rooms.[37] The key records for the purposes of this work are the minute books of these courts. These handwritten notebooks detail the daily sittings of the courts and record information relating to defendants, prosecutors, witnesses, court and other officials as well as providing information about examinations, outcomes and sentences. There is a wealth of information contained within these minute books that has never been systematically subjected to analysis.[38] This is in part because the minute books have suffered from the pressures of space that threaten all archival sources. While the minute books of both courts combined cover a period of nearly 70 years (1752–1821) only 128 books survive in total and given that each book covered approximately two to three months there would presumably have been something in the region of 300–400 books originally. In addition to this the books that do survive rarely overlap in their coverage of the two courts making a comparative study of the Guildhall and Mansion House somewhat problematic.

As will become evident in the course of this study the two courts operated similarly but also had certain distinct differences in the types of business they dealt with. The information contained within the minute books also varies in terms of its quality and usefulness. Some minute books are very detailed in the descriptions of examinations whilst others are marked by their brevity. The role of the clerk of the court may well have been crucial in some instances whilst in others the nature of the offence and whether it was being sent on through the criminal justice system may have occasioned a more detailed entry. For the purposes of this study two key samples have been taken. In the period 1784–85 and 1788–89 it has been possible to use minute books from both courts that overlap to some extent.[39] The main quantitative information on offenders and offending has therefore been extracted from these records. In addition three minute books from the Guildhall court in the 1790s have been used both quantitatively and qualitatively to provide a useful comparison.[40] Throughout the study extensive use has been made of surviving minute books from across the period to ensure that the sample slices taken are not in some way extraordinary.

In addition this study has also drawn on a number of other primary sources. The records of the Chamberlain's court in the City provides detailed information about the relationship between City apprentices and their masters;[41] the Bridewell Court records, the Repertories of the Court of Aldermen[42] and other documents generated by the corporation have also been used. Old Bailey trial records and the sittings of the Sessions for the Peace for London have been consulted, as have the very limited surviving records of the Poultry and Wood Street compters.[43] Because the minute books can be somewhat cursory in the way that they detail hearings and examinations the London newspapers have been sampled to provide more qualitative data in places. Naturally newspaper reporting has to be treated with some caution; reporters were much more likely to write up cases that they felt would interest their readers or that met the editorial needs of the paper. Similar caution is also necessary in the use of the evidence of the various parliamentary committees of the late eighteenth and early nineteenth centuries. Those appearing as City officials or contractors engaged to 'farm' the City paupers, for example, might be expected to display a degree of self-interest in answering questions. However, the reports of several committees in the early nineteenth century regarding the police, prisons and poor of the City usefully reflect views of past practice that are not always available for the second half of the eighteenth century. Finally, the justicing manuals of Richard Burn have provided an invaluable insight into how magistrates were supposed to discharge their duties.[44] Once again, it is apparent that on occasions these manuals were treated as guidebooks rather than rule books.

Outline of the chapters

The City had several non-jury courts and disciplinary institutions, which will be discussed in Chapter 2. The chapter will also explore the way in which the summary courts worked and look at the level of business they dealt with and at the social make-up of those using them. The cost and availability of justice at these courts will be considered, and the style of these proceedings will be explored. Through an analysis of the outcomes of hearings at the Guildhall and Mansion House this chapter will suggest that while these courts were primarily arenas for the resolution of interpersonal disputes they also played an important disciplinary role in the administration of authority.

In Chapter 3 the focus of attention will move from the operation of the summary courts themselves to the role of the various policing agents that served them. It will examine the nature of policing in the City before the arrival of professionals in 1839[45] and consider how effective these agencies were, and how they operated. Who made up the members of these policing organisations, and what were their motivations? Were they in existence to serve all of the City's community or did they function to uphold the rights and interests of one section of society over another? The City was served by a layered and connected system of policing that was thought by contemporaries to be superior to comparable systems elsewhere in England and was exempted from legislation in both 1792 and 1829. To what extent was this simply an example of the City's independent spirit rather than a vindication of its policing network? In order to assess this Chapter 3 will look at the levels and distribution of policing. It will also explore the nature of policing by looking at the role and function of the ward constables, watchmen and the City patrol as well as considering the policing of the busy Thames quayside. Using trial reports from the Old Bailey, the summary court minute books and the London press we will consider how proactive these policing agents were. Chapters 2 and 3 will therefore contextualise the summary courts and establish how these courts operated and how offenders were brought before them.

The chapters that follow will analyse the types of offences that came before the summary courts in greater depth. By looking in turn at property crime and interpersonal violence, before turning to what we might usefully describe as the regulation of everyday life, we can explore the key themes of this study. In Chapter 7 I explore a little-known popular pastime of Georgian London, bullock-hunting, and the ways in which the summary courts dealt with this problem. Chapter 8 considers the courts' role in the regulation of trade and working practice and looks at the work of the Chamberlain's Court with regard to City apprentices. It then considers the administration of poor relief at summary level. Finally I will draw together work from the early chapters and compare this with the recent historical work on property crime, interpersonal violence and regulation.

2
Locating the Summary Courts

In the second half of the eighteenth century the City of London was served by two summary justice rooms: the Guildhall justicing room situated within the old Guildhall building on Basinghall Street, and the Mansion House court at the lord mayor's residence at the junction of Cornhill and Poultry. Each operated at the geographical and administrative heart of the City. The centrality of these courts was crucial, for it was their accessibility to a range of different users, and their close association to the governance of the City, that made them such a vital element in the lives of Londoners. The City's population had little distance to travel to bring their grievances before a magistrate, a luxury not afforded to a large proportion of people living in rural areas. The very size of London – that is the greater metropolis and not just the City – meant that the level of crime and social tension was higher than elsewhere while toleration of disorder was lower, making the role of the City courts particularly important to our understanding of summary process during this period.

This chapter will first provide an overview of government of the City of London and its various non-jury courts in order to contextualise the work of the summary courts. Second it will analyse how the summary courts functioned by looking at the nature of these courts and how they operated. Here, by looking at the costs, style and frequency of these hearings, at the types of cases heard before them and at the number of cases that were transferred up to the higher courts, and at what kind of justice, arbitration-based or criminal law based, was offered, we can better understand their wider role in eighteenth-century society. Equally we need to know more about the individuals that presided over the justicing rooms in the City: how many justices served the City, who were they and how often did they sit?

The corporation of the City of London

The Corporation was the administrative centre of the City of London. Fiercely independent, institutionally conservative and wealthy, its influence reached into every inch of the 'square mile'. Joanna Innes has described it as a 'multi-functional overarching body'.[1] The City was divided into 26 wards. The size and population of these wards varied considerably and included those, such as Farringdon Without, that bordered onto the rapidly expanding and less-heavily regulated wider metropolis. Each ward was represented by an alderman, elected for life by the freemen of the ward to sit on the Common Council that administered the City.[2] These aldermen then in turn elected one of their number annually to serve as lord mayor. The lord mayor and aldermen formed the basis of the administrative government of the City. The aldermen themselves were the representatives of the City's 1000 freemen, as it was their responsibility to elect the aldermen and the members of the Common Council. To qualify for a vote a freeman had to be a householder, paying Scot and bearing Lot[3] in the ward and paying £10 a year in rent for 12 months or paying at least 30s in local taxes.[4]

To become 'free' an individual had to follow one of two routes. One could be made an honorary freeman but most individuals would have first been admitted into one of the 89 municipal companies or guilds that operated in the City. Only freemen were entitled to practice retail trade within the City and this helped to endow the City with a sense of self-confidence and even self-importance in the sense that 'outsiders' were excluded. However, the growth of greater London gradually began to erode this situation. Some of London's merchants chose not to take up their freedoms because the changing geography of London made it possible for them to follow a wholesale business or to work in the financial trade without the necessity of obtaining a freedom.[5]

Twenty-four of the wards returned one alderman each; the Farringdons (Within and Without the walls) sent one between them, while the final alderman represented Southwark on the south side of the River Thames (see Figure 2.1).[6] The elected alderman sat in the Court of Aldermen, which supervised the election of future aldermen along with other officials and post holders. In addition the court licensed all the brokers in the City and was authorised to spend the City's money.

The main legislative body of the Corporation was Common Council, responsible as it was for the election of the great majority of the City's functionaries. Here the City's 26 aldermen were joined by 240 common councillors. Finally, the Court of Common Hall was made up of freemen who also served as liverymen in one of the City's companies to elect

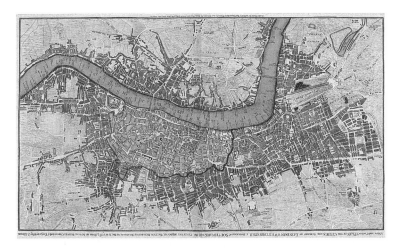

Figure 2.1 Map of Westminster, the City of London, Southwark the River Thames and the surrounding areas leading out to the countryside, by J. Gibson. (1763) © Guildhall Library

those City officers not covered by the courts of Aldermen and Common Council. By the early nineteenth century the court became more closely involved in policing matters, a situation that was rooted in the 1790s when the City authorities became concerned about the impact of Patrick Colquhoun's proposals to police the river Thames, and in particular the extension of powers of arrest within the City proper.[7] However in the eighteenth century it would appear that the court was rarely involved in day-to-day responses to criminal activity in the City.

This then was the underlying administrative structure of the City, a multi-layered civic administration that linked the City's merchants, traders and ratepayers together in a network formed upon local ward politics. This civic superstructure allowed the process of law to operate in a structured and cohesive manner, whether for civil or (as we shall see) criminal matters. Its members had first-hand knowledge and experience of the problems of crime and disorder in the capital. Naturally their discussion of these problems, in council and on social occasions, must have helped direct some form of concerted policy towards particular types of activity (such as prostitution or gambling) on occasions. At the top of this administrative structure sat the lord mayor who attended all these courts and so enjoyed an overall understanding of the functions of governance. The position of lord mayor was central to the nature of authority in the late Hanoverian City. As chief magistrate he was able to influence policing initiatives and target areas or offences that he considered important. Before we explore the role of the City magistrates it is important to place them in context with other legal institutions within the jurisdiction of the Corporation so that their function can be understood within the larger picture of regulation and adjudication within the City.

Civil courts

There were two important civil courts in the City of London at the end of the eighteenth century and a number of ancient smaller courts that were in decline and rarely used.[8] The lord mayor's court was presided over by the Recorder in his position as the principal judge of the Corporation (the Recorder sat in judgement on City cases at Old Bailey) and its advisor on legal matters. The court was essentially a court of arbitration: mainly dealing with trade disputes, breaches of contract and non-payment, and those infringing City by-laws.[9] Anyone discovered to have used fraudulent means to obtain their freedoms risked being disenfranchised at this court. Apprentices wishing to be released from unsatisfactory indentures could plead their case in front of the Recorder and, if successful, could apply to recoup their premiums, with the court awarding costs to the successful party.[10] The mayor's court had several attorneys-at-law attached to it who also played a part in the summary process.

While the mayor's court heard employment disputes the Sheriff's court was concerned with disputes that arose out of debt and non-payment. This court was divided into two sections each presided over by a judge appointed by the Common Council. Cases of debt were heard before a jury made up of 'substantial householders'[11] and unsuccessful defendants retained the right to take their cases before the lord mayor in person who had the power to alter the judgement of the court if he saw fit, by reducing the amount of the claim or by varying the terms of repayment. In addition to the mayor's and Sheriff's courts there was the little-used Court of Record, which heard civil pleas, and two Courts of Requests (one for the City and one for Southwark) which dealt with small claims for debt amounting to 40s or less.[12] The City Court of Requests, established in the reign of Henry VIII, pioneered a system of summary justice in relation to small claims. This was a response by the lord mayor and aldermen to the rising costs of civil litigation in the higher courts in London that was to occur in other metropolitan areas in the period between 1680 and 1750.[13] Debt was a feature of eighteenth-century society, as the tragic story of Robert May illustrates, and it would seem that the lord mayor and aldermen were closely involved in regulating and negotiating the many disputes that arose as a result. There were two other courts worthy of mention. The Chamberlain's court and the Bridewell were integral to the exercise of power and authority. However, since the former dealt almost exclusively with disputes between employers and employees it can better be dealt with later in this study. Bridewell as the City's house of correction had close links to the Chamberlain's court and was the disciplinary institution used, amongst other things, to punish those disobedient and unruly apprentices who mainly appeared there.[14] Having briefly dealt with the related civil courtrooms of the City we can now focus on the key arenas of negotiation in this period, the summary justice rooms at Guildhall and Mansion House.

The City justicing rooms

By the mid-1750s the summary courts divided the City between them. Offenders arrested to the east of Queen Street were brought to the Guildhall justicing room where an alderman sat in judgement while those from the west came before the lord mayor at Mansion House, although this arrangement was not set in stone and these boundaries were not always adhered to in practice. Defendants waiting for their hearings were held in either of the two holding prisons, or compters, at Wood Street or Poultry. The existence of the twin courts owes much to the death, in 1737, of Sir Richard Brocas who had been a particularly active magistrate in the early eighteenth century. Eighteenth-century justices were notoriously varied in their caseloads with some diligently convening meetings weekly or more often while others hardly ever discharged their judicial responsibilities except to turn up to one of the four annual quarter sessions.[15] Brocas' death created a void and the authorities had to take action to prevent the City's summary system from falling into chaos.[16] All City aldermen were automatically sworn as Justices of the peace (JPs) when they were elected to office so at any one time there were 26 of them to call upon.[17] Following Brocas' death the remaining aldermen magistrates agreed to sit 'in rotation' in the Matted Room of the Guildhall from 11 a.m. to 2 p.m., five days a week. In 1778 the Old Council chamber was redecorated so that it could be used as a justice room.[18] Initially each alderman served for one day at a time, assisted by a clerk and an attorney from the mayor's court, but after 1784 the Court of Aldermen unanimously resolved that justices would sit for a week at a time.[19] At first the lord mayor was included in the rotation cycle but after the building of the Mansion House as his residence in 1753 the lord mayor convened his own court in tandem with the Guildhall office.

The creation of the rotation office in 1737 was important in establishing the first permanent summary court in London.[20] Its example was followed in 1740 by the arguably more famous Bow Street Office – situated outside the City in Middlesex – run by De Veil (and later the Fieldings) and marks an important change in the dispensation of local justice. In rural England plaintiffs seeking a hearing with one of a number of local Justices often faced a journey of several miles, a time consuming and expensive exercise that caused some to choose not to pursue their grievances. This situation, while it had its disadvantages also allowed plaintiffs to choose between justices in order to better achieve the outcome they desired.[21] Distance in the City was rarely, if ever, a problem. However, the establishment of the capital's first magistrate court did mean that plaintiffs could no longer so easily pick and choose which justice to take their case before. The close-knit world of City government and commerce may also have worked against those that wished to exploit cracks in any ruling hegemony as their rural counterparts seem to have been able to do.

The rotation system in the City was not without its critics. John Wade writing in the 1820s complained that visitors to the Guildhall court would often be frustrated to find it closed or that no alderman was on duty. He slated the service claiming that:

> The time of the magistrate's attendance is uncertain; or he comes too late to get through the business of the day; or, as sometimes happens, he never comes at all, nor appoints a brother alderman to come for him: in which case after waiting four or five hours in fruitless expectation of his worship's arrival, witnesses, accusers and accused, clerks, door-keepers, reporters, etc are obliged to retire with a kind of 'call again tomorrow', and the whole business of the day, night charges included, is postponed to next morning.[22]

Wade may have been correct in observing the situation in the late 1820s but this was not the case in the late eighteenth century. By this period the Guildhall justice room was well established, with City dwellers used to its function and aware of its existence. The minute books show that aldermen magistrates were clearly available on all working days throughout the second half of the eighteenth century. The offices were closed on Sundays and for the public holidays but were open and operational at other times. In 1788, the Court of Aldermen noted that all

aldermen were required to inform their colleagues if they were plan-
ning to attend the sessions at Old Bailey to ensure that justice room
'may always be duly attended'.[23] Perhaps the situation changed after the
creation of the police offices in 1792 but the records suggest otherwise.

Not only were these courts geographically convenient, the cost of
using them was fairly modest. Unlike the notoriously avaricious trading
justices of Middlesex, the charges payable in the Guildhall or Mansion
House were made to the clerk of the courts and not to the magistrate.
A printed tariff described the cost of justice in the City. A warrant to
arrest a suspect for assault or theft, or to search premises for stolen goods,
would set you back a shilling.[24] A shilling was not beyond the means of
most working Londoners. Wages were difficult to measure in the eighteenth century because they were often supplemented by customary
perks and fluctuated with trade cycles and other factors. Nonetheless,
in the period 1765–93 labourers in London were paid between 9 and
12s weekly with journeymen taking home slightly more.[25] Those in
more skilled or profitable work could have earned considerably more.
Finding a shilling or two for a court hearing would not have been too
difficult, especially as many plaintiffs stood a good chance of recovering
this fee, and some poorer prosecutors had their costs waived. While the
expense of using the summary process was not prohibitive, it was also
notably cheaper than pursuing the suit into the jury courts. If a case proceeded to the quarter sessions or Old Bailey the prosecutor would have
to pay for the indictment, the costs of any witnesses, and lose time away
from work.

Justice at summary level had the attraction of being relatively cheap
by comparison and prosecutors often recovered the costs of the court
actions if they were successful. Constables prosecuting those that broke
City regulations relating to trading or traffic were allowed to keep all
or part of the fees and fines, supplementing the costs of policing without putting an increased burden on the ratepayer. Fines were sometimes
redistributed, indirectly via City institutions, to the poor. Confiscated
short-weight bread helped supplement the prisoner's diets in Newgate.
Other more worthy causes benefited from the charges and fines, such
as the Marine Society that worked to offer young men and boys a route
out of crime and onto the high seas.[26] The court fees therefore partly
funded the prosecution and regulation process whilst also being redi-
rected to help the poorest elements of society, a not unusual practice in
the country at the time.[27]

The centrality and availability of the City magistracy has consequences for our understanding of the use of the law in this period. The

costs of these courts did not represent a barrier to the lower ranks of City society; the fees were not unduly high and could often be recovered by prosecutors. This made the summary courts of more immediate use to the broad mass of citizens than the sessions of the peace and King's Bench where the recent attention of historians interested in restorative justice has been focused.[28] As we will see, City dwellers used them in their hundreds.

An overview of types of cases heard by the courts

A huge range of different types of case came before the summary courts in this period. Tables 2.1 and 2.2, which sample all cases brought before the JPs in the City for two rare periods in the 1780s for which overlapping records survive, illustrate this massive diversity and the high workloads of the courts.

Table 2.1   Types of case heard at the City summary courts, November 1784–March 1785 and November 1788–March 1789

Type of case	Guildhall	Mansion House	Total
Property offence	132	331	463
Violent offence	110	310	420
Regulatory offence	121	290	411
Total	363	931	1294

Source: The minute books of the Guildhall and Mansion House justice rooms.[29]

Table 2.2   Other business before the City justice rooms, 1784–89

Action	Mansion House	Guildhall	Total
Affidavit	983	108	1091 (35%)
Certificate	789	0	789 (25%)
Warrant (general)	251	61	312 (10%)
Powers attested	219	0	219 (7%)
Order of removal	179	0	179 (6%)
Letters of Attorney	118	0	118 (4%)
Backed warrant[30]	66	17	83 (3%)
Warrant (Bastardy)	61	1	62 (2%)
Other	35	13	48 (1.5%)
Set parish poor rate	43	0	43 (1.5%)
Parish order	34	0	34 (1.0%)
Precept for election of official	19	1	20 (0.5%)
Warrant – desertion[31]	19	0	19 (0.5%)
Acknowledgements	17	0	17 (0.5%)

Hoards	14	0	14 (0.5%)
Warrant (peace)	13	1	14 (0.5%)
Warrant (search)	13	3	16 (0.5%)
Indenture of Apprentice	9	0	9 (0.3%)
Warrant (distress)	9	0	9 (0.3%)
Exhibits	7	0	7 (0.2%)
Certificate	6	0	6 (0.2%)
Totals	2904	205	3109

Source: The minute books of the Guildhall and Mansion House justice rooms.[32]

In this sample of 24 'court weeks' the minute books of the two City courts indicate that over 4324 hearings/adjudications took place before the City magistracy. This suggests that these courts heard on average about 180 cases per week, meaning that between them these courts dealt with over 700 cases each month.[33] Although comparison with local magistrates and petty sessions in other areas is difficult because different summary courts used different recording practices, this suggests that the City courts were busier than their rural counterparts.[34]

The majority of these hearings dealt with relatively routine matters, such as the issuing of warrants, which were minimally recorded in the minute books. However, in 1294 cases a longer record indicates that a full hearing took place leading to an adjudication when the names of the participants, the nature of the offence/dispute and some sense of the outcome was recorded. Amongst these 1294 cases property offences formed the largest subsection of the courts' business accounting for 35.7 per cent of the hearings. The prosecution of violence, chiefly inter-personal assault, formed almost as great a caseload (32.4 per cent). Theft and violence accounted for 68 per cent of all hearings but the relative weight of these two types of cases is interesting. Beattie's work on the 1730s indicates that hearings involving violence outnumbered those involving theft by nearly two to one, 50 years later theft cases slightly predominated.[35] If Beattie's data is comparable this would imply a considerable change towards a greater emphasis on theft accusations. This might reflect the growing use of the summary process to deal with minor property offenders and thus re-emphasise the importance of summary proceedings to our understanding of the wider criminal justice system. However, it is possible that the courts changed their recording practices in relation to, for example, preliminary requests for warrants in assault disputes, and therefore such conclusions must be tentative.[36]

These courts also dealt with a variety of regulatory disputes and prosecutions that reflect the day-to-day confrontations and disputes of Europe's largest city. Traffic offences including dangerous driving and unlicensed vehicles, the obstruction of the streets; trading violations; immoral behaviour; drunkenness and disorder; master/servant disputes and a host of other petty infringements of City regulations came before them. In addition to the hearings and examinations of property crime, interpersonal violence and regulatory disputes, a considerable amount of administrative and other business was being undertaken. A small amount of poor law business came through the summary courts, although most of those seeking help or found begging were dealt with by the clerks. Some vagabonds and beggars were examined before the magistracy, often to be 'passed' to their place of lawful residence via the Bridewell for a brief reminder of the City's hospitality lest they chose to return. Bastard bearers and absent husbands or fathers were similarly ordered to take the necessary steps to prevent their families' upkeep falling upon the ratepayers. The Mansion House court also swore in new constables and other officers of the City and set the poor rates. Numerous affidavits were sworn each week before the lord mayor and considerable numbers of warrants were issued in both courts. This guaranteed that these courts were busy arenas of adjudication and negotiation in the eighteenth century. Large numbers of Londoners were appearing here as prosecutors, witnesses, defendants and policing agents, many more indeed than were passing though the doors of Newgate and Old Bailey.

The City summary courts were not simply criminal courts but almost certainly played a host of other important roles in London society. Warrants were issued to churchwardens and overseers of the poor against the purported fathers of illegitimate children and for those men who abandoned their families causing them to become dependent on poor relief.[37] The primary aim of bastardy warrants and warrants for desertion was not a moral one but rather a more pragmatic device to reduce the overall costs of the parish community. Warrants were also issued at the request of complainants after a brief investigation by the magistrate into the circumstances of the complaint.[38] Once the warrant had been issued the City's constables and marshals could act upon it, by arresting the person named on it and bringing them to court.[39] Most of the warrants labelled as 'general warrants' in Table 2.2 were for assault or potential felonies. Search warrants were also issued which specified the place of search and the reason given. Such warrants were issued only when there was sufficient grounds for suspicion and particular named goods were specified as being missing. It was not a general invitation to rifle through a person's property looking for suspicious items.[40] To what extent magistrates and executing officers complied with this is open to question.

Thus a large amount of courtroom time was taken up with administrative business, especially at the Mansion House, but both courts dealt with a great deal more than just petty crime. In part this is because of the multi-faceted nature of magistracy in the eighteenth century in which justices acted as the *de facto* leaders of their communities, the lynchpin of social relations. While community ties may have been of less significance in London the centrality of these courts allowed them to play a very similar role. They were an integral part of the complex meshing of local government business that touched the lives of Londoners in a multiplicity of ways. They certainly dealt with many more defendants, witnesses and prosecutors than the higher courts of assize and quarter sessions that served the City, but what sort of justice did they offer?

The style and outcome of hearings at the City justice rooms

What form did the hearings before the magistrates take in this period? The scene in the Guildhall justice room is illustrated by Hogarth in Figure 2.2, as Jack Idle is brought before his more industrious former

Figure 2.2 The Guildhall Justice Room, by William Hogarth © Guildhall Library[41]

workmate. The image is not necessarily accurate in all respects but conveys the essence of the open court.

The courtroom depicted by Hogarth was a public space. The justice sat with a clerk who noted down the proceedings and issued any required paperwork. The courts were attended by one of four attorneys from the mayor's Court; for most of this period George Rhodes appears to have been the principal attorney but Thomas Beach, William Windale and William Nash each earned just over £43 a year for their work in the justice rooms.[42] The accused was brought in from the holding compter by a constable (or by an arresting officer or prosecutor from the street if the offence occurred whilst the court was sitting) or was summoned by a warrant. The case was then presented by the prosecutor and an examination by the magistrate of the accused and any witnesses ensued.[43] This could be detailed and exacting or cursory and straightforward, depending on the offence itself.[44]

In December 1789, Elizabeth Austin was brought before the lord mayor charged, on the oath of a constable, with being an idle and disorderly person. On the strength of the evidence presented and the constable's willingness to swear to the veracity of the charge Austin was sent to Bridewell for a month. The next day Jane Pearce accused Elizabeth Walden of abusing her five-year-old son. A witness for Pearce described the fatal assault on the child and his subsequent examination by a doctor. Walden was remanded in custody in the Poultry to allow more evidence to be presented which might have resulted in a murder indictment. On the following day the coroner reported that the child had died of natural causes and Walden was discharged.[45] On the 19 November 1761 Ann Bewry was charged by Edward Read with picking his pockets after he had spent the night with her. The clerk recorded the evidence presented by Read and his cross-examination by the alderman. Read said that he had taken her into custody soon after the theft but she had escaped with the help of some friends. Bewry was undoubtedly one of the capital's many prostitutes and Read was trying to keep his involvement with her as quiet as possible, however the questioning of the court made this difficult. He admitted that he had fallen asleep 'after he had lain with her' and that it was 'when he awoke [that he] missed his money'. Bewry had substituted his money with worthless counters. However, when pressed by the justice he admitted 'that he remembered not what time of the day he saw his money'. Perhaps infuriated with Read's behaviour or frustrated by his lack of clarity the magistrate dismissed the case and released Ann to carry on her precarious existence.[46]

These cases reflect the brevity of the recording of some cases in the minute books and the rich detail in others. In some instances the records of the courts are much more forthcoming, recording detailed exchanges between witnesses and the court that are, in effect, depositions. We can see the full workings of the summary court in an arson case from March 1779. On the 17 March Henry Washington, a parish constable, gave an account of several suspicious circumstances relating to a fire in Cheapside. The detailed recording of this case runs for several full pages in the minute books of the Guildhall court.[47] A fire had broken out at the home of Thomas Hilliard, a substitute constable in the City. Hilliard had alerted the watch who had hurried to the scene. However, the cause of the fire was disputed and Hilliard himself was suspected of arson, as an insurance fraud or for some other more heinous purpose. The case unfolds in the minute books. On the first day Washington came before the court with a number of persons including Hilliard under his care. He described the events of the night of the fire from his position as duty constable at the watch house. The court then heard evidence from Hilliard, his wife and servants, another couple that lived in the house and from members of the watch and constabulary that attended. The actual exchanges are recorded in the minute books. To give an example:

> Thomas Hilliard was called in and said that after supper last night he went down into the kitchen and the cellar – he was going into bed when he smelt the fire – he then pushed into the maid's room, and also knock'd on the wainscot – he shoved the maid's room open, and said 'Molly have you any lighter here, or is your candle safe, for I believe the house is on fire' He thought the shavings were in a blaze – he passed the closet where they lay, but did not examine it – nor did he smell the key hole – he said, he could not give a reason for not looking to the shavings.[48]

Hilliard was remanded so that more evidence could be gathered and more witnesses could be interviewed. He was held in custody at the Poultry compter (as illustrated in Figure 2.3), where he initially admitted arson before subsequently retracting his confession. The thorough nature of the examination before the magistrate is illustrated by the involvement of an 'expert' witness in the person of William Payne, in his capacity as a carpenter. Payne was questioned about the construction of a closet (which was identified as the place where the fire started) and its combustibility. At the end of the hearing Hilliard was committed to Newgate to await trial.[49] Arson was an extremely serious offence in

THE POULTRY COMPTER. (*From an Old Print.*)

Figure 2.3 The Poultry compter, from an old print (from 'Old and New London' c.1875). Author's personal collection

the metropolis given that the risk of fire spreading and consuming adjacent property was a very real one.[50] The detailed examination of this case and the way it is was recorded shows that part of the function of the summary process was to prepare cases for trial at the higher courts. It is clear, therefore, that while some, if not many, of the hearings that occurred at these courts were brief and cursory, others were careful and considered.

The outcome of some summary hearings involved the imposition of a fine, the sentencing of the culprit to Bridewell or another prison, or some other penalty. However, the style of the court was often deeply influenced by a more civil mode of proceeding in which the emphasis was on restorative justice. As we shall see many cases that came before the magistracy ended in some form of agreement between the prosecutor and accused. Some cases were dismissed because the prosecutor failed to make an appearance or because the justice considered there to be insufficient evidence to proceed. However, it is worth noting that, theoretically at least, magistrates were supposed to refer all serious (i.e. indictable) offences to the higher jury courts of quarter sessions and assize.[51] However, the summary courts in London (in common with the actions of JPs elsewhere in this period) sent very few cases on to the higher courts, preferring to deal with offenders at this stage of the justice system where possible.[52]

As we have seen with Richard Hilliard, the accused could be remanded in one of the local compters or Bridewell while witnesses were sought or goods suspected to be stolen were advertised in the newspapers.[53] Suspects could be re-examined several times before being discharged, summarily punished or committed for a jury trial.[54] This practice of 'further examination' was potentially a prosecution strategy, exploiting as it did the criminal justice system of the time. With scant evidence the accused could be thrown into gaol for a short (but very unpleasant) period before being released. If the procedure was repeated more than once (and there are several instances where it was), the accused could easily spend a week or more in prison. It also gave the magistrate an alternative to committing the accused to trial.[55] Remanding for further examination was therefore a multifaceted tool of the summary bench, allowing as it did for the punishment of minor offenders, the terrifying of young delinquents and the more careful examination of others. Once again it reminds us that magistrates used statute law as a moveable feast rather than as a regimented set of rules; offenders were supposedly only liable for detention for three days but by re-examining suspects at regular intervals justices could flout the principle of *habeas corpus* if not the letter of the law. This is particularly apposite in property cases and will be discussed further in Chapter 4.

Table 2.3 shows that nearly 60 per cent of offenders brought before the two summary courts were discharged or dismissed by the sitting justice. Large numbers of defendants were dropping out of the criminal justice

Table 2.3 The nature of outcomes of the City summary courts, November
1784–March 1785 and November 1788–March 1789

Outcome	Guildhall	Mansion House	Total
Settled & discharged	214	455	669 (59.4%)
Summarily punished	69	208	277 (24.6%)
Sent on	36	143	179 (15.9%)
Total known outcomes	319	806	1125 (99.9%)
Outcome unknown	44	125	169
Total	363	931	1294

Source: The minute books of the Guildhall and Mansion House justice rooms.

system at an early stage and so have been overlooked by most histories
of crime. The explanations behind these discharges and dismissals will
be examined as we look in turn at the prosecution process and the way
in which the courts dealt with property crime, interpersonal violence
and the regulation of trade, the streets and public morality. In addition
to the 59.4 per cent of defendants that were released by the magistracy a
further 24.6 per cent received some form of summary punishment. The
courts were able to imprison and fine offenders for a number of crimes
as well as having the less formal sanction of persuading them to enlist
in the armed forces. Some were imprisoned by the magistrates, usually
in Bridewell, others were fined before being released and a small number
were ordered out of the City under the settlement laws.

A significant percentage of cases were processed without any formal
punishment being given. JPs had wide discretionary powers and they
used them to act as mediators within their communities. The settling
of disputes to the satisfaction of both sides in this way was both less
expensive and less divisive to community relations. Operating as they
did in London, with higher incidents of criminality and greater pressure
on the criminal justice system, City justices were perhaps minded to
deal with a greater proportion of petty offences summarily than might
have been the case outside of the metropolis. It is therefore not surprising to see that many cases were settled at the summary level and filtered
out of the justice system early on. When the figures for those hearings
that were settled are combined with those that were summarily punished we can see that in cases where the outcome is known 84 per cent
of defendants were being dealt with by the City justices without the
need for the further involvement of the wider criminal justice system.[56]
Therefore it is important to remember that when we look at crime rates

(or more properly, *prosecution rates*) for the eighteenth century, we have to take account of the number of cases that are discharged at this initial phase in the system. The growing body of work on the history of crime has for the most part concentrated on the relatively small number of cases that were serious enough to reach the higher courts of the land but has not always shown an awareness of the vast number of cases filtered out lower down the system.[57]

Prosecutors: An overview of social status and gender

Much of the historiography of crime has been concerned with the perpetrators of crime rather than their victims.[58] Indeed, studies that have concentrated on the prosecution of property offenders have tended to view the prosecuted as the victims of a harsh criminal justice system. The victim was central to the prosecution process in the eighteenth century and this is clearly evident at the summary courts in the City.[59] By analysing the minute books of the City's justice rooms it is possible to begin to ask questions about the men and women that used the courts to seek redress, justice or recompense from those that insulted, assaulted, disobeyed and stole from them.

Identifying the social status of prosecutors from the court records is fraught with difficulty. In many instances no specific occupational data is recorded at all, only the names of those involved are recorded. Added to this the court records themselves are incomplete, with many missing volumes. However, despite these problems it is possible to attempt an analysis of the social status of prosecutors. If a sample of minute books is taken from the second half of the eighteenth century we can construct a table of occupations for prosecutors that can be compared to some recent work on the social status of prosecutors.[60]

The prominence of officials (primarily constables, watchmen and street keepers) is to be expected given the regulatory nature of the courts' business. Additionally the large proportion of unknown occupations creates problems for analysis. So for the present these two categories as well as 'others' will be removed from the findings to produce Table 2.5.

Clearly, where we have an idea of social status tradesmen and artisans form more than a third of prosecutors. This table omits the 765 cases for which we have no known occupational data and this could affect the figures in a number of ways. For example, the occupations of persons of lower status were less likely to have been recorded by the courts and, if this is the case, the numbers of the labouring poor will be under-represented. Despite this the labouring poor still account for at least

Table 2.4   Prosecutors at the City justice rooms, 1761–1800

Occupation	Number	Percentage
Gentry/Wealthier merchants	6	0.6
Masters/Professionals/Merchants	78	5.0
Tradesmen/Artisans	133	8.6
Poverty vulnerable trades	85	5.5
Labourers/Poor	65	4.2
Other category	29	1.8
City officials	371	24.1
No known occupation	765	49.8
Totals	1532	99.6

Source: The minute books of the Guildhall and Mansion House justice rooms.[61]

Table 2.5   Prosecutors at the City justice rooms, 1761–1800 (Unknowns and officials omitted.)

Occupation	Number	Percentage
Gentry/Wealthier merchants	6	2.7
Masters/Professionals/Merchants	78	21.0
Tradesmen/Artisans	133	35.8
Poverty vulnerable trades	85	22.9
Labourers/Poor	65	17.5
Totals	367	99.9

Source: The minute books of the Guildhall and Mansion House justice rooms.[62]

17.5 per cent of prosecutors. There are also a significant percentage of tradesmen and those employed in poverty vulnerable trades (weavers and Hackney Coachmen, for example). What little comparative work we have on the social status of prosecutors at summary level suggests that in Essex 31 per cent of victims at petty sessions were tradesmen and 22 per cent were described as 'poverty vulnerable'.[63] These figures are therefore similar to those in the City of London.

The proportion of prosecutors drawn from the higher levels of society are slightly greater in the City than was the case in Essex, with the gentry, professionals and richer middling sorts accounting for nearly a quarter of the prosecutors for whom an occupation can be identified. The possible under-representation of the labouring poor and the slightly higher figures for the urban elites may well be a result of the omission of the cases for which we have no identifiable occupation. It could also be caused by the relationship between good occupational data and certain sorts of offence. For example, property offending was much better recorded in the court minute books than assault, because of the court's role as a pre-trial forum. In this role the court was required to judge which cases should be sent on to the higher courts and part of the process of the pre-trial hearing involved the swearing of evidence from victims and witnesses. Assault hearings were often settled at summary level, without the need for the diligent recording of evidence with the result that it is much more likely for occupational data to be mentioned in a property hearing than in one for assault. Secondly the victims of property crime were much more likely to have been drawn from amongst the ranks of the propertied, and therefore would have had a tendency to tilt the statistics in their favour. We will be able to learn more about the people using these courts as we explore the prosecutions of specific offences in subsequent chapters.

The summary courts facilitated the hearing of disputes, they dispensed warrants and forced those accused of a variety of offences and infringements to attend. They were a semi-civil, semi-arbitrational arena for the settling of disputes and arguments rather than a criminal court. However, they had the power to punish as well as to arbitrate and this is an important dimension of their role. The men that sat in these courts were the justices of the peace for the City of London. These were powerful and, for the most part, wealthy individuals and it is necessary to understand something of their lives and motivations in order to appreciate the way in which summary justice functioned in this period.

The City magistrates

The magistrates of the City were, as Rudé noted, 'almost without exception men of wealth'.[64] They had risen to positions of influence and been voted into office by their respective wards and parishes. To become lord mayor one had to have served as alderman and be nominated by the Court of Common Hall. Apart from the wealth and power that was part and parcel of aldermanic office several of these individuals had experience of Parliament. In the period 1770–1809 between 18 and 20 per cent of London aldermen served as MPs, not all of them as representatives of the City.[65] John Sawbridge was an MP between 1774 and 1795 and his support of the radical politician John Wilkes' nomination for the mayoralty in 1774 (in return for his own smooth election as MP for London) hints at the cosy patronage of City politics. Indeed Sawbridge succeeded Wilkes as lord mayor in the following year.[66]

Independence and an attention to the vested interests of the corporation characterise the careers of several City MPs. Sir Watkin Lewes demonstrated his understanding of the City's long tradition of independence by resisting the intrusion of press gangs into the City.[67] This determination to defy government intervention in City affairs had been evident during the American Revolution and again in 1787 when the sitting lord mayor, John Burnell, 'declared his resolution not to back any press warrants' bringing him into direct confrontation with the Prime Minister, first Lord of the Admiralty and the Lord Chancellor.[68] The City may have only returned three members of parliament but several other aldermen made it to the national stage as representatives of seats outside. Alderman Townsend served as MP for West Looe in 1767 and Calne in 1782 and the wealthy Jamaican planter William Beckford served for Shaftsbury from 1747–54 before he fought and won his London seat.[69] National politics and City politics were closely linked but City MPs were primarily concerned with representing City interests.

London aldermen were a distinct group in the second half of the eighteenth century. While many of them invested in land outside of the capital few chose to exchange their metropolitan lifestyles and careers for that of country gentlemen.[70] They remained rooted in trade and the accumulation of wealth in the urban centre. Many derived their personal fortunes from trade or from the financing of trade. Alderman Newnham began life as a sugar-baker but moved into banking on gaining his inheritance. Bankers, financiers and merchants accounted for 63 per cent of the aldermen serving in the City between 1738 and 1762 while in the years 1768–74 of 43 aldermen 12 were bankers, at least three were major merchants, several were 'gentlemen of leisure' and 'only a handful followed the more common City crafts or trades.'[71] Some 20 per cent were wholesalers and were intrinsically linked to the wharfs and warehouses of London. Others were successful self-made men like John Boydell, who rose from impoverishment in Derbyshire to make his fortune by purchasing the copyrights in the re-prints and paintings of artists.[72] Boydell's legacy can still be seen in the collection of the Guildhall Art Gallery.

City interests, predominately trade and finance, must have informed decision-making at Guildhall and Mansion House. This does not mean that individual interests and personal predilections should be discounted. Boydell, the son of a vicar, was steward of the Marine Society in 1785 and this may have affected the way he discharged his magisterial responsibilities. It is also likely that these men shared their thoughts and opinions with each other in the numerous social gatherings open to them. Meetings, civic ceremonies, balls and investitures would have brought these men together while marriage and friendships would have created further links between them. Nick Rogers has observed that approximately 'one third of the Georgian aldermen were related to former City dignitaries or to their fellow members.' They formed what Rogers has termed a 'City patriciate', bound together as they were 'by interlocking ties of kinship'.[73] This further emphasises their metropolitan focus and is suggestive of their ability to administer a layered and connected system of civic government. This close network of power in the urban context may also have reduced the labouring class' ability to manipulate the summary and welfare process in the way in which their rural counterparts seem to have been able to do elsewhere.

Amongst the aldermen of London were 'some of the richest commoners of England.' Few surpassed Richard and William Beckford whose enormous wealth was accrued from their West Indian plantations, or Sir Charles Asgil who headed a banking house and died with assets worth around £160,000.[74] Harvey Christian Combe, who died leaving an estate of £140,000, reveals the 'social and political range of London's super-rich brewing fraternity in the late Georgian period.' Combe was close friends with the Whig politician Charles James Fox and the Prince of Wales, demonstrating the way in which these City patriarchs were interlinked within London society and national politics.[75]

It would be unwise to generalise about the character of the individuals that dispensed justice in the square mile throughout the late eighteenth century. They were, however, representative of a mercantile elite. Most had made their money from business or by making crucial alliances with those that had. These men served the City in a variety of ways; as national representatives of the City in Parliament, as local politicians as aldermen and lords mayor, and as Sheriff and Chamberlain. They sat on boards of governors at the Bridewell and Bethlem hospitals, the Marine Society and various other organisations.[76] They were a *metropolitan* elite, influenced by their experience of the urban centre and its particular needs. While many may have chosen to reside outside the City, most lived within the greater metropolis (in the fashionable parts of Westminster) or commuted from their opulent properties along the banks of the Thames.[77] Along with the various talents and abilities they brought to the office of magistrate they must also have been able to add a good understanding of City affairs and City politics which would have informed their actions. While some may have had moral issues uppermost in their minds others may have been more concerned with furthering or protecting their business interests (or those of their supporters) while others had their wider political careers in mind. At least one of their number had direct experience of crime. In July 1790 Alderman Curtis was on his way home when his coach was stopped by highway robbers. A London newspaper reported that:

> When they stopped the coach he was asleep, and was awakened by finding a large horse pistol on each side of his breast. They robbed him of three guineas, a gold watch, and of the Newgate Calendar, which he happened to have in his pocket. We hope the latter will be of use to the gentlemen.[78]

This was the classic highway robbery and we might expect the experience, which echoes that of the lord chief justice earlier in the century, to have had some bearing on the way in which the alderman discharged his magisterial duties.

Concluding remarks

The City of London contained a layered network of arenas of negotiation that were connected administratively, at the heart of which were the summary courts. The Guildhall and Mansion House justice rooms individually and collectively dealt with the majority of all civil and criminal prosecutions in the City of London at the end of the eighteenth century and as such formed an essential part of the fabric of Georgian London's social relations. These courts were accessible, affordable and used by a significant proportion of the population of the City.[79] They dealt with a very wide range of business, from theft to domestic violence to the regulation of the streets. They touched the lives of thousands of Londoners in a way that Old Bailey never did. Our understanding of the criminal justice system and its impact upon eighteenth-century society therefore has to involve an appreciation of the role of the summary process. The following chapters will explore this process, in the City of London, in much more detail to emphasise the importance of this key tier of the judicial system.

3
Policing and Personnel: Constables and the Watching System

In the early hours of 28 November 1770 three men burgled the *Wheat-sheaf* alehouse in Fleet Market. The landlady, Mrs Poole, was woken by the noise and demanded to know who was there. One of the intruders warned her to remain quiet or else they would 'blow her brains out'. Undeterred Mrs Poole threw open the nearest window and cried out 'Watch, Thieves, Murder!' However, there being no watchman nearby one of her lodgers crept out undetected and ran to the watch house for help. Before he returned, the 'fellows had taken upwards of £8 out of the till, and made off'.[1] This is a typical example of the reporting of crime, and more importantly, policing, in the late eighteenth-century London press. However, in the spirit of balance let us turn to another example of 'police' behaviour from the newspapers.

> On Saturday Mr Catchpole, one of the Lord Mayor's Marshalmen, assisted by Messrs. Sanderson and Clarke, constables, took in a house near Golden-lane two men, charged with breaking open the same morning an alehouse, the sign of the City of Canterbury, the corner of Primrose-street, Bishopsgate-street, and stealing out of the bar 17s in silver, a bag of halfpence, a watch, wearing apparel, and various other things, which were found in their lodgings; they were carried before Alderman Hart, who committed both men for trial.[2]

These examples illustrate the differing and sometimes contradictory views of policing in London in the 50 years or so before the creation of professional forces.[3] Many newspaper reports condemned the ineffi-ciency, idleness and corrupt nature of the men charged with protecting the lives and property of those living and working in the capital. In doing so they echoed the thoughts of some driven individuals – men such as Patrick Colquhoun, John Wade and William Blizzard – who argued for a better-organised and paid police for the capital. These contemporary viewpoints served as the backbone for early historians of the police who used them to point to the transformation the Metropolitan force made to policing in the mid-nineteenth century. However, in recent years we have been well served by several studies that have qualified such Whiggish tales of progress. The story that has emerged is a more complex one of gradual evolution rather than dramatic change. The history of policing in the City represents another example of this new orthodoxy. The courts at Guildhall and Mansion House were filters in a judicial labyrinth that covered the square mile. As such the summary process was an integral part of the government and policing of the City of London. However, it is clear that by the time issues reached the summary courts, they represented the later or final stages of the policing process and were in many respects a reflection of it. As we will see the magistracy and the various policing agencies in the City were tied together.

The prosecution process of the Hanoverian period has been widely accepted to have been 'victim-led' in which the role of policing agents was a supporting one. However, there is good evidence to suggest that in the period between 1780 and 1839 a more 'professional' form of policing evolved. This evolutionary process can be explored by looking at the nature of policing in the City at this time. It can be argued the City was well policed prior to the Metropolitan Police Act. This will be shown in terms of manpower per head of population and geographical area, specialist functions such as the policing of the Thames Quayside, proactive and reactive policing and the nature of the personnel involved. Indeed, the overall picture that emerges is that of communal, or rather, community policing. Naturally, this system was not without its problems. Not everyone wanted to fulfil their civic duty and perform the role of constable, and payments for successful convictions may have influenced prosecution processes unfairly. Nonetheless, as this chapter will demonstrate, the nature of policing in the City had evolved from within the community and remained very close to the day-to-day experiences of City life. In this respect, the nature of policing and the role of the summary courts were very much in tune with each other.

Until 1829 England had no professional police force as we would understand it and there was considerable debate about the creation of such an institution, with powerful arguments from both sides. Contemporaries certainly believed that society had a problem with law and order, and this problem was perceived to be growing in the immediate aftermath of the wars with revolutionary and Napoleonic France. Historians have suggested that professional policing emerged in the late eighteenth century, particularly in London, with a series of localised initiatives by organisations and individuals.[4] Others have reflected on the development of a 'disciplinary society', as conceived by Foucault, which views the police as a corrective tool of the elites. Alternatively it is possible that the creation of professional police forces in the 1830s represented a desire to minimise risk: a form of insurance against increasing incidents of crime and criminality.[5]

All of these theories are persuasive and it would seem that we need to view the development of professionalism in policing as an amalgam of a number of factors. Professional policing in London did not begin with the creation of the 'Peelers' in 1829, but was well established before Peel's initiative bore fruit. The City of London was excluded from Peel's plans and retains its own separate police force to this day. This chapter will examine how effective policing was in the City in the years before 1829: how large an area in terms of population and geographical spread did they cover, were they proactive or reactive to City problems and how did they practise their policing? Traditionally the policing agents prior to 1829 have been seen as amateurish and incompetent but this chapter will support recent arguments for a more balanced interpretation of their role and effectiveness.[6]

The structure of policing in the City

Some contemporaries believed that the City of London was well policed in the late eighteenth and early nineteenth century (at least by comparison with the wider metropolis). An 1812 parliamentary select committee concluded that:

> The City of London, from the nature of its Magistracy, the description of its various public offices, the gradation and subordination of their various classes, the division and subdivision of its local limits, affords an example of that unity, and of that dependence of parts on each other, without which no well constructed and efficient system of police can ever be expected.[7]

In the City, policing and the administration of criminal justice, in common with all other aspects of daily life, were heavily influenced by the individual ideology of the sitting lord mayor. Outside initiatives, as Pitt and Peel both discovered, were not welcomed if they infringed the City's special status or privileges. The City fiercely guarded its independence and, in the realm of 'police', it had some justification in believing that it had no need of the reforms that were being called for elsewhere. Part of the justification for this view lay in the structure of policing in the City: a structure that was organised on a tripartite model (of public, private and community policing) while at the same time being coordinated from the centre of City government.

At the heart of the City's policing system sat the magistracy, in the shape of the lord mayor and aldermen. Below, and directly answerable to them, were the City marshals. Underneath the marshals the City employed small numbers of men as patrols, whilst at ward level watchmen were recruited to police the streets at night. Each ward also elected a number of householders to discharge the office of constable on a rotational basis. Finally the various commercial interests of the City employed policing agents to protect their property, most notably along the long stretch of the river Thames that flowed through the capital's centre. This system of policing therefore had three branches: public, community and private that together formed a tripartite policing network. We will now consider each arm of this system in turn.

Public policing: The marshals and patrols

The marshals were responsible for ensuring that the system of police operated smoothly and effectively, that order was maintained and that the decisions and reforms of the mayor, aldermen and Common Council were enacted and executed. These were salaried positions that had been in existence since the 1750s.[8] To assist them in their duties the marshals had six marshalmen who were also salaried and had similar responsibilities to the marshals but also served warrants across the City's jurisdiction.

Throughout the 1770s and 1780s the office of under marshal and (after 1778) upper marshal, was held by Thomas Gates and it is evident from a handful of cases that reached the Old Bailey that Gates performed a variety of policing roles in this time. In 1772 he was protecting the lord mayor from an angry mob that had gathered in Guildhall Yard and had to defend himself from the attacks of the crowd as they tried to get at the lord mayor's coach. He struck out at one individual with his ceremonial mace and 'broke his head' and was then pelted with mud by the mob in the riot that ensued (a riot caused by the decision of the Court of Aldermen to overlook the candidacy of the populist

radical politician John Wilkes). In the following year, Gates successfully coordinated the arrest of three coiners, searching their properties
and gathering evidence that he later presented at their trials to secure
their conviction. One of Gates' duties was to execute search warrants
when directed to do so by the lord mayor, and in 1775 he appeared
at Old Bailey to give evidence against Fanny Hart for burglary. In the
course of his search, Gates discovered a pair of muslin lace ruffles that
proved vital in Hart's trial. These searches appear to have been very thorough. Gates was at the home of one of the coiners for two hours and
he found the missing ruffles in a drawer in a lower room of a shared
house. Thus Gates was acting very much as we might expect an investigating police officer to act. However, Gates did not just have to deal
with petty crime, during the Gordon riots he attempted to quell the disturbances and persuade individuals he knew to stop attacking private
property.[9]

We should of course be wary of seeing Thomas Gates as a professional crime fighter. Gates appeared at Old Bailey on just ten occasions
between 1770 and 1780, many of his other duties would have been
largely ceremonial (processing with the lord mayor, attending Guildhall
and Mansion House and at executions), but it would seem that Gates
was a proactive Marshal. He has been credited with transforming the
small force of marshalmen into 'an effective crime-fighting force' and
this demonstrates that policing reforms in this period were possible, if
driven by determined individuals.[10]

Across the capital at Bow Street the Fielding brothers had developed
their own force of crime fighters, the Bow Street Runners. This organised body of thief-takers, partly funded by government, represents the
first real attempt to use detection to solve crime and to apprehend
criminals. Whilst its model was rejected by Peel in 1829 it must have
influenced and inspired men such as Thomas Gates in the last quarter
of the eighteenth century. In 1784, the Common Council debated the
creation of a patrol that was similar to the Bow Street horse patrol that
had been established by the Fieldings earlier in the century.[11] Council
agreed to allocate the sum of £300 for the employment of ten officers
who would carry out a variety of duties that included the supervision
of the night watch.[12] Over the next 30 years three patrols developed
out of this initiative so that by 1828 a day patrol of 23 men patrolled
the City streets from 10 a.m. to 8 p.m., while a 16-men night patrol
came on duty at 6 p.m. and stayed on until 1 a.m.[13] These patrols were
paid, and in addition to apprehending 'thieves, rogues and vagrants',
they reported back to the marshals on the conduct of constables and

watchmen as well as the state of taverns and bawdy houses.[14] The press had been urging other areas to follow Bow Street's example for some time. In January 1770, the *General Evening Post* noted that, after the wash-house of Mrs Jenner had been raided – and a brewing copper made off with – it was 'a pity that the inhabitants do not appoint a patrole [*sic*], as it would be the means of detecting a set of loose fellows who have lately infested that place'.[15] Gradually other areas of the metropolis hired men to form patrols, recognising that they could be a useful addition to crime prevention and detection in London. They may have been small in number but, like the Runners of Bow Street, the City marshals and patrols demonstrate that paid policing agents operated on the streets of the capital well before 1829. How effective they were is hard to determine but what is clear is that they had an important supervisory role to play in the public policing of the City and this was a role that helped integrate the various policing agencies that served the mercantile centre.

One of the important responsibilities of the Marshals was to supervise the night watch, an organisation that came in for considerable criticism in the late eighteenth century. This criticism needs some revaluation and so we now turn our attention to the City's watchmen and their effectiveness or otherwise in protecting the residents and businessmen of the late Hanoverian capital.

The watching networks of the City

Watchmen have a long tradition in English history, dating back to 1285.[16] The role of the watch was to protect the property of the City's population after dark. Watchmen were detailed to keep an eye out for disreputable characters, to check for open doors and unlatched windows, and to have an ear for unexpected sounds that might suggest break-ins or other criminal activity. A regulated watching system had been established in the City in 1705. Common Council awarded funds for the building of watch houses in wards where there were none and enshrined the practice of watchmen being deployed in 'stands' and on regular 'beats' in City law.[17] After several years of debate and wrangling caused by the problems of financing and supplying men for the watch the City finally succeeded in obtaining an act of parliament to reform the watch in 1737.[18] However, a lack of sufficient funds ensured that the operation of the watch still varied from ward to ward.[19] Despite this, the reforms did bring some uniformity to aspects of the watch system. Wages were set at £13 per year which went some way to countering the complaints of those who felt that low pay was a disincentive to recruitment. Additionally the hours of service were established, and all watchmen were issued with a five-foot-long staff. By 1806 there were 765 watchmen operating across the 25 City wards but with the individual wards retaining their localised control.[20]

Watchmen have suffered greatly from contemporary depictions of them as incompetent, old and decrepit. This report, from the *General Evening Post* in 1770, is typical: 'It is observable, that there is a watch-man's box very near several of the houses that have been broke open last week; a melancholy proof of the negligence or inefficiency of these guardians of the night'.[21] Fifteen years later another correspondent complained that after a prostitute had been brutally attacked outside a Fleet Street inn bystanders rushed to her aid but 'the watchmen, neither moved with compassion or their duty, remained in their boxes'.[22] This view of the watch as a confederation of incompetents is repeated time and again in the London press: watchmen are reported as absent from their stands as householders are burgled or gentlemen are assaulted and robbed in the streets.

Watchmen were an easy target for newspapers and they delighted in offering up titbits to their readers of watchmen who were embarrassed, or made fools of by the criminal elements of the City. While a watch-man ('half asleep') near Drury Lane was crying the hour 'a pyramid of lights fell on his head, and set fire to his hat and wig' one reported.[23] In another incident a watchman who attempted to arrest a streetwalker on the Strand was invited to stand toe-to-toe and box with her. After 'beating him well, she broke his lanthorn to pieces, ran off with his staff and made her escape'.[24] Young men enjoyed the 'sport' of baiting watch-men and knocking over their stands or stealing their lanterns while they dozed and the *Whitehall Evening Post* warned these young 'Bloods, as they call themselves', that they faced the prospect of being charged with theft if they did so, despite 'it appeared to be more of a frolic than done with any felonious intent'.[25] The theft of a watchman's lantern in 1775 by Thomas Hayford was dismissed by John Wilkes sitting as magistrate at Guildhall because 'it did not appear to be done feloniously'.[26] Clearly then these policing agents suffered from a widely held negative image of their usefulness, and a perception that relatively minor attacks upon them would go unpunished.

There was an ongoing debate about the merits of a more organised and professional police force that had arguably commenced in the wake of the Gordon riots of June 1780 and indeed continued past the intro-duction of the Metropolitan Police in 1829. The 50 or so years between these two events can now be seen as an evolutionary period in the transition towards a modern paid police service. As we shall see, many watchmen – along with constables and other policing agents in the late eighteenth-century City – were much more effective than some of their contemporary detractors would have us believe. I shall return to this later.

While some individual watchmen may have been lazy or inefficient or simply too old – like 'Bandyleg' Charles Chapman who died in post aged 84 – it is far too generalised a view of the watch as an institution.[27] By 1822, all watchmen were appointed by Common Council and had to provide a certificate of good behaviour signed by two 'respectable' householders, a sign that at least by the nineteenth century the importance of having reliable watchmen had been established.[28] It is impossible to be sure about the quality of the watchmen that served the City wards. The truth is probably somewhere in between these conflicting views of efficiency and incompetence. Particularly bad cases of elderly or corrupt watchmen are more likely to have been reported by the newspapers than the majority of men who performed their duties competently. For a more official viewpoint we need only turn to the parliamentary commission of 1812 who noted that the watch system in the City was not a 'dead letter',

> [but] is kept alive and in action by the constant superintendence of the Marshals of the City, with their Assistants, who every night visit the different Wards and Precincts, and take care that the Constables, Beadles, and Watchmen of all descriptions are alert and do their duty.[29]

So how might we view the watch in the 50 years or so before they were replaced by full-time professionals and to what extent does the criticism they received seem justified?

Whether they were patrolling their set beat, returning to their box or stand at regular intervals, or merely calling the hour, the presence of watchmen was evidently of some comfort to City residents. Watchmen stopped and searched suspicious persons and were 'expected to intervene in fights and thefts and investigate disturbing noises in the night' and in general terms act as 'assistants to the victim of a crime.'[30] However, while this is undoubtedly the main purpose of the watch in most circumstances, it is clear that many of these individuals took a much more proactive role in policing their areas. That this is the case is born out by reference to those same London newspapers that carried stories of absent, corrupt and inefficient watchmen. A burglar, emerging from a window of a house he had just robbed, was discovered by a patrolling watchman. The thief tried to avoid arrest by shooting the watchman who managed to call for help and catch up with the crook. In another report a watchman found an unattended hackney coach and horses at four in the morning. He noted the number of the coach and restored it to its rightful owner. In a particular sorry tale a watchman on patrol heard the despairing cries of two 'blacks' that had taken shelter under a building in Lincoln's Inn. As he was calling the hour at four 'he heard the groan of a man, and on his searching under the building; found the two poor distressed objects; one of them just dead, the other so far exhausted that he died before the least assistance could be given him'. In a similar case the actions of a watchman who had found a man lying at the foot of Blackfriars bridge stairs, presumed to have been the victim of a street robbery or assault, probably saved his life.[31]

All of these examples could be supplemented by others that indicate that negative views of watchmen, whilst not infrequent, are matched by as many positive reports of their behaviour. Watchmen checked up on empty properties, gave early warnings of fire, made sure that warehouse doors were secured and alerted householders to open windows and suspicious persons. In other words, they policed their communities; communities that they were familiar with. Which leads us to revaluate these amateur crime fighters: one way we might do this is by looking at their behaviour in the light of Bruce Smith's recent research into the prosecution of the theft of lead.

Smith has argued that 'public officials played a larger role in the process of prosecution than has previously been appreciated'.[32] Under legislation passed in 1756[33] Smith shows that, at least by the 1820s, 'police officers' were regularly bringing suspected lead thieves before the Police Offices of the metropolis (those created after 1792) having stopped and arrested them on the streets. Indeed the act of stopping and searching can be seen as proactive engaged policing even if it did not lead to a prosecution. Such preventative policing was exactly the model that police reforms envisaged in the debates leading to the creation of the Metropolitan Police in 1829.[34] In 1771 Robert Cleghorn and Richard Aldrich had just robbed the home of Luke Currie in Cheapside and were making off with a considerable haul when they were seen by James Wright, a watchman. Wright suspected them of some crime because of the bundles he saw them carrying and chased them. Although they split up, Wright, and another watchman he called to help, caught Cleghorn and questioned him. After jettisoning the bundle in an abortive attempt at escape, Cleghorn was eventually taken to the watch house to be searched. Wright gave evidence at his trial at Old Bailey where both men were convicted and sentenced to be transported.[35] In a similar incident Robert Briant stopped Elishia Collier and two others as they passed near him in the street. At first he thought Elishia had a child with her but after noticing that she was 'not carrying it like a child, I asked her what it was? She said, linen to wash; I opened one corner, and found it was not; and we took her to the watch-house'. It turned out to be printed calico that she and her two accomplices had stolen earlier.[36] In both cases the actions of the watch were independent of any call for assistance from victims. What Smith has described for metal thieves is undoubtedly the case for many other property-based crimes and for an earlier period. The availability of the summary process to prosecute suspects swiftly was a crucial adjunct to the actions of City policing agents. We shall return to the prosecution of minor property offenders in the next chapter.

Considerable numbers of individuals were prosecuted because watchmen or patrols on the streets of the City apprehended them. Individual watchmen and patrols were acting upon instructions to question those out at night without good cause or those carrying bundles of goods (like Elishia Collier) that might not belong to them. This indicates that watchmen were taking a clear *proactive* role in the prevention of crime and the apprehension of criminals without being directly called in to assist by members of the public. This is suggestive of a system of policing that was more efficient than some contemporaries suggested. The court records at Old Bailey frequently describe the actions of watchmen who came to the help of colleagues, or responded to cries of 'stop thief!' or simply 'heard the rattle sprung'. There are links between watchmen on the quays and those patrolling the riverfronts and streets leading into the City proper and considerable evidence of collaboration and mutual assistance. This collaboration and the discretion available to these police agents was a concern for some contemporaries who were worried about corruption, but in reality, probably allowed watchmen and others to police their areas thoughtfully and effectively and in much the same way as the reformed police were able to in the late nineteenth century.[37] We need to be sceptical of notions of a corrupt and inefficient body of incompetents in need of reformation in the early nineteenth century; the watch was far from perfect but neither was it as useless as some people insisted.

The watch and the City Marshals that oversaw them were not the only policing agents that served the City of London in this period. They represent what we might usefully term the 'public' or 'central' element in a multilayered system of policing. We can now turn to the 'private' and 'communal' policing networks to better understand how the City responded to the many and varied problems of crime and criminal behaviour.

Policing the Thames waterfront

Before considering the communal policing of the City wards, we can explore the private initiatives that protected the financial interests of City merchants and other businessmen. The river Thames stretched the entire length of the City's southern boundary, from Tower ward in the east to the large ward of Farringdon Without in the west. Hundreds of wharfs, docks, quays and warehouses lined the banks of the river and the waterway was congested with shipping. All this amounted to a vast financial enterprise worth millions by the end of the eighteenth century.[38] It also represented a huge opportunity for theft and pilferage. In 1711 the Excise, alarmed at widespread pilfering from the docks and quays, appointed their own special constables. These men were paid a salary of 10s a week and gained a bonus of an additional 5s for each criminal they prosecuted to a successful conviction. These 'constables of the quays' often acted from strong financial motives, and quite possibly came to rely upon the prosecution of offenders in order to support themselves and their families.[39] The riverfront was peppered with alehouses and brothels, which served as information centres and employment exchanges as well as entertainment venues. Quayside constables were familiar faces here and were well practised in developing informers to assist in catching and prosecuting felons.[40]

However whilst they sought the co-operation of those working and living close to the docks area, these quayside constables were less keen to co-operate with the other policing elements in existence at the time such as the 'Charlies' hired by merchants to protect their goods. One can speculate that they resented the intrusion of other 'outside' security men on to their 'patch', particularly if it interfered with their own chances of profiting from any rewards (or undermined their own appropriation of their employer's goods). Indeed, some of those working in and around the quays and landing points of the Thames were open to corrupt practice, or at least took the notion of legitimate perquisites to extreme lengths. A publican, who also served as an 'officer of the Custom House' was caught out by an honest carman for his involvement in selling sugar without paying the required duty. In a tale reminiscent of modern tobacco smuggling, the publican was in league with a grocer and two dockyard coopers. All were summoned before the sitting magistrate at Guildhall but there was insufficient evidence to warrant further action. The alderman

> lamented the want of proof to commit the grocer, to whom he administered a reproof, and remarked that it was a long lane which had no turning: he therefore hoped this escape would operate as a warning – With respect to the publican, he should have care to have him deprived of his place in the Custom house, and his license stopped.[41]

In May of the same year another excise officer was prosecuted for taking rum: his excuse was his own drunkenness, which did not go down well with the alderman on duty.[42] Undoubtedly the temptation to filch from the quaysides was great and relatively easy, which is why merchants and others were so keen to protect their investments. However, the lack of professional full-time watchmen on the riverfront probably meant they were fighting a losing battle against determined depredators.

Most dockyard watchmen, men such as William May, probably only operated as part-time police. May stripped tobacco as he watched and others held jobs related to the quays and used watching as a means to supplement their income.[43] The problem of quayside pilfering persisted throughout the eighteenth century and neither the presence of the constables of the quays nor the 'Charlies' seems to have deterred those Londoners who were unable to resist such an abundant array of removable goods. Policing the river represented a serious problem both for the merchants that used the quayside and the City authorities within whose boundaries it lay. Here law enforcement was outside the direct control of City government, being *private* rather than *public* policing. This section of the City was probably not as well policed as some would have liked, and this led to further reform at the turn of the eighteenth century.[44]

The final element in the tripartite system of policing of the City of London was the 'communal' policing of the wards.

Constables and the policing of the City wards

Throughout the eighteenth century there was a clear and certain link between local 'independence' and civic duty. In the absence of professional full-time police, the communities elected or selected individuals to serve in rotation in a number of roles. The underlying principle was that these roles were unpaid, that they were performed by the community and *for* the community. In doing so individuals acted as a 'community of self-governing citizens, who gain[ed] their freedom by engaging in government themselves'.[45] These public servants were expected to be respectable men (women were not deemed suitable for the responsibilities of policing their communities even if they qualified by property ownership), men who had a direct interest in their community and had sufficient social status to place them above those they were to police. This was consistent with a patriarchal society in which the natural leaders of a community policed the morals of its inhabitants to control the spread of vice and corruption, just as the head of a household was expected to supervise and direct the behaviour of his family and other dependants. Thus, in principle all those serving as parish constables in the eighteenth century were expected to be men of some means, independent (in that they served no master) and able to act without prejudice. In reality many of those acting as constables in the English capital were men of much lower social status, having been hired as substitutes or deputies by wealthier men who no longer wished to sign up to this neoclassical notion of civic duty.[46] This is a process of change that others have identified as one of the reasons for the gradual evolution of professional policing in the early nineteenth century.[47]

The 26 wards of the City were subdivided into precincts for the purposes of policing. The householders of each precinct chose one of their number to serve as constable for 12 months.[48] In addition each of the City's wards elected a 'respectable citizen' to serve as Beadle. The Beadle was responsible for setting the nightly watch, supervising the ward constables and ensuring that the streets were cleaned and all 'nuisances' regularly removed. The administrative centre of the ward was the annual Wardmote, where all local officers (beadles, constables, inquest men, street keepers and scavengers) were formally appointed, having been selected from among the inhabitants of the ward at parish or precinct meetings. All these positions were unsalaried and thus, in principle at least, invoked the ideal of civic duty. While constables could claim back their expenses, they were not reimbursed for their time. It is perhaps not surprising that, as elsewhere in the metropolis, many of those elected to serve as constables hired substitutes or deputies to undertake the work for them.

Substitution and the avoidance of serving as constable

All substitutes, and appeals against serving, had to be approved by Common Council and those elected to serve were liable to a fine if they failed to take up their office without finding a substitute. Whilst the Court of Aldermen had the power to excuse individuals from service on grounds of ill-health or ineligibility, it rarely agreed to do so.[49] Indeed, even when what might appear to the modern reader to be quite reasonable grounds were presented the City's governors often rejected them. In 1723 John Dibble pleaded with the Court of Aldermen to be excused service because he was in ill-health and his apprentice had absconded. He set out his dire position in an impassioned appeal: 'I have no body to work but my Self: So being Constable at this time will be the ruin of me and my family'.[50] Similarly William Brown, an impoverished barber, asked to be excused because 'through the decay of trade he does not make on average more than five shillings a day for the maintenance of himself and his family'. Brown was also 'troubled with two Ruptures, for which, he wears a double truss, and which complaint subjects your petitioner to a faintness and weakness so much so that he is frequently obliged to lay down for two or three hours at a time'.[51] Brown appears to have been an entirely unsuitable candidate to have served as an active police agent, a situation that must have been repeated on many occasions. William Payne, by contrast an active and highly motivated constable, also suffered from his civic duties. Soon after his death his widow, Elizabeth, asked Common Council for financial help because his activities had caused his business to suffer, with the result that his son, William junior, 'made only a poor living'.[52]

The records of the City's quarter sessions and Court of Aldermen are liberally interspersed with requests for exception from office or indictments against those refusing to undertake the position of constable.[53] In 1790 four individuals applied to the Court of Aldermen to be relieved of the duty of serving their wards as constables: William Mountain argued that because he owned a property that spanned two wards, Cripplegate and Farringdon, and had served as constable for the former he should be excused. James Hammond wanted to be excused because he only rented a business property in the ward (and therefore did not have a *direct* interest there). Two other men tried to avoid serving by arguing that they had undertaken previous forms of civic service, one as a militiaman and the other as a common councilman. None of these appeals were successful.[54]

The failure of these appeals may well have had as much to do with the desire of the City governors to raise funds as it was to ensure that the principle of collective communal engagement was upheld. Those failing to serve or to provide a deputy in their place were subjected to a fine and the money extracted from those bent on avoiding their civic duty was used to supplement the upkeep of the poor. Indeed it has been suggested that in the first half of the eighteenth century there was a deliberate attempt to put forward richer individuals for the position of constable with the express purpose of raising extra revenue.[55]

Whatever the motivations of the civic authorities, historians have been keen to emphasise the problematic nature of the constable's position.[56] The parish constable from the early modern period onwards was caught between his duty to the state and to his community. Good will and neighbourliness were important and, as constables had to continue to work in the parish in which they served, this restraint upon them should not be underestimated. Many constables were also artisans and risked alienating their customers and losing valuable trade. In 1784, in the ward of Cripplegate Without, the positions of constables were filled by a broker, a baker, a carpenter, chaser, packman and two shoemakers; all trades that were reliant upon customers.[57] It may be correct to note that within the ideal of public service constables would not 'mix with or be an associate of the common people' but in reality it would have been almost impossible to separate the 'public man' from his community; his activities as a constable would therefore have had implications for his business.[58] This would have been in addition to the observation by Daniel Defoe that the duty of constable was one of 'insupportable hardship; it takes up so much of a man's time that his own affairs are frequently totally neglected, too often to his ruin'; a position clearly illustrated by the appeals of John Dibble and William Brown.[59]

The nature of the criminal justice system in the eighteenth century did allow individuals to find other ways to avoid public service as parish constables. Under the terms of an act of William III in 1699 those successfully prosecuting horse thieves to conviction could receive the so-called 'Tyburn ticket' that exempted them from most forms of civic duty. These tickets could also be sold on to others and so had a value in their own right.[60] The issuing of such tickets was a part of the reward system that had come into being to encourage the prosecution of felony.[61] The reward system, much criticised by contemporaries concerned about corruption, undoubtedly led to the development of more targeted crime fighting by those motivated by a desire to earn a living from the successful prosecution of offenders. Some of these reward seekers (such as the notorious 'thief-taker general' Jonathan Wild) were certainly corrupt, but others simply chose to make policing their primary means of employment. Thus, given that substitute constables could expect to be paid in the region of £8–£15 per year by those that they deputised for and were able to earn additional fees and rewards for their policing activities, it is unsurprising that many individuals chose to serve in this way.[62] Some commentators felt that the use of substitutes undermined the principle of a 'community of self-governing citizens'. The magistrate and pamphlet writer Patrick Colquhoun was scathing about the use of substitutes.[63] He objected on the grounds that substitution produced constables who were less diligent in their duties and who were open to corruption; 'It is of the highest importance that an Office invested with so much power should be executed by reputable men, if possible of pure morals, and not with hands open to receive bribes' he thundered.[64] However, Colquhoun was trying to hold back a tide that had already begun to erode this principled position. In the City of London substitution was widespread with over half of all constables being substitutes.[65] Many of those serving for other men did so over a number of years and, given the stipulation that their appointment had to meet with the approval of the lord mayor and the Court of Aldermen, this suggests that broadly speaking the wards were happy with this situation.

It is possible to explore this situation more deeply by analysing the returns sent to the lord mayor by the wardmotes of the City in the last quarter of the eighteenth century.[66] Of the 244 constables named on the returns for 1784 over half (131) were serving as substitutes for other men. Not only this, but if we look across the period 1783–86 it becomes evident that the same names appear again and again. For example, three men – Thomas Wood, Thomas Perkins and Seth Clinton – acted as paid substitutes with the ward of Langbourn, each time deputising for different ward members. Five others substituted for 3 years in succession and two others for 2 years. No one elected as constable for Langbourn actually fulfilled his civic responsibility in 1784 and Langbourn is by no means exceptional. In the smallest ward, Bassishaw, James Prior substituted for three different individuals between 1783 and 1785 and in Tower ward William How did likewise, with four others substituting for 3 years in a row. Between 1771 and 1789 more than half of all those who filled the position of constable were deputising for someone unwilling to take on the role themselves.[67]

The extent of substitution is neatly illustrated by Table 3.1 below:

Table 3.1 Substitute constables for all City wards who served at least twice in their chosen ward, 1771–89

Number of Years Service	Number of Constables
Two Years	103
Three Years	59
Four Years	30
Five Years	26
Six Years	18
Seven Years	8
Eight Years	1
Nine Years	1
Ten Years	1

Source: Wardmotes 1771–1812.[68]

Clearly substitution was a regular practice in the City and it was not uncommon for substitutes to serve more than once. Individuals who deputised over a period of years would have built up a considerable experience of policing. They would have had the opportunity to familiarise themselves with the inhabitants of their area, to identify criminal elements – the local prostitutes, drunks, beggars and vagrants and other potential 'troublemakers' – in much the same way that professional policemen were to do in the nineteenth century. They would have been familiar to local innkeepers, traders and residents who would have known where to find them if they needed them. Naturally it is possible that such familiarity bred contempt or facilitated bribery or the abuse of power, as Colquhoun had warned. However, the reselection of these men at the Wardmote would also suggest that a degree of confidence and trust rested in them.

Bryan Chandler served Aldersgate ward as a substitute constable for every year between 1776 and 1785, an unbroken run of 10 years. In Billingsgate Benjamin Lepine appears in the returns for 1776 and 1777 but not again until 1784. He served in 1785 and 1789. This may simply reveal gaps in the records or inaccuracies in the returns but it may also mean something else. It is possible that Lepine used policing as a supplement to his main occupation or turned to policing when work was scarce. Stephen Wallinger served as a substitute for Broad Street ward between 1783 and 1789 by which time his fellow citizens had chosen him to take on the role of beadle, demonstrating that he was seen as a capable and 'respectable' individual. Finally, Edward Burton served as a constable in Cripplegate from 1783 to 1795. During that time we would expect him to have developed a good knowledge of his area, and to have been well respected in his position to be continually accepted by the ward.[69] It is therefore reasonable to view these as examples of experienced men, serving their communities and holding the respect and confidence of the inhabitants.

As we saw from the examples of Dibble and Brown and others who appealed against their election, not everyone could afford to pay some-one else to serve in their stead. Elaine Reynolds has questioned how widespread the practice of substitution was in Westminster, given the costs involved.[70] However, it may be that the relative wealth of the City's population or the willingness of men to serve as constables allowed sub-stitution to become more widespread than elsewhere in the metropolis. It seems plausible, given the numbers of substitutes that operated there, that in the City those wishing to avoid serving as constables could do so by hiring willing substitutes and that these substitutes were able to make a decent living from fees and the rewards system that accompanied the policing of their communities. In order to determine whether serving as a substitute constable was a viable occupation in itself we need to con-sider the sort of money that these individuals could earn in a year and compare this to average wages in London at this time.

In the period 1780–90 carpenters were paid an average wage of 19s a week or £49.4s a year if they were in regular work. Bricklayers earned slightly less, about 18s a week, while bricklayers' labourers were paid just 12s a week, amounting to £31.2s a year. However, all wages in London fluctuated throughout the eighteenth century, affected by trade cycles and war.[71] Coal-heavers were paid 10s a week during the Napoleonic wars while at the end of the conflict an 'ordinary labourer' could take home 18s for a week's work.[72] This was dependent, of course, on these workers being able to secure a regular job or waged labour, something that was by no means guaranteed.

By contrast those who worked as constables on the quays were paid 10s a week which, while it only amounted to £26 annually, could be supplemented by fees of 5s for each successful prosecution.[73] If they only managed two prosecutions a week this would have doubled their salary and made them better off than carpenters. Since men like William May (whom we met earlier 'watching' while he stripped tobacco) may have acted as quayside constables on a part-time basis, their salary from policing was merely a part of their annual income. Likewise it is diffi-cult to place too much emphasis on wage rates as those working in the building trades would have been subject to periods of unemployment or underemployment when they may have turned to some other form of work to avoid slipping into debt or poverty.[74] Therefore one of the advantages of acting as a paid-law enforcement officer (either as a substitute ward constable or as a private constable on the quays) may well have been the guaranteed income, however small, it brought in.

In addition to the fees for prosecuting that constables received there were fees to be gained for prosecuting specific offences (such as vagrancy) and substitutes were entitled to an annual fee which varied from ward to ward but could be somewhere between £10 and £20 per year.[75] It is therefore possible that being a constable, was, if not a lucrative occupation, at least a viable alternative to other forms of semi-skilled or unskilled work. It was steady work and as such may well have appeared attractive to London's male population. The notion of unpaid amateur policing in the late eighteenth century is therefore in need of some reassessment. Substitutes were not salaried policemen (at least not in the modern sense) but they may well have viewed themselves as such. They were at the call of their community, they were paid for a number of activities that would become the job of the 'new' police, and they were well placed to earn rewards offered by the criminal justice system. Substitute constables therefore represent an historical bridge between a parochial constabulary and nineteenth-century professionals.

So far I have outlined the structure of policing in the City in the late eighteenth century. A tripartite system was in place, which owed its underlying principle to long-held notions of communal self-government. However, this principle was being eroded throughout the eighteenth century, within London and outside London. We can see in the example of the City an overlapping combination of public, private and community policing that was gradually evolving into what we might term a more 'modern' professional police force. At this point we need to return to the question of whether this tripartite system represented an effective system of crime fighting and prevention. This is not an easy task to achieve but by looking at two key factors we can at least make an attempt at it. First the role and duties of these various policing agents need to be established. What is it that these men did? Were they proactively fighting crime and catching criminals, or were they predominantly there to assist victims in the prosecution process? What about their role in controlling morality and vice in their communities, did they act purely on instruction or were some of them imbued with a sense of righteous indignation at the immoralities of their fellow citizens? Simply put, how did these men carry out their duties and how closely do their activities resemble those of the professionals that ultimately replaced them? Second we need to have some idea of how many patrols, constables and watchmen served the City in this period and how this compares with the numbers of police after 1829. This chapter will now go on to assess both these important questions.

The role and duties of the police of the City

The primary duty of the parish or ward constable was to keep the peace, they were therefore 'peace officers'.[76] They could be called upon by individual members of their community to assist them (in making an arrest or in serving a warrant, for example). They could also act independently against certain types of offender. Indeed it was their duty to arrest vagrants and the 'idle and disorderly' as well as those working on Sundays, along with anyone that infringed the licensing laws or who breached economic or social regulations concerning the maintenance of the highways, buildings, swearing and the market place.[77] Watchmen could also stop and search anyone they found out on the streets between sunset and sunrise who could not give a good account of themselves. There are numerous examples of this activity in the minute books and newspapers.

In October 1789 George Marr was arrested by constable Leman Caseby for being a 'loose, idle and disorderly person wandering abroad in the open air and having no visible way of living.' Marr was sent to Bridewell for 10 days and ordered to be passed from the parish on his release.[78] Catherine Thompson suffered a similar fate when she was brought in by John Clarke for 'behaving riotously on the Sabbath and misbehaving herself in the time of the divine service'.[79] The vagrancy act was a wide ranging piece of legislation that could entrap (amongst others) beggars, tramps, peddlers, travelling players, minstrels, jugglers, quack doctors, runaway husbands and gypsies. After 1784 this legislation was extended to allow the arrest of anyone who was believed to be about to commit an offence by defining those persons who could be viewed as suspicious – for example, someone in the possession of a picklock or crowbar – as a 'rogue and vagabond.'[80] This 'stop and search' legislation effectively allowed the watch, patrols and constables of the City license to question anyone they held suspicions about. Given that constables were entitled to a 10s reward for the successful prosecutions of such 'rogues' (and could be fined the equivalent if they neglected this duty) anyone sleeping rough, begging, soliciting or hawking in eighteenth-century London risked being arrested and sentenced to a short period of correctional imprisonment in Bridewell.[81]

However financial recompense (and the fear of being fined) was just one motivating factor behind the actions of City constables. William

Payne, who was a prominent participant in the Gordon riots despite his position as a City constable, was also a member of the Reformation of Manners movement.[82] His determined campaign to rid the City streets of prostitutes is entirely consistent with his membership of that movement (and we shall encounter the aptly named Payne again later in this study).[83] Other constables may have held similar strong personal views that influenced their approach to their duties. However, the motivations of policing agents are not always easy to determine from the brief notes that constitute many of the entries in the court minute books. If we wish to understand how these individuals acted it is necessary to supplement our evidence by using additional qualitative sources such as the trial reports from the Old Bailey and the many London newspapers of the period. By looking at the actions of constables, patrols, watchmen and others it is possible to discover where these men were and what they were doing. We can also consider whether they were proactive in their duties or were merely reacting to requests for help from the public or others.[84] These findings give some indication of the different roles of these early City policing agents as well as the way in which the different branches of the watching networks supported each other in attempting to keep the peace and reduce crime and criminality. Thus it is possible to argue in support of recent historiography that in the City of London policing was neither as rudimentary nor as inefficient as contemporary critics suggested, and to support work that has argued that, for certain offences at least, the state – through its officials – was much more involved in the prosecution of property crime than was previously believed.[85]

Table 3.2 Descriptors of 'police' appearing before Old Bailey, City of London juries, 1779–1820

Descriptor	Number	Percentage
Constable	277	67.7
Watchman	61	14.9
Patrol	26	6.35
Constable of the Night	13	3.17
Marshalman	10	2.4
Watchman on Quay/Merchant's Watchman	9	2.2
Constable on Quay/Custom House. Constable	7	1.7
Extra Constable	3	0.7
Street Keeper	2	0.4
Market Constable	1	0.2
Total	409	

Source: The Old Bailey Proceedings Online.[86]

The diversity of descriptors in Table 3.2 demonstrates the different types of police agents operating within the City.[87] Unsurprisingly constables and watchmen dominate the results as the most commonly used terms. 'Patrol' – more properly the City Patrol – represents the public policing system discussed earlier, which was separate from the wards, but as will be seen, worked closely with the watchmen. On the quays private watchmen served the merchants and East India Company while the customs and excise employed their own watchmen and constables to police the Thames.[88] The proliferation of constables at the courts illustrates the crucial role that ward constables played in bringing offenders before the courts once they had been arrested. Each of the City's watch houses had a constable on duty at night, whose role was to take charge of and question those suspects brought in by watchmen. Furthermore, nearly all those taken before the magistracy were accompanied by a named ward constable. Evidently the ward constables had an important function within the City's justicing system. By contrast the City's watchmen had set rounds, or beats, and once they had arrested a suspect and taken him or her to the watch house they would have returned to their box to continue their rounds. These differences in part explain the disproportionate number of constables in the records of Old Bailey trials. So where were these various police agents when the crimes under investigation at Old Bailey were committed and what were they doing? By using the testimony of these individuals it is possible to arrive at some interesting analysis.

Even a cursory reading of the newspapers in the period reveals that the constables and watchmen of the City carried out their duties with a varying degree of dedication and success. Some merely reacted to situations or individual requests for help, while others were much more proactive and investigative, and some clearly fell well short of what contemporaries felt was their duty. The majority of watchmen and other police agents were on the streets (or at least insisted in court that they were), which is where they were expected to be. Once again this is hardly surprising, especially given the frequency of critical contemporary newspaper reports that suggested that watchmen were absent from their posts as burglaries were taking place. Others declared that they were 'beating their round', 'on my round', 'on duty' or 'calling the hour' as justification of their actions and proof that they were where they should be. Readers familiar with the reformed Police created in 1829 will recognise that the policing agents giving evidence at the Old Bailey were performing very similar duties to those of Peel's professionals in the nineteenth century, suggesting once more, continuity in policing practice.

George Shirley aroused the suspicion of Edward Chapman as he was on his way to Leadenhall Market.[89] Shirley was carrying a large cut of beef and there was something about his manner or appearance that concerned him. As he walked in the direction that Shirley had come from Chapman soon bumped into an acquaintance, William Cook, a butcher's servant, who was unloading a delivery cart. Chapman asked if he had missed anything. Cook soon realised that he had lost some meat and the two men chased after Shirley and made him return to the butcher's house where the meat was identified. Presumably aware that he was now in serious trouble Shirley claimed that he had found his prize behind a water pump and was merely taking it to Whitechapel to find its owner. A constable was called and Shirley was taken into custody to appear at the summary courts the next day. This demonstrates one of the roles of ward constables: to assist victims of crime in their attempts to arrest and bring to justice those that robbed or in other ways offended against them. Policing agents were not always available or so willing to help. Indeed, one correspondent to the press (who signed himself 'Castigator') noted that watchmen were ill-equipped to deal with determined, and often armed, robbers:

> I think watchmen perfectly justified in avoiding as they possibly can to encounter housebreakers. It is ridiculous to suppose one or two such beings can contend with those that are better fed, better taught, and better armed than themselves, and have besides a desperate cause to support, [this latter presumably being their freedom and indeed their lives].[90]

Given that there are several reports of watchmen being threatened, shot at or even killed by armed criminals resisting arrest it is clear that this was dangerous work. However, this did not deter some from 'doing their duty'. Across the metropolis a watchman was shot through the thigh while attempting to arrest a burglar but managed to call for help and catch the thief who was taken before Sir John Fielding at Bow Street.[91]

The constable of Candlewick ward, John Ellis, arrested Patrick Egan because he became suspicious of him when he found him trying to sell a roll of cloth to a Jewish trader.[92] He questioned Egan who told him that he had been given half a crown to carry the goods to the trader and sell them but was unable to identify the man who had charged him with this task. Ellis arrested him and took him before the lord mayor, who demanded clarification of Egan's story and committed him to the Poultry compter in the meantime. Ellis' suspicions seem to have been well founded for when Egan was re-examined it transpired that he had left his previous job at a dyer's just three months earlier, after which his employer had missed a quantity of cloth. Egan, alias McGrab, was committed for trial at the Old Bailey and transported for seven years.[93] Constable Ellis had acted as one would expect an alert policeman to in preventing a crime in his community and was not merely reacting to a request for help from a prosecutor. The example of Joseph Gabitas also shows a constable who clearly knew his community well. Gabitas went to the scene of a disturbance where Benjamin Solomon had attacked and knocked down Elizabeth Carpenter.[94] Gabitas knew Solomon well, and knowing that he was a troublesome character with a violent reputation he arrested him for the assault.

We might also point to the swift actions of watchmen and others who prevented break-ins and fires (a real concern for the communities of London) as evidence of efficient localised policing. A watchmen patrolling near Fleet Market noticed a burglar enter the house of a glover and quietly alerted the householders who saw off the thieves; another equally alert watchman discovered a lighted torch that had been thrown on to the roof of a public house and 'immediately alarmed the family, or probably the whole neighbourhood would soon have been in a general conflagration'.[95] Evidently while some watchmen dozed in their stands or refused to come to the assistance of victims of crime, others risked their lives and saved others by their prompt and occasionally heroic actions. Ward constables similarly acted in a variety of ways, some merely reactive – doing the minimum required to discharge their civic duty – while others used their experience and knowledge of their communities to act as determined crime fighters.

These variations in levels of activity might have been affected by age, health and other personal commitments (such as work or family) or they may well be closely related to the position of the individual within the community. Substitute constables, who were likely to have been of lower status (since they seem to have been quite willing to take on the burden of office for a financial recompense) may well have made more active policemen, especially in the prosecution of vagrants, beggars and other 'street' offenders. Watchmen, because they were usually on the streets, were more likely to encounter suspicious characters at night. Ward constables were more frequently involved in the prosecution of these offenders at the summary courts and above, because they would have been called in to assist citizen arrests and to bring along offenders swept up into the compters and watch houses by the trawling of the patrols and watch overnight.

The action of these men does, however, point to a functioning and broadly effective policing network that operated across the City. In order to try and establish the efficacy of the City's policing networks it is necessary also to determine how many men served as policing agents. This will help to indicate the depth and breadth of policing in the square mile in this period.

Levels of policing: The number of policing agents in the City 1776–1818

If the eighteenth-century press reports of crime are to be believed there was a dearth of police across the capital and this situation was the cause of much of the lawlessness and property crime that occurred. Thus, in 1770 the *Middlesex Journal* reported the highway robbery of a gentleman in St. Paul's Churchyard and lamented the fact that 'there was only one watchman on that side of the church from Cheapside to Ludgate Street.'[96] In 1790 *Lloyd's Evening Post* complained that despite a watchman's stand being 'within three yards of [the] door' a pastry cook's shop, also in St. Paul's Churchyard, had been plundered of 'money and plate to the value of £150'.[97] Naturally we should be cautious of evidence from the newspapers, especially as the press has a long history of twisting the reporting of crime to fit its own agendas.[98] While the second report reflected a view that the watch, in particular, was fairly ineffectual if not corrupt and useless the first comment revises the age-old complaint that there are not enough police to deter and catch criminals. Fortunately we can be fairly sure of the numbers of constables, substitutes and extra constables and watchmen operating in the City in the late eighteenth and early nineteenth centuries because a variety of records survive for this period.

Let us consider the levels of constables, substitutes and extras for the time being before returning to the numbers of watchmen, patrols and others later. At the annual Wardmote local officers recorded the names of those elected to serve in the various civic positions. These returns were then passed onto the lord mayor for approval. Therefore we can use these records to count levels of constables in the City wards. Alongside the wardmote returns we also have the evidence presented to the select committee of the House of Commons in 1818 in its investigation of law and order in the metropolis.

Table 3.3   Distribution of constables, substitutes and extras by ward, 1771–89[99]

Ward	Constables	Substitutes	Extras	Total
Aldersgate	3	4	0	7
Aldgate	3	3	3	9
Bassishaw	0	2	0	2
Billingsgate	6	4	0	10
Bishopsgate	2	5	3	10
Bread Street	5	7	0	12
Bridge	5	7	0	12
Broad Street	2	8	0	10
Candlewick	3	4	0	7
Castle Baynard	4	5	3	12
Cheap	2	9	0	11
Coleman Street	2	4	0	6
Cordwainer	4	4	0	8
Cornhill	1	3	0	4
Cripplegate	9	7	2	18
Dowgate	4	4	0	8
Farringdon Within	4	11	1	16
Farringdon Without	10	5	1	16
Langbourn	3	9	1	13
Lime Street	1	3	0	4
Portsoken	2	3	1	6
Queenhithe	4	5	0	9
Tower	5	7	0	12
Vintry	4	5	0	9
Walbrook	3	4	0	7
Total	91	132	15	238
Average Per Ward	3.64	5.28	0.6	9.52

Source: Wardmote Papers 1771–1812.

Table 3.3 reveals that in the period 1771–89 there were, on average, 238 constables operating throughout the City wards in any one year. Given that the City of London's population in this period was approximately 82,500 each constable nominally served 347 persons.[100] This is a relatively high ratio of constables per head of population, representing less than one person a day for a year of service. However, the number of constables, substitutes and extras serving in each ward varied considerably. While there were 24 in Cripplegate in 1785 the ward of Bassishaw returned only three. Partly this was because of the differing size of the City wards and the number of precincts they included (since each precinct chose one constable to serve). This force of 238 men is almost identical to Beattie's findings for the earlier period.[101] Thus it would seem that the numbers of constables present in the wards were stable and consistent across the eighteenth century. The effectiveness of this force can, in part, be assessed by determining how stretched it was. The actual distribution of constables varied between the wards as can be seen by reference to Table 3.4.

Table 3.4 Distribution of constables by ward in the City of London, 1771–89

Ward	Precincts[102]	Parishes	Constables	Houses[103]	Houses per constable
Aldersgate	8	6	7	1035	148
Aldgate	7	4	9	1089	121
Bassishaw	2	1	2	142	71
Billingsgate	9	5	10	398	40
Bishopsgate	7	3	10	2038	204
Bread Street	13	4	12	331	28
Bridge	14	3	12	385	32
Broad Street	10	6	10	785	79
Candlewick	7	5	7	286	41
Castle Baynard	10	4	12	784	65
Cheap	9	7	11	367	33
Coleman Street	6	3	6	611	102
Cordwainer	8	3	8	367	46
Cornhill	4	2	4	180	46
Cripplegate	13	6	18	1894	105
Dowgate	8	2	8	369	46
Farringdon W/I	16	10	16	1368	86
Farringdon W/O	18	7	16	4278	267
Langbourn	12	7	13	530	41
Lime Street	4	2	4	209	52
Portsoken	5	3	6	1385	231
Queenhithe	9	8	9	488	54
Tower	10	4	12	782	65
Vintry	9	4	9	418	46
Walbrook	7	5	7	293	42
Total	225	114	238	21625	91

Sources: of Common Council 1663, C.L.R.O: Alchin MSS, E/57, C.L.R.O. Wardmote Present-ments 1680–1853; C.L.R.O. 266B Box 2 Wardmote Papers 1771–1812, and J. Smart, *A Short Account of Several Wards, Precincts, Parishes, etc. in London* (1741) as used in Beattie, *Policing* Table 4.2 p. 195.

Table 3.4 shows that, on average, each constable's 'patch' was approx-imately 91 houses. However, there was a considerable discrepancy between the best-served wards of Cornhill and Bread Street and the worst, Farringdon Without. It would have been much easier to find a constable to respond to your problem if you lived in one of the 'inner' City wards such as Bread Street or Cheap than it was in the outlying wards of Bishopsgate or Cripplegate. The numbers of constables serving Aldersgate, Bishopsgate, Cripplegate and Portsoken had increased by the last third of the century. By this period there were more constables per household in these larger outer wards, perhaps in response to a fear of rising crime from the expanding metropolis outside the City's boundaries or indeed to the catastrophic impact of the Gordon riots in 1780.[104]

The population of the City was in decline throughout the eighteenth century. By 1795 there were just 13,921 houses in the City.[105] This represents a fall of one third in household numbers, which, if accurate, means that the numbers of houses for which each constable would have been responsible would be significantly reduced. It would also create a smaller pool of individuals from which to select the constables as the century progressed, perhaps increasing the reliance upon substitutes and the recruitment of extras (and a concomitant move towards professional policing). Both these points have implications for our understanding of policing in the City. If there were proportionally more constables per head of population at the end of the eighteenth century this might explain the contemporary opinion that the corporation was well policed, at least in terms of coverage. Secondly if the wards increasingly relied upon substitutes then the pool of experienced policing agents is likely to have grown, further enhancing a view that this was a semi-professional organisation.

The wards could also appoint 'extra constables' to deal with a variety of problems. After 1737 all the watchmen of the City were sworn as 'extras', as were all beadles after 1763.[106] Extra constables were partly useful to the wards because, as Harris has suggested, it allowed them 'to tailor local policing to the ward's particular concerns, without obliging inhabitants to carry the permanent burden of another ward constable.'[107] The beadle, as a long serving and unpaid servant of the community, represented a cost-effective addition to local policing.[108] Some of these extra constables were sworn in for special occasions or particular purposes, such as Lord Mayor's Day or the Sessions, executions and the reading of the lottery.[109] Given that there was no provision to increase the number of ward constables, the City marshals appear to have used the appointment of 'extras' as a way to increase 'police' numbers.

The Wardmote returns are fairly unhelpful in determining why certain wards had more constables than others but we may reasonably speculate about the presence of particular factors. Firstly the proximity of some wards to the river Thames, with its opportunities for pilferage and theft, might indicate that levels of crime were likely to be higher. Similarly, those wards that bordered the wider metropolis of London may have been, or may have viewed themselves as, more exposed to crime and disorder. Nine of the City's wards had embankments on the Thames, and all of these wards had at least nine constables operating within them.[110] The great market of Billingsgate, the old London Bridge, Customs House and Bridewell were all situated within these riverside wards. They all posed problems for policing that were additional to the pilfering that was prevalent on the quays. Seven wards shared borders with greater London, notably Farringdon Without, Cripplegate, Bishopsgate and Portsoken, and all list larger numbers of constables.[111] Cripplegate had 18 constables on average, which reflects the need to protect property in a ward that was adjacent to the wider metropolis and one that contained a larger proportion of the City's poorer inhabitants. In the centre of the City lay several much smaller wards, Bread Street, Cheap, Cordwainer, Walbrook, Langbourn, Lime Street and Bassishaw, which had quite different levels of policing. Cheap and Bread Street had 11 and 12 constables respectively, while Bassishaw had only two and Lime Street just four. Cheap and Bread Street contained more domestic housing, and so more individuals that were liable to serve as constables, while Bassishaw and Lime Street were business areas rather than residential ones.

The 1818 Parliamentary survey showed that there had been some adjustment in the exact distribution of constables throughout the wards but the pattern was broadly similar. The two Farringdon wards and Cripplegate still had the most constables as might be expected given that they were the largest wards. Overall levels of policing are much the same as before with 240 regular constables. However, there were more than twice as many extras by the early nineteenth century (39 in 1818 as opposed to 15 for the earlier period), but given that this figure includes an extra five from Aldgate (who were selected particularly to represent the City's central synagogue in Bevis Marks) the increase is not dramatic in a period of heightened concern about law and order.

Throughout the eighteenth century the system of community policing in the wards relied upon the constables whose numbers remained fairly static although there was some increase in the numbers of extra constables who were often recruited for specific events but afterwards retained. This suggests to me that the community was generally happy with the level and cost of ward policing and saw no particular reason for reform, a situation repeated in the 1830s, while the evidence shows that local magistrates were at best lukewarm about police reform. This point is perhaps more clearly emphasised if we look at the numbers of men serving in the watch during this period, which will provide a more comprehensive picture of policing in the City.

Beattie calculated that there were 672 watchmen in 1737, Rumbelow noted that there were 736 watchmen employed in 1775 and Patrick Colquhoun estimated that there were 765 by 1806.[112] Andrew Harris has noted the flexibility of the watch and its ability to expand when necessary.[113] According to the official report of the 1818 committee there were at least 570 watchmen employed across the City plus around 20 or more additional supporting officers, a body of over 600. With a further 72 patrolmen and 29 reserves this meant that some 700 men were employed daily in policing duties. The City therefore would seem to have had an estimated force of 650–800 watchmen and about 250 constables during our period, meaning that overall the wards were policed by approximately 1000 men serving a resident population of about 82,500: a ratio of one 'officer' for every 80–90 persons. Naturally the City's population was swelled by large numbers of workers coming into the City during the day but this still represents an impressive ratio of police to population. In 1839 the 'new' City police numbered just 500 men (although the population was less by then) and the Peelers in the wider metropolis after 1830 each served over 300 persons.[114]

This detailed analysis of the numbers of policing agents deployed in the City demonstrates that London was far from being *unpoliced* before the arrival of professionals. In terms of distribution and numbers the City seems to have employed a large body of men for the purposes of policing. Indeed when the new police arrived outside the City borders the proportion of those actually patrolling the streets was greatly reduced.[115] So it would seem that simply in terms of numbers the old City constabulary, watch and patrol network that existed throughout the Hanoverian period was considerably larger than the professional force that replaced it.

Concluding remarks

Clearly we can no longer accept that proper and effective policing began in the early nineteenth century. Certainly Peel's reforms helped to give a definite structure to the policing system. But this was a system that had been evolving over a long period. Changes in policing and prosecution were happening in advance of legislation as Reynolds has shown.[116] Gradual change was also occurring in the City with small increases in the numbers of policing agents. The flexibility of the system of policing meant that extra constables could be deployed when and where necessary. The structure of City government from parish, through ward to Aldermanic court and the lord mayor allowed for a multi-layered and supervised system of policing, in both an eighteenth-century and modern understanding of the word 'police'.

Importantly the experience of the City also allows a challenge to be made to those that see increased policing as the inevitable response to urbanisation and population growth. As Harris argues;

> The City of London, while creating some new and more aggressive forms of policing before many other parts of England, underwent neither rapid industrial change nor population growth in the early nineteenth century.[117]

Neither did it experience the rampant urbanisation that characterised many areas of eighteenth and early nineteenth-century England. The City's policing was a 'dynamic' system that evolved in response to the needs of its inhabitants.[118] The combination of day and night watches, constables and beadles, and Marshalmen provided a seemingly adequate level of security for the City's inhabitants. This may well have been insufficient to deal with outbreaks of unprecedented disorder such as the rioting of 1780, or indeed capable of halting all depredations from the river trade, but even modern police forces struggle to prevent all criminal activity or to deal with sporadic rioting. It is perhaps accurate to see the level of policing in the eighteenth-century City as better than that in the greater metropolis or the country as a whole.

In Westminster opponents of the existing system complained that,

> The present establishment [of police in Westminster] for the protection of our houses from nightly depredation, is now become, not a security, but a public imposition; to be obliged to pay a quarterly rate for supporting a feeble old fellow, who thinks it sufficient to disturb your rest, by croaking out the hour of the night in a lamentable, unintelligible voice, is one of the numerous absurdities, to which John Bull submits with his usual Patience and Folly.[119]

The men who served as constables and watchmen in the City were a mixture of those fulfilling, perhaps grudgingly, their civic duty and others who carried out their duties with care and due diligence. Many of these individuals, notably those serving as constables in the wards

and on the quays, may well have had other jobs but knew that policing was a regular employer and as such it represented a viable means
of earning a living. The majority of substitute constables were regulars,
holding their positions for several years, some in excess of a decade. The
evidence from the City minute books and the Old Bailey Proceedings
also supports recent research that has attempted to undermine the long-
held viewpoint that in England prosecution was, unlike many states
elsewhere, simply the preserve of the victim of crime.[120] In the City, as
elsewhere in London, constables, patrols and watchmen were detecting
crime, arresting suspects and prosecuting them through the summary
courts.

These men represent an evolutionary bridge between the old
parochial system of rate-paying constables and the salaried ranks of the
Metropolitan police. Therefore, the experience of the City supports the
findings of Paley who argues that it 'is highly unlikely that the new
police really were more efficient than the old' when we consider either
numbers of men employed or how they operated.[121] The City possessed
an integrated, tripartite system of policing that was flexible, respon-
sive and answerable to local, public, private and community bodies.
A fierce critic of the capital's policing system, John Wade, noted in
1829 that, 'Though the police of the City is better conducted than in
any other division of the Metropolis, it is neither pure nor perfect.'[122]
It was certainly not perfect but, perhaps due to the peculiar nature
of City government, it was in many ways better than the system that
operated outside of the square mile. The actions of the various policing
agents resulted in prosecutions before the summary courts. Constables,
watchmen and patrols all appeared before the justices as witnesses,
prosecutors, guards and, occasionally, defendants: their duties were
interlinked to the workings of the summary courts. This will be clearly
demonstrated as we consider the operation of the courts in relation to
property crime, interpersonal violence and the regulation of other types
of illegal and immoral behaviour. Prosecution *was* a personal business
in the eighteenth century but City policing agents played an important
role in assisting and, in some instances, directing this process.

4
Property Offending in the City of London

At half past eight on an April evening in 1784 Samuel West was walking in the east of the City of London, close to the borders of Whitechapel. As he turned to a corner a man armed with a drawn sword confronted him and demanded his money. As West pleaded for his life two other robbers came up and rifled his pockets, removing his gold watch, chain and carnelian seal. West called for help, and a nearby patrolman – James Gabetus – arrived as the gang attempted to escape. After a desperate struggle, which required the help of several policing agents, two members of the gang were arrested. They appeared before the alderman at Guildhall and were committed to take their trial at Old Bailey. On the 21 April Joseph Hawes and James Hawkins were found guilty of highway robbery and were sentenced to death.[1] This case and its outcome conform to a widely held view of the eighteenth-century criminal justice system. The courts were concerned with property crime and the archetypal offender in this period was the highway robber. The fate that awaited those highwaymen that were unfortunate enough to be caught was death, and so determined attempts to resist arrest were common. However this view can obfuscate the reality of most property crime in the Hanoverian period. Many thieves avoided 'dancing the Tyburn gig' and most property crime never reached a jury trial at all.[2] A concentration on the trials conducted at Old Bailey, and the executions of felons at Tyburn and outside the debtor's door of Newgate, has in some ways created a false impression of property offending and its prosecution in the long eighteenth century.

A careful analysis of the minute books from the Guildhall and Mansion House justicing rooms reveals that the summary courts of the City of London were regularly used for the examination of trivial and serious property offenders. While the majority of individuals were accused of stealing relatively paltry amounts, a great deal of this appropriation *could* have been indicted as felony. Although it has been argued that justices of the peace 'had no power to dismiss felony charges for insufficiency of the evidence', this seems to be exactly what the City aldermen were doing.[3] They used their discretion to discharge some defendants who could have been sent on for jury trial, while imprisoning others summarily for short periods in the City gaols. This had the result of removing considerable numbers of property offenders from the criminal justice system at a very early stage. This has important implications for our understanding of the judicial process since most studies of property crime have focussed on the courts of assize and quarter session and the rituals of the adversarial jury trial that occurred there. If in fact most potentially indictable crime was dealt with at summary level then historians may need to re-orient the direction of their research if they wish to fully comprehend the nature of crime and prosecution in the late eighteenth century.

This chapter will explore the nature and amount of property offending that came before the summary courts and analyse the ways in which the justices dealt with it. One aspect of this understanding is the importance of gender and its affect upon decision-making. This chapter will confirm that women were far less likely to be prosecuted for theft (even for petty theft) than men during this period. It will also suggest that, in the City, magistrates were much less inclined to commit female offenders for jury trial at Old Bailey.

Number and gender of offenders

The eighteenth-century criminal justice system was concerned with the protection of private property. From 1688 to 1820 the number of offences that carried the death penalty grew from around 50 to more than 200, and almost 'all of them concerned offences against property'.[4] Between January 1750 and December 1800, 95 per cent of the trials at the Old Bailey related to property crime.[5] However, a great deal of property offending was prosecuted at a lower level than this, much of it at summary level.[6]

Table 4.1 represents just over a year's business at the Guildhall and Mansion House justice rooms.[7] In that time these courts heard 859 prosecutions for a variety of property-related offences. The figures shown are drawn from a sample of justice room minute books from the City's two courts.[8] The 859 cases of property crime they reveal underestimate the real figure of prosecution across this period. This is because the data is

Table 4.1 Statistical analysis of property offenders before the City
justice rooms, c.1784–96

Offence	Male	Female	Total
Theft	265	73	338
Suspected felonies	210	50	260
Common pilfering	121	19	140
Fraud	24	6	30
Picking pockets	8	3	11
Burglary/Robbery	12	4	16
Forgery	19	6	25
Pawning	7	12	19
Uttering/Coining	3	4	7
Embezzling	5	0	5
Receiving	6	2	8
Totals	680(79%)	179(21%)	859

Source: The minute books of the Guildhall and Mansion House justice rooms.

drawn from two overlapping periods where there are records for both
courts but also from three periods (between 1793 and 1796) when only
the Guildhall justice room's minutes are available. The corresponding
period for the Mansion House would increase this sample by at least
150–200 cases.[9] Therefore, an estimated 1000 property offenders were
brought before the City magistrates annually in the late eighteenth
century. How does this compare with prosecutions at the Old Bailey?

Table 4.2 Property cases heard by the London jury at Old
Bailey, 1784–96

Offence	Male	Female	Total
Theft	260	59	319
Theft with violence	16	1	17
Forgery	10	1	11
Fraud	10	2	12
Coining	5	1	6
Totals	301(82.5%)	64(17.5%)	365

Source: The Old Bailey Proceedings Online.[10]

In 14 sessions the London jury at the Old Bailey dealt with 365 'found'
indictments to which should be added 53 others to allow for cases
thrown out by the Grand Jury, making a total of 418.[11] The Old

Bailey dealt with fewer than 250 property accusations for the City in a 12-month period.[12] Thus more than four times as many property offenders were being processed by the summary courts as were prosecuted at Old Bailey.

This can be explained in part by their role and function as pre-trial hearings for a variety of offences, and I shall return to this later. What is very clear from Table 4.1 is that the summary courts were extensively used by Londoners to prosecute offenders for theft or suspicion of theft. Given that property crime dominated the criminal justice system in this period this again emphasises the importance of the summary courts to any understanding of that system.

The majority of those appearing as defendants at the summary courts were men. In London, as elsewhere in this period, men were much more likely to be prosecuted for theft than women.[13] In Tables 4.1 and 4.2 women account for just 21 and 17.5 per cent of the accused respectively, and these figures are slightly lower than the roughly 24–25 per cent prosecuted at the Surrey assizes between 1660 and 1800, or the north east circuit in a similar period.[14] Moreover, in certain sorts of property crime the percentage of male defendants rose even higher, to 93.5 per cent for robbery and 87 per cent for burglary.[15]

Prosecutors in property offences

Victims of property crime regularly appeared before the magistracy to report incidents of theft, missing items or to ask for search warrants.

Table 4.3   Occupations of prosecutors in property cases at the City justice rooms

Occupation of prosecutor	Number of hearings	Percentage of prosecutors in occupational category
Gentry/Wealthier merchants	3	2.5
Masters/Professionals/ Merchants	17	14.6
Tradesmen/Artisans	62	53.4
Poverty vulnerable trades	15	12.9
Labourers/Poor	19	16.3
Totals	116	99.7

Source: The minute books of the Guildhall and Mansion House justice rooms.[16]

Additionally, ward constables and watchmen brought in suspected offenders for examination by the court. Disputed goods and items were advertised for identification and suspected felons were detained while this process was undertaken. Alongside the victim/prosecutor the central figure was always the magistrate who played a multiple role. While arbitration between depredators and their victims was discouraged it still occurred. Many victims simply wished to see their property returned, as we shall see.

Perhaps unsurprisingly, given the nature of London's commercial economy, the largest proportion of prosecutors were tradesmen or other artisans. Shopkeepers and publicans in particular were especially vulnerable to theft. Employers bringing accusations of theft against employees were also fairly common, as were prosecutions by those working on the busy quayside. Shopkeepers and their servants prosecuted thieves operating in their stores while tavern keepers sought to convict those that stole their pewter pint pots. These were small businessmen (and women) who were trying to protect their property – property which was exceedingly vulnerable to opportunist crime.

Masters, professionals and merchants all had reason to use the courts. Indeed seven out of ten prosecutors of property crime at the justice rooms were members of the top three occupational groups as shown in Table 4.3, albeit of varying means. Not all these prosecutors were determined to see these petty thieves stand trial for their crimes however. Jonathan Vaughan was suspected by his master of stealing two watchcases from his workshop, a potentially 'capital' crime.[17] However, once he had retrieved his property Vaughan's master showed no desire to pursue the prosecution. He simply dismissed Vaughan from his employ. The servant had lost his position, which was perhaps deemed punishment enough.[18] This case, and others like it, represents an example of petty pilfering by employees, an activity that must have been quite common in the period. However, once goods had been returned, and an apology made or the servant dismissed, the need for further costly prosecution was removed.

When members of the lower orders of society appeared as prosecutors in property cases it was often on behalf of their employers. In the autumn of 1780 an alert shop assistant – Jonathan Jennaway – prevented the theft of jewellery from his master's shop in St. Paul's Church Yard.[19] While William Cheetham attempted to distract Jennaway's attention, his partner tried to steal some items from a glass display case. However, the case was a different one from those he had encountered previously and opened from the side instead of the top. In trying to open it he broke the glass lid and alerted Jennaway.[20] Mary Fisher, the wife of a drayman, was involved in the prosecution of a brewer's servant accused of stealing a barrel of porter. Mary was a witness and came to court with the brewer to prosecute.[21] However there were occasions when members of the labouring class appeared to prosecute those that stole their own property, as John Houghton, a labourer, did when he charged John Marshall with stealing his handkerchief.[22] Thus these courts were not used exclusively by the middling sorts and above when it came to the prosecution of thieves and pilferers.

The nature of property offending in the City

This chapter will now look in some detail at the types of offences that were heard at this level and at how gender affected this, before considering how property offenders were dealt with by the City magistracy. Common theft, or petty larceny, constituted the most prevalent property offence in this period. This was the theft of goods or property valued at less than 1s.[23] It has been suggested elsewhere that this type of petty theft in the metropolis was routinely being filtered out of the wider criminal justice system. Petty larcenies were not being sent to the Sessions, as was often the case outside of the capital, because these jury courts were too busy.[24] Instead petty larceny was largely dealt with at summary level. The 338 prosecutions for theft identified in Table 4.1 covered a wide range of appropriations as we can see below.

Table 4.4 The nature of theft prosecuted at the summary courts, c.1784–96

Goods stolen	Male	Female	Total
Personal property	84	44	128
Goods from docks	58	6	64
Clothing	47	13	60
Foodstuffs	27	7	34
Industrial goods/Tools	34	0	34
Money	7	2	9
Livestock	8	1	9
Totals	265	73	338

Source: The minute books of the Guildhall and Mansion House justice rooms.[25]

The largest categories of stolen goods were items of personal property stolen from homes, businesses and the streets. Pewter pint pots from inns, jewellery and watches, shoe buckles, ribbons and a cornucopia of other possessions were separated from their owners. Susannah Cook was remanded in Wood Street compter after being accused by three different publicans of stealing their tankards.[26] Clothing was routinely stolen; being easily disposed of in the capital's many pawnbrokers and secondhand shops and stalls.[27] On the 24 January 1785 Thomas Sawyer was brought before Justice Crosby accused of stealing a shirt, neck cloth and handkerchief and was fully committed for trial at the Old Bailey.[28] Sawyer had taken the items from a stationary whiskey (a type of horse and cart) but had been seen doing so by the victim. Joseph Garlin claimed to have found William Howard's missing coat in the street and no witness was able to gainsay him.[29] An unnamed journeyman butcher helped himself to some clothes out of a box in Fleet Market.[30] Much of this theft was opportunistic: congested streets and crowded markets were perfect hunting grounds for would-be thieves, with carmen and porters transporting all sorts of goods and property across the City.[31] Cheeses and sides of beef were removed from carts (as we recall from the example of George Shirley in Chapter 3) and from the fronts of shops, while some thieves contented themselves with stealing small portions of food to eat. The theft of money and livestock were less frequently prosecuted at the summary courts but the former was often a feature of larcenies committed by prostitutes and servants. As he made his way home one evening William Dickie was accosted by a streetwalker who tried to pick his pocket under pretence of unbuttoning his breeches; he lost some silver but couldn't prove she took it.[32] John Price spent the night with a prostitute only to wake and find her and all his money gone.[33] The constable of Bishopsgate ward brought 'two notorious offenders' before the alderman 'for decoying a young lad into house of ill fame in Angel alley, Bishopsgate Street, and taking from his person three half crowns and a sixpence'.[34] Much of this theft was felonious and should properly have been dealt with by the quarter sessions and assize but, as will be shown later, a considerable amount of prosecutions for property offences were resolved at the summary level.

As well as theft by prostitutes there are other gender factors that affect property crime. Men, while they stole clothing, were more likely to steal goods that related to their gendered sphere. So it is not surprising to find that men account for 100 per cent of the prosecutions involving industrial goods. Men were accused of stealing hammers and irons, nails, lead pipe and canvas, and other everyday items that they could use or sell on. In June 1784 Michael Fitzpatrick was charged with stealing two wood planes, a pair of iron pinchers, a chisel, an old hammer and an iron adze, belonging to two journeyman carpenters. All these items had been found on him when he was stopped by the watch.[35] In February 1788 Thomas Barnwell was accused of stealing 46 lbs in weight of lead from a house in the City belonging to an Essex victualler. Barnwell was a lodger there and had been systematically stealing the lead and selling it on for over a number of days before he was caught.[36] The London press reported a similar case across the metropolis. A watchman spotted a man on the roof of a house at one in the morning and 'sprang his rattle' to alert his colleagues. The thief slipped back into the house through an open window but was seen and a nearby patrol entered the building to investigate. On being informed that there was a lodger that slept in the garret,

> They immediately went up stairs and knocked at the garret door, which not being opened to them, they burst open, and there found the prisoner in bed, apparently asleep; and in another bed, which was in the same room, they discovered, concealed, a large quantity of lead, which had been stolen.[37]

Thefts of industrial goods included both opportunistic larceny, as Barnwell's case indicates, and workplace appropriation as in Fitzpatrick's. Men were also much more frequently prosecuted for stealing goods from the docks and City warehouses. Much of this appropriation was of tea, coffee, sugar and other imported luxuries that were landed from the merchant fleets of the capital.

The taking of small amounts of these luxuries, along with offcuts of wood or 'shavings' or 'thrums' from the workplace might not be have been viewed as theft by the perpetrators or the wider labouring classes.[38] London dockyard workers had a long tradition of supplementing their wages with the by-products of their labour, but this practice of taking home the 'perks of the trade' was increasingly proscribed in the eighteenth century. Therefore, some of those prosecuted at the Mansion House or Guildhall were the victims of the changing definition of customary rights as a more capitalistic logic began to govern the changing nature of the wage.[39]

One of the more ambiguous categories of property crime highlighted in Table 4.1 were those acts labelled as 'common pilfering'. The courts appear to have used the term 'common pilfering' to mean the stealing of small quantities of low-value goods or produce from the storehouses and

wharves which concentrated along the banks of the Thames and its surrounding networks of streets and alleys.[40] Pilferers commonly took small
quantities of easily disposable goods: tobacco, indigo, coals and so forth.
Many probably did so considering them to be 'perks' of their poorly paid
labouring in London's docks and warehouses and much of the detection
of these petty thieves fell to the part-time quayside watchmen and merchant constables. We can be reasonably confident in suggesting that
much pilfering went either unnoticed or did not result in prosecution.[41]

Pilfering was a petty crime that continually agitated the merchants
and ship owners that used the long stretch of docks and quays along the
City's southern border. The proximity of the docks represented a serious
policing issue for the authorities; watchmen in these areas may have
been more diligent in bringing forward suspected thieves and pilferers,
thereby increasing the numbers of prosecutions.[42] Porters transported
goods from the Thames to warehouses, shops and private addresses
throughout the City and beyond, and anyone operating without the
means to identify themselves as legitimate left themselves open to arrest
by the watch or the constables. This was further complicated by traditional notions of perquisite and privilege. Defendants at the Old Bailey
frequently argued that the goods they had taken were damaged or soiled
in some way and were for their 'own use' and for resale, justifying the
appropriation as reasonable. This may have been the excuse used by
those appearing before the lord mayor at Mansion House but the records
of pilfering cases are seldom detailed enough to support this suggestion. However, some dockworkers were prepared to deliberately damage
goods so as to be able to justify the appropriation of them.[43] Quayside
constables took a different view of this acquisitive behaviour by dockworkers and made efforts to search men as they left the area. All sorts
of goods could be concealed about the person, in over-large trousers,
coats and under hats. Goods could also be secreted safely for collection
at a later date. On many occasions individuals must have successfully
arrived home with this ill-gotten bounty intact, a useful supplement to
their household budget, at other times a quick-witted constable or ware-
houseman may have acted to thwart the theft. Such was the unfortunate
experience of Daniel Debarge in 1789. Whilst working in an East India
warehouse, Debarge attempted to remove a quantity of nails but was
suspected by a warehouse keeper who followed him home and 'found
him emptying his pockets of some articles which proved to be nails.'[44]

So, as we have seen, pilferage and petty theft formed by far the bulk
of all property offences heard at the summary level. Male offenders typically stole industrial and consumable goods and tools, but also took

food, personal property and money. Women were more likely to be prosecuted for stealing personal property, clothing or food, items consistent with their gendered sphere. Thus, Mary Fox stole a petticoat by attempting to hide it under her apron, but was seen and sent to Bridewell for ten days. Similarly, Jane Mountain was accused of ransacking the drawers of Mary O'Clancy's house after she had taken her on as a washerwoman.[45]

In the period from 15 February to 24 March 1796 there were 28 cases of theft that were examined before the magistrates at Guildhall.[46] This excludes those listed as suspected felonies and omits repeat appearances by those remanded for further examination (which will be addressed presently). Of these 28 cases, 17 were for the theft of property, four of food, three of industrial goods, while three represent items taken from lodgings and one for the theft of a pair of dogs. Some beef was taken from a butcher in Grub street and veal from another whose cart was en route for Chelsea, as were three loaves of bread from a baker's yard and a basket of potatoes. Mary Jones took various items such as bed linen and an iron from her lodgings but agreed to return them and was forgiven; Rebecca Davis absconded with her landlady's linen from her lodgings in Drury Lane. Those stealing industrial goods took coal, lead and pewter.[47] The remaining 17 persons stole other items of property. It is possible to look at a few of these cases in detail to see what they tell us about the nature of property appropriation in the City.

If we follow four individual cases committed to Newgate to await trial at the Old Bailey, the survival of more expansive records allows us to explore these thefts in greater detail. We are able to obtain a deeper sense of the motivation and context of these offenders and of the opportunism, desperation and the material contexts that could lead individuals into property crime. Joseph Davison stole 13 hempen bags so that he could set himself up in business as a potato dealer.[48] He was caught red-handed but his employers spoke up for him in court, perhaps believing that he had intended to return the sacks when he had established his small business. Samuel Edwards was accused of taking a pair of silver shoe buckles, some stockings and a pocket map of London. John Allnutt, had lost the items amidst a move from lodgings in Coopers Row to Mark Lane, and suspected that one of the workmen employed on the site was responsible. He made some enquiries and 'in consequence of some information' he received Edwards was arrested and carried before Alderman Newnham at Guildhall. Allnutt's enquiries must have taken him about five days given he noticed the loss on the 12 or 13 of February (he was unsure on this point). A constable was despatched to accompany Allnutt to the prisoner's lodgings in East Smithfield where the missing items were discovered. The stockings were in a drawer, the map in a cupboard and crucially the buckles were in his wife's pocket. Because the lodgings were shared by other tenants, as was common at the time, there was insufficient proof to convict Edwards.[49] Edwards was lucky; as a workman employed in building or repairing houses he had taken advantage of his position and made away with a small amount of goods that he could use or sell to supplement his wages. Without clear sworn testimony that he had actually stolen the items from Allnutt's lodgings it was very hard to prove his guilt. The fact that he was employed and had a wife probably helped his situation in court.[50]

Again we can see that opportunism was one of the most common factors in property crime in this period as the case of William Buckthorpe illustrates. Buckthorpe was loitering near a calico glazer's shop in Bartholomew Close near to the sprawl of Smithfield Market early one morning. While the owner, Mary Rutter, was busy inside Buckthorpe slipped in through the window and stole a roll of cloth valued at £3 6s. Unfortunately for Buckthorpe, George Heeley had noticed the young man acting suspiciously and ran after him and 'caught [him] with the piece under his great coat'.[51] In another case James King, a flamboyant character who worked as a shop man for a haberdasher and milliner in Bishopsgate, was prosecuted at Guildhall. Over a period of 11 months his mistress, Sarah Jackson, had become suspicious of her assistant on account of his extravagance in clothes. Jackson presumably felt that he was dressing beyond his means, and believed it might have been at her expense. King was dismissed from her service and later arrested on suspicion of theft. His lodgings were searched and various items, mainly ribbons, that Jackson was able to identify were found. However, the jury seem to have been unsure of the extent of King's guilt and so while he was indicted for stealing various items valued at over 30s, he was in the end only found guilty of stealing to the value of 1s.[52]

Opportunism and greed were two clear motivations behind three of these incidents of theft. Smithfield may have provided a ready market to dispose of the roll of cloth that William Buckthorpe removed from under the nose of the shop keeper and a pair of silver buckles may well have been usefully traded for food, alcohol or tobacco to improve the circumstances of Samuel Edwards and his wife. James King, if he did indeed help himself to Sarah Jackson's stock of ribbons and other goods was perhaps more interested in keeping up with the latest fashions in an increasingly consumer-orientated society. Eighteenth-century shops used visual display as their prime method of marketing to tempt the passing customer, and so it is not surprising that they attracted less-welcome attention.[53] In Joseph Davison's case, the motivation was different. A desire to improve his and his family's situation (he had a wife and three small children) by starting a business was undermined by his lack of capital. His theft of sacks therefore feels more like an act of desperation than one of greed. Thus, if as seems likely, these cases are not untypical, the motivations for theft in this period would seem to be mixed but largely related to need and opportunism rather than representing organised crime or large-scale appropriation. This may not have been the case for forgery or robbery that were more likely to attract people with a higher commitment to a semi-professional criminal lifestyle.

So far this chapter has concentrated on the nature of relatively petty theft and while this represents the overwhelming majority of property crime heard before the City courtrooms it is important to note that other, more serious, offences were also examined at this stage. The courtrooms at Guildhall and Mansion House occasionally heard accusations of burglary, forgery and street robbery. These were capital offences that have usually been associated with the higher courts. There were 25 cases of forgery in the sample covered in Table 4.1 and 16 cases of burglary or robbery of which at least 35 per cent were dealt with at summary level. Table 4.2 shows that just 11 individuals were accused of forgery and 17 were accused of theft with violencebefore the London jury at the Old Bailey in the 14 sessions sampled. Again it would appear that the summary courts are an important source of information about all property crime, not just petty or less-serious offending.

Next to 'theft' the largest category of offences listed in Table 4.1 is 'suspected felony', an open definition that covered a wide range of activities. Many of those brought in for suspected felonies were examined on more than one occasion by the justices and this re-examination process needs to be understood as more than just an operational function of the City courts.

The re-examination process employed by City magistrates

In order to understand the re-examination of defendants it is necessary to comment briefly on the pre-trial process in this period. One of the roles of the eighteenth-century magistrate was to assist prosecutors in bringing cases before the jury courts and as such they were given powers to issue warrants to search suspect's premises and to arrest them and bring them in for questioning.[54] This questioning took the form of an examination before one or more magistrates. At an examination the justice attempted to understand the facts of the case presented; he questioned the prosecutor, the accused and any witnesses including policing agents involved in the detection or arrest of suspects. At the end of this examination he might bind over prosecutors to appear at the next sessions to present their cases before a judge and jury, and his clerk might help (for a fee) with the writing of a formal indictment.[55]

It seems to have been common practice for those arrested for property offences to have been examined on more than one occasion and often to have been kept in one of the City's compters in the meantime. This can be viewed in two ways. First it represents an attempt by the justice to ascertain the facts of the case and to establish whether a crime has been committed. On several occasions the clerk of the court simply recorded that a particular constable believed an offence had taken place because he either saw the defendant loitering without good cause or because he was in possession of some item (such as a piece of clothing, a trunk or foodstuffs) that raised his suspicions. This practice of arresting individuals on suspicion was a part of the duties of watchmen and other policing agents as outlined in Chapter 3. Sometimes the magistrate was happy with the explanation given and released the defendant while in other situations the individual was detained for further examination a few days or so later, while the goods were advertised to see if anyone came forward to claim them.

Sir John Fielding developed the practice of holding prisoners suspected of offences while advertising stolen items and using his 'Runners' to investigate and seek out potential witnesses and victims. He convened his meetings in the nearby inn, the *Black Bear*, and his intention appears to have been to build and strengthen prosecution cases, a strategy in keeping with the Marian pre-trial process.[56] However, this might also have allowed the defence a chance to fashion a more robust counter case as Sir John recognised. Fielding set aside one day a week to hear these examinations. On Wednesdays all prisoners committed in the preceding week were re-examined before a bench of 'three or more' justices, a process which Beattie suggests 'must have helped to clear up other offences and at the same time, if other victims of these defendants came forward with further charges, to bolster the prosecution's chance of success when the trial came on at the Old Bailey'.[57] Fielding, it would appear, was redefining the pre-trial process by using his magisterial discretion to interpret his powers in a way that he saw fit. He used the vagrancy laws to hold suspected persons for up to six days before formally indicting them or releasing them. In doing so he was probably exceeding his authority and this systematic abuse of legislation designed to deal with beggars and vagrants, coupled with the unwelcome side affect of this action in the appearance of numerous lawyers drew a significant chorus of opprobrium in Fielding's direction. William Augustus Miles complained that Fielding was more intent on cementing his reputation as an examiner than serving the cause of justice.[58] Beattie's conclusion is that we should understand this re-examination process as Fielding's ongoing mission to develop and refine the criminal justice system in London.

However, it is possible to view the re-examination process as a way of dealing with petty crime without recourse to a jury trial. Frequently City offenders were remanded and re-examined two or more times, and would have ended up spending perhaps three to seven days (or more) imprisoned at the Wood Street or Poultry compters. In this way the magistrates were able to punish casual offenders with short periods of imprisonment, perhaps as a way of taking them out of circulation and deterring them from further offending. The process also allowed the sitting magistrate to pressurise offenders into joining the armed forces.[59] The City's aldermen were themselves under pressure to provide troops for the wars of the eighteenth and early nineteenth centuries and famously resisted the use of press gangs within the square mile.[60] Offering petty thieves such as Thomas Donsdon – who was arrested after stealing a quantity of beef from a stall in Fleet market – the chance to avoid a visit to Old Bailey may well have informed this treatment of casual offending. In 1796 Alderman Clark allowed Donsdon to join the Loyal South Volunteers despite there being ample evidence of his guilt.[61]

While male suspects were not routinely *forced* to join the armed forces as an alternative to a jury trial, they may 'have found the pressure to enlist virtually impossible to resist'.[62] The practice of judicial impressments allowed justices to 'do their duty' by the king without undermining the independence of the City and its determination to resist the activities of press gangs. Peter King has used both parliamentary reports alongside newspaper and journal sources to argue that

> many other offenders who might otherwise have been indicted were put in to the armed forces without ever being taken to a summary hearing. Second, some of those who were committed to gaol to await trial were later allowed to avoid formal indictment by agreeing to enlist.[63]

In both instances this would help to explain why some suspected felons disappear from the records of the summary courts after being remanded for further examination.

The re-examination of offenders can also be seen as a way of dealing with the problem of vagrancy. Anyone found wandering abroad without the apparent ability to support themselves or able to give a good account of their behaviour was liable to be arrested and charged as a 'suspected felon'. Indeed the watch and parish constables were liable to a fine of 10s if they did not apprehend such individuals and could earn a reward for prosecuting them as 'idle and disorderly' and we should not discount this factor in the prosecution process.[64] Many of those arrested as 'suspected felons' may, like Henry Rolaston, simply have been unfortunate in being on the streets at the wrong time. Rolaston was attempting to make his way home rather the worse for drink on a December night in 1800. He was stopped by a constable who was suspicious of the bundle he was carrying. He was held in the watch house overnight and brought before the lord mayor in the morning. Fortunately for Rolaston the chief magistrate was satisfied that the goods were his own and discharged him.[65]

Many other suspected thieves were released after a short spell in the compter and after an attempt had been made to establish whether the goods they had in their possession were ill-gotten or not. Not all were as fortunate as Rolaston. Sometimes a lack of evidence was seemingly irrelevant if no one was prepared to vouch for them. Three costermongers caught taking a little bit too much of an interest in the windows of a silversmith in Barbican were arrested and searched by a constable. He found some knives on them, which although in itself was not necessarily damning evidence in the late eighteenth century, they were still remanded in custody. When they came up before the alderman on the following day they were all sent to Bridewell for 14 days as pilferers, despite the clerk of the court noting that 'no other evidence' had been produced.[66]

The re-examination process in the City also functioned in much the same way as that at Bow Street, as a method of building a prosecution case. Thomas Pruden appeared before Sir Francis Sanderson at Guildhall in May 1794, accused of stealing two casks containing peppermint and bitters. He claimed he had been asked to carry the goods to the *Antigallican* public house in Dark House Lane in return for sixpence. The magistrate remanded him and noted that the casks were marked. On the following day a distiller named Read and his partner identified the casks from these marks and Pruden was committed for trial at Old Bailey. At the trial Read told the court that he became aware of the theft only when the constable from Guildhall told him of the arrest. He checked his stock and found the casks missing. Pruden, despite a bold and lengthy denial was found guilty and sentenced to a public whipping and a year's confinement in the house of correction.[67]

These examples of re-examination show the discretionary nature of the practice. Sometimes, as in Rolaston's case, the examination process allowed those swept up by the watch to be vindicated – especially if a person could be found (often an employer) who would vouch for them. By contrast it also enabled a more rigorous investigation to take place, as with Pruden, whereby any goods detained could be advertised or leads (such as a dealer's mark on goods suspected to be stolen) could be followed up and victims alerted. Finally if the magistrate believed an individual was guilty of *something*, even if evidence was ambiguous or even non-existent, he could use the vagrancy laws to send suspects to Bridewell if the re-examination process failed to provide more concrete grounds for prosecution.[68]

It would seem therefore that the practice of re-examination by magistrates in the City shared similar characteristics to the pre-trial process that was created by Fielding at Bow Street, even if the latter's was more extreme. While Fielding seemingly overstepped the mark and found his practice curtailed, in the City re-examination continued throughout the eighteenth century. It was certainly used to help build cases against thieves and also to allow the innocent to prove the facts of their stories. It may be the case that the City aldermen had noted the practice at Bow Street, since the newspapers regularly reported the activities of the 'blind beak' and it is unlikely that the controversy of Fielding's actions escaped their notice. It is possible that they adapted the principle to suit their own needs in the square mile, once again demonstrating their firm grasp of their discretionary powers and the grip that the authorities had on everyday life in the City.

Outcomes

In the first half of the eighteenth-century City justices rarely sent petty larcenists to trial before a jury, choosing instead to deal with them summarily by imprisoning them in the Bridewell.[69] Did this practice continue to the end of the century and what implications this might have for our understanding of the criminal justice system of the period?

Many of those accused of common pilfering from the City's wharfs and warehouses in the 1780s were dealt with in just the way that Beattie outlines in the earlier period. As was established earlier, 'common pilfering' was an ambiguous term. It appears to come under the umbrella of petty larceny but seems to have been prosecuted by justices utilising the wide powers they had under the vagrancy laws. In his 1785 edition Richard Burn states that:

> Any person...found in or upon any dwelling-house, warehouse, coach-house, stable, or out-house, or in any inclosed [*sic*] yard or garden, or area belonging to any house, with intent to steal any goods or chattels:- shall be deemed a rogue and vagabond within the meaning of this statute of the 17 G.2.[70]

This allowed magistrates to lock up minor property offenders as 'idle and disorderly pilfering persons' even if they had stolen a specified item from an identified victim. As Beattie suggests

> it seems reasonably clear that such committals resulted from the magistrates' decision to take advantage of the grey areas on the borderland of larceny and of the vagueness of the vagrancy laws to punish those suspected of small thefts by sending them for a brief period of hard labour and perhaps corporal punishment rather than committing them for trial at the quarter sessions or assizes.[71]

The practice was common in Surrey in the early eighteenth century and throughout the first half of the Hanoverian period in the capital, and indeed persisted to the end of the century as we can see from Table 4.5.

Table 4.5 Overall outcomes of examinations of property offenders before the City justice rooms, c.1784–96

Outcome	Number	Percentage
Discharged	248	36.7
Dealt with summarily	237	35.1
Committed for trial/Bailed	190	28.1
Total known	675	99.9
Remanded destination uncertain	184	
Totals	859	100

Source: The minute books of the Guildhall and Mansion House justice rooms.[72]

Table 4.5 demonstrates that over 70 per cent of those accused of property offences at the summary courts (485 out of 675) were dealt with summarily. It was not simply pilferers who were being treated in this way;

a variety of defendants accused of theft had their cases handled by the justices. A very considerable proportion, 36.7 per cent, of all property offenders were being discharged after an examination (or series of examinations) before the sitting justice of the peace. Only 28.1 per cent of those accused of a property crime before the City magistrates were fully committed for trial at Old Bailey or the London sessions. This demonstrates that the summary courts were playing a vital role in the wider criminal justice system in London by filtering out large numbers of property offenders at an early stage.

Suspects were sometimes discharged for 'want of evidence' or because no prosecutor appeared against them, or because the case was 'settled' or 'agreed'. On occasions defendants were discharged at the will of the prosecutor, who perhaps had satisfied his or her desire to establish ownership of certain goods or their authority over a recalcitrant employee. The settlement could be a simple one, the return of stolen goods or the payment due. When John Wiley was accused of trying to defraud George Steel and his partner of the price of 66 pairs of shoes, he produced the money and was released.[73] Indeed, we should view this use of the courts as an arena of negotiation with the summary process and the authority of the magistracy being used as a lever to persuade non-payers to settle their bills. Judicial discretion is often hard to read from the sparse records of cases that do not progress beyond the summary level but there are occasional flashes of illumination. William Willis stole some pieces of timber and was chased and arrested by a local constable who took him to the watch house and then to the Poultry compter. His father heard of the arrest and meted out his own punishment on the lad. Hearing this, the presiding lord mayor released William without further sanction.[74]

Table 4.6   Nature of outcomes for property offenders dealt with summarily before the City justice rooms, c.1784–96

Nature of Outcome	Number	Percentage
Imprisoned	149	62.8
Reprimanded	37	15.6
Settled	26	10.9
Other	25	10.5
Totals	237	99.8

Source: The minute books of the Guildhall and Mansion House justice rooms. 'Other' includes those sent to sea or into the armed forces or to the hospital (in the case of two female offenders).[75]

As can be seen from Table 4.6 a significant proportion of minor property offenders, 16.4 per cent, were imprisoned by the magistrates: usually in Bridewell but occasionally at the Poultry or Wood Street compters. By the 1820s the compter at Giltspur Street was home to a large number of minor property convicts whose place of birth reveals the cosmopolitan nature of the capital.[76] Most of those imprisoned were pilferers but there were 29 thieves as well as a number of pickpockets (probably all young offenders) and a receiver in the City's various prisons. The normal period of confinement was between seven days and one month and usually involved a beating. The short length of imprisonment coupled with the harsh treatment that awaited inmates allowed the courts, the magistrates and of course, the prosecutor/victims to punish some and deter others without entering into great expense. Sometimes the decisions to imprison defendants or let them go can appear somewhat arbitrary from the brief notes in the minute books. Jasper Fors found himself sent to Bridewell for being in possession of six handkerchiefs despite there being 'no direct evidence' that he had stolen them while Ann Turner escaped a similar fate because a deponent gave her an excellent character.[77] Such discretionary decision-making was informed by the perceived status of the accused, as much as by the nature of the offence committed. Both Fors and Turner had clearly been picking pockets, but the young man was much more of a concern (and a more suitable object of summary punishment) to the justices than was Ann. Bridewell, along with the other compters and lock-ups of the metropolis, was an important part of a disciplinary machine that was there to meet the needs of the mercantile class, allowing as it did for the swift administration of a cautionary reminder of the power of the ruling order.

Other defendants were more fortunate, especially if their victims were prepared to let the matter drop. In October 1821 a man and his son distracted a shoemaker and his shop assistant and made off with a pair of boots valued at 44s. The culprit was a bookbinder who had found work hard to come by and had been working as a milkman. He told the court he 'had an ailing wife and six children, of whom the boy with him was the eldest but one, and he earnestly entreated mercy for the sake of his family, alleging this was his first and only offence'. The shoemaker 'humanely joined in this request, expressing his willingness to forego prosecuting, if the Magistrate should think it proper to overlook the offence'. The alderman agreed to consider the matter and, while the shoemaker enquired into the truth of the man's story, he remanded him for further examination.[78] In a second example, two boys were charged with stealing from the luggage on the Northampton wagon. It was established, after the boys had been remanded, that they had good characters and no history of previous misconduct. The prosecutor, the newspaper reported,

> very humanely, said that he should be sorry to prosecute them, as probably they might never offend again, and begged that they might be discharged. The magistrate said, fortunately for the prisoners, the Waggoner's evidence was not so conclusive as to make it impossible for him to discharge them, and hoped that, as this was their first offence, it would be their last. The prisoners, after receiving an impressive admonition from the magistrate, were discharged.[79]

Clearly then property cases, even those that were felonious (and so should have been sent on for jury trial), could be settled before the magistrate if an apology, payment or the return of goods was forthcoming. In these cases the worst the culprit could expect was a reprimand from the justice and a warning as to their future behaviour.

As I noted earlier some property offenders could be persuaded to enter the armed forces. George Parsons stole a three-penny cheesecake from a pastry cook in Red Cross Street and was sent into the Marine Society. Tom Williams was suspected of stealing from his roommate and the justice sent him to sea.[80] Both were teenage boys and appropriate objects for judicial discretion. In February 1784 a 'young man belonging to a reputable family in this City' was accused of stealing a gold watch, a serious offence. However, instead of the Old Bailey, 'in consideration of his family, the Alderman, with the consent of the parties, sent him to serve the East India Company as a soldier'.[81] Thomas Whittington was sent to the Philanthropic Society, his theft of a coat and a large sum of money (from a 'person who out of humanity took him out of the streets'), seen as a 'shocking Instance of early Depravity' by the magistrate. Once again a more serious outcome might have resulted had the prosecutor, or the justice, pressed the case.[82]

Some prosecutors came to an agreement with those they had accused (who were sometimes their employees), while others were simply discharged with an admonition to behave better in future. Without more detailed qualitative information it is impossible to be conclusive about the motor for magisterial decision-making at the summary courts. But it is reasonable to suggest that youth, previous conduct, available evidence, and character all affected the way in which the City justices arrived at their judgements. To what extent did gender affect this process? Women were five times less likely to be prosecuted before the summary courts for property offences than men. Did they also receive more lenient treatment when they got there?

Table 4.7 Outcomes of examinations of property offenders at the City justice rooms, c.1784–96, by gender

Outcome	Male	%	Female	%	Total
Discharged	175	32.8	73	51.4	248
Committed	158	29.6	20	14.0	178
Bailed	9	1.6	3	2.1	12
Imprisoned	126	23.6	23	16.1	149
Reprimand	24	4.5	13	9.1	37
Settled	18	3.3	8	5.6	26
Other	23	4.3	2	1.4	25
Total known	533	99.7	142	99.7	675
Destination unknown	151		33		184
Totals	684		175		859

Source: The minute books of the Guildhall and Mansion House justice rooms. 'Other' includes those sent to sea or into the armed forces or to hospital (in the case of the two female offenders).[83]

Table 4.7 would suggest that they did. Women were much more frequently discharged by the courts than men and twice as likely to be set free with merely a reprimand. They were more often able to settle their disputes over property (items pawned or otherwise 'borrowed') than were males. Crucially women were able to escape a jury trial almost twice as frequently as male property offenders, a finding that partly explains why fewer women appear at the Old Bailey (as shown in Table 4.2). Women were not, of course, impressed into the armed forces but this lack of judicial resource did not mean that more female property thieves were incarcerated. Imprisonment was used for both sexes but more men were sent to these institutions as pilferers and petty depredators. In 1821, there were just 76 women in the Giltspur for property offending in comparison to the 200 men that were detained.[84] So since only 27.5 per cent of the thieves, receivers and fraudsters in the Giltspur at this time were female, the magistracy was clearly treating male offending more seriously.

It is of course possible that female property defendants are under-represented. The sorts of offences that females typically committed, such as shoplifting, pick pocketing and pilfering by servants were extremely hard to detect or to prove in court and the victims of prostitutes who removed their pocket books and watches while they were sleeping or otherwise engaged would often have been too embarrassed to prosecute.[85] The numbers that do appear in the summary courts probably represents a fraction of those women that committed property crime in the City. However, while women accounted for just over 21 per cent of all property offenders in Table 4.1 they were responsible for 34 per cent of accusations of the theft of personal items in Table 4.4 even if many of them were simply 'getting away with it' by being discharged here. It does, however, imply that women were not as lacking in criminal activity as some indictment-based work implies.

It has been argued that the second half of the eighteenth and early nineteenth century saw a decline in female criminality.[86] However, because Feeley and Little did not look at the summary courts they are unable to discuss all the possible shifts in jurisdiction in trying to account for the decline in the proportion of women indicted for property crimes. We have seen that in the City women were accused of committing a variety of property offences but relatively few of them were sent on to face a jury trial. So while Feeley and Little suggest that it was not until the nineteenth century that 'many of the less serious cases were shunted off to the lower courts' the evidence here demonstrates that the summary process was routinely dealing with these offences in the last quarter of the eighteenth (and, we might speculate, possibly earlier).[87]

Female thieves were certainly active in the City, possibly for the reasons that Beattie has suggested: unemployment, poverty and the lack of supervision.[88] Susannah Corbet stole the clothes from a hairdresser while he slept off his evening's drinking. Susannah appeared at Guildhall and was sent for trial having been arrested by a patrol because 'she appeared very bulky' (she had hidden the stolen items under her own). Her victim, naked apart from 'his drawers' took refuge in the watch house where he was given a watchman's coat to cover his embarrassment. Corbet was caught with clear evidence of her crime and the hairdresser identified her and his missing effects; in this case she had little chance of escaping justice and was sentenced to three months imprisonment at Old Bailey and was fined a shilling.[89] Susannah was unlucky. When they came before the summary courts, women were much more likely to escape punishment than their male counterparts. As elsewhere in this period, City justices frequently exercised their discretion to release females accused of property crime and sent very few of them to face a jury.

Clearly discretion was also available to prosecutors, and the summary process allowed a fast resolution of disputes. But it is judicial discretion, as wielded by the magistracy, which matters here. Supposedly justices of the peace had limited formal options available to them when presented by a property offender. If the prosecutor failed to appear or refused to press charges a defendant could be released. If neither of these eventualities occurred then the justice was obliged to send the case for trial, even if the offence only amounted to petty larceny. As has been shown, however, the majority of property offenders were being dealt with at summary level, with a significant number being released without further action. Given this level of discretion by magistrates and grand juries, along with the notable use of discretion by prosecutors it is apparent that there were considerable opportunities for escaping a trial for a capital felony in the late eighteenth-century metropolis. While annually there were around 250 property trials at the Old Bailey under City indictments in the 1780s and 1790s there were many more hearings at the summary courts. A significant proportion of these property offenders were arrested on suspicion of committing crime and subsequently released after a period of incarceration. This procedure may have been used to help build a prosecution case or it may be indicative of a disciplinary process in which minor property criminals were punished with a view to deterring them from future, more serious, offending. It is likely to have been a mixture of both and also an important way of removing some of the burden of work from the higher court system. This informal use of carceral punishment by the magistrates suggests that we need to be wary of reading judicial practice from contemporary manuals. As recent work on the Refuge for the Destitute has highlighted, Old Bailey judges used informal imprisonment as a sentencing option in the early nineteenth century even though no such option formally existed in law.[90]

Concluding remarks

Five key points emerge from this chapter. Property crime was an overwhelmingly male preoccupation. This has been established by previous studies of the higher courts and remains true at the summary level; women were less-frequently prosecuted for property crime than men. It is also the case that property crime was gendered. Men stole goods related to their work and life experiences while women stole items such as clothes and bedding that related to their occupation as servants. More serious property theft by women was often closely linked to their activities as prostitutes. Which highlights the next point that can be made by this study; property crime was for the most part occasioned by need and opportunity. The theft of goods from lodgings and workplaces as well as the pilfering of commodities from the docks and warehouses of the Thames points clearly to petty appropriation as a way of supplementing a meagre existence. Of course, we cannot ever be sure why some chose to steal while others did not but it is possible to suggest that London presented a vast array of opportunities for those with a mind to commit crime.[91]

Third, the summary courts exercised a huge degree of discretion in relation to property offending. While justicing manuals such as Burn's were adamant that *all* theft (felonious or otherwise) had to be considered before a jury this was ignored by the aldermen of the City. Less than 30 per cent of all property cases that were examined by City justices were sent on by them to Old Bailey. Those bringing defendants also had a large discretionary role to play in this process and their decisions were affected by their relationships to those that stole from them. Servants and apprentices could be forgiven or admonished, the court could use the Bridewell to discipline them, and the experience of prison could serve as a warning to their future behaviour. The magistrates had discretion in abundance. By using the re-examination process they could frighten petty thieves, persuade them to join the armed forces or take pity on their difficult circumstances and release them. Many of these justices would have served on Grand juries or had other direct input into the criminal justice system of the capital and it is evident that they believed that they had the right and the power to filter property cases out of the system at this early stage and so keep the wider criminal justice system clearer for more serious offences.

The fourth point to note is that the discretion of the courts seems to have been of most benefit to female property offenders. Considerable numbers of women were being accused of theft in the City but were then removed from the criminal justice system at summary level. Proportionally more women were discharged, released with a reprimand, made a settlement with, or were forgiven by their accusers than was the case with males. This would necessarily have reduced the numbers of female thieves that appeared at the Old Bailey and so suggests that we should be wary of believing that the numbers of female property offenders was falling in this period based on research carried out from the records of the higher courts.

The final point that can be made follows from this filtration process. There was simply much more crime being examined and many more criminals, witnesses and victims involved at summary level. Four times as many cases were heard at the City justice rooms than were dealt with by the London jury at Old Bailey. This necessitates a reflection on our understanding of the criminal justice system in this period. The terror of the gallows was not evident in the matted gallery of the Guildhall, even if its threat is implied by the presence of the justice of the peace in his robes of office. The arrest, trial and execution of the highway robbers we met at the beginning of this chapter was in fact atypical of the nature and prosecution of property crime in the late eighteenth century. Instead the summary courts operated for a very wide range of the City's population, and the magistracy acted to some degree as mediators who practised restorative justice in reuniting victims with their property. It is, however, true that it was those with property to protect or reclaim that prosecuted here, and this may have excluded the poorest of London's populace from the process.

5

Settling their Differences: The Prosecution of Interpersonal Violence

In August 1785 the *Public Advertiser* carried a story of domestic violence. It was rare for the London press to print stories of non-lethal violence unless it was exceptional, involved the theft of property, or was in some way amusing. This case fell into the first category:

> A man was carried before the Lord Mayor, charged with beating and stabbing his wife in the neck, and otherwise ill-treating her. The Lord Mayor recommended it to him to be reconciled to his wife, and to use her better for the future. This he promised to do: but they were no sooner in a public house but he beat her again, whereupon he was brought a second time before his Lordship, who committed him to the Poultry Compter till he can give security for his good behaviour to her for the future.[1]

What is immediately shocking to the modern reader is the seemingly casual way in which this case is viewed by the magistrate. It would appear that while actual violence had been inflicted on the wife the lord mayor's concern was to bring the two parties to reconciliation rather than to punish the husband for his cruelty. Even when this attempt ends in failure, and a subsequent beating, the emphasis of the law is still on resolution rather than repudiation. We cannot know the exact circumstances of this case and it may well be, as I have suggested, exceptional but it does tell us a great deal about the treatment of non-lethal violence by the summary courts in this period. Assault (a term that covered a wide range of violent actions) was fundamentally regarded as a dispute between two individuals; it was a civil matter not a criminal one. Thus, the summary courts did not see it as their role to punish those brought

before them for petty violence. Instead the magistracy acted as mediators, brokering settlements and in some cases using the power at their
disposal to force reconciliations. This chapter will explore the quantity
and nature of assault prosecutions in the City and analyse the circumstances in which they arose. It will consider how these accusations of
petty violence were dealt with, what proportion of the City's population
had cause to use these courts and how this affects our understanding of
social relations and the use of the criminal justice system in this period.
What it will reveal is that the records of the City courts offer important
insights into the ways interpersonal violence was dealt with at the end
of the eighteenth century.

Much of the previous work on violent crime has been focused upon
lethal violence.[2] However, both murder and manslaughter were rare
occurrences in late eighteenth-century London. On average only around
12 indictments for homicide were heard per annum at the Old Bailey
between 1780 and 1830.[3] Clearly, this does not represent the majority
of prosecuted acts of violence in the City. Once again I will argue that
only by looking at the summary courts and the adjudications of the City
justices and, more importantly, in the discretionary decision making by
the victims of violence can we understand fully how the criminal justice
system operated with regard to interpersonal violence.

In recent years historians have begun to explore the treatment of
assault at the quarter sessions.[4] However, this approach has its problems
not the least of which is that so few cases of interpersonal violence actually made it to court. As King has written, the 'dark figure of unrecorded
crimes is so huge that it engulfs the relatively small number of acts that
reached the courts'.[5] While it has been evident that most petty violence
was dealt with by the magistracy the relatively poor survival of summary
court records has made historical research here difficult.[6] Fortunately the
minute books of the City's two justice rooms give us an opportunity to
explore the nature and prosecution of assault and to reach some useful
conclusions.

The frequency of assault prosecutions in the City of London

The first important observation that can be made about assault is that it
took up a considerable amount of the business of the summary courts
in the late eighteenth century. Of 2429 cases sampled for the period
1784–96 there were 693 cases of assault. This represents 28.5 per cent

of the offences heard before the City summary courts. However, percentages are not the most significant guide to the quantity of assault prosecutions in the City. As demonstrated in Chapter 4, a considerable amount of minor property crime was being dealt with by the summary process, which would necessarily reduce the proportion of violent offences recorded as would the large amount of regulatory business that was coming before the City magistracy. Therefore it is more useful to look at the actual numbers of assault prosecutions.

The City courts were hearing more than 20 cases of assault each week, which equates to over 1000 annually. Given that there were around 14,000 households in the square mile by 1801 suggests that perhaps as many as one in seven were involved annually in an assault prosecution in some capacity or another. However, the term *assault* was a very loose one and covered a range of violent actions in the eighteenth century. It could be as apparently serious as the domestic assault that opened this chapter but could equally refer to a show of force involving the waving of a fist; indeed anything 'done in an angry threatening manner' could constitute an assault.[7] Thus, simply shoving someone aside could result in an assault prosecution if the victim chose to press the matter. John Cullum was imprisoned overnight in Wood Street compter while the magistrate considered the details of his alleged assault on a pet dog. The 'Lap Dog' was owned by a 'very querulous, garrulous' Lady, who considered charging the man with theft. Fortunately for Cullum there was no evidence of this and Alderman Combe decided that his confinement (for 'striking the Dog – which was a yelping cur') was punishment enough and discharged him.[8]

Prosecutors in assault hearings at the summary courts

There are acute problems with identifying who brought assault prosecutions before the courts because the available occupational data recorded at summary level is so poor. There are just 15 hearings where occupation is clear and these are set out in Table 5.1. Even in such a small sample it is notable that the largest proportion of prosecutors came from within the ranks of artisans and tradesmen. This was also reflected in the occupations of prosecutors appearing at the quarter sessions for the peace in the City.[9] However, there are a significant number of prosecutors from the labouring poor or poverty-vulnerable trades. This is in line with findings from outside the City.[10]

Given the paucity of information from either the summary courts or quarter sessions the Old Bailey was also considered as a source of assault

Table 5.1 Occupations of prosecutors in assault cases, 1761–1800

Occupation	Number
Gentry/Wealthier merchants	0
Masters/Professional/Merchants	1
Tradesmen/Artisans	10
Poverty vulnerable trades	2
Labouring poor	2
Totals	15

Source: minute books of the Guildhall and Mansion House justice rooms.[11]

prosecutions. However, the Old Bailey is not without its problems as a source.[12] Just 18 assault cases were heard before the London jury between 1778 and 1810. Several cases involved the use of firearms, indicating the serious nature of these assaults, while the prosecutors were drawn from a wide cross section of London's population and members of the poorer class (broadly defined) appeared in significant numbers.

The nature of assault in the City of London

While the paucity of qualitative information available makes the identification of relationships between victims and prosecutors in assault cases extremely difficult, it is possible to analyse assaults by placing them in the one context that can be identified thoroughly – that of gender.

Table 5.2 Nature of assault charges at Guildhall justice room, 1784–96

	Number	Percentage
Male on male	289	41.7
Male on female	163	23.5
Female on female	153	22.0
Female on male	36	5.2
Assault on official	52	7.5
Total	693	99.9

Source: The minute books of the Guildhall and Mansion House justice rooms. NB. Most attacks on officials were carried out by men, although a few women were involved.[13]

Analysing assault prosecutions by gender shows that men were responsible for the overwhelming majority of assaults prosecuted at the summary level. This comes as no surprise as men have always dominated statistics of interpersonal violence in the past and continue to do so in the present. In the City, in this period, men carried out approximately 70 per cent of all assaults. This is not to say that women did not have a significant presence in these statistics. What is noticeable is that women tended to assault other women and were rarely prosecuted for attacks made on men, although this may well reflect the reluctance of men to prosecute female aggressors.[14] The reverse is unfortunately not the case and nearly a quarter of prosecuted assaults were made by men on women, some – but not all – of which represent examples of domestic violence.

Unfortunately the court records are at their least informative when recording the events that led to prosecutions for assault. Many entries simply give no information other than the name of the accused, victim and the constable that brought them to court. On other occasions there is the merest scrap of additional information that helps to define the attack. Many of these assaults were trivial affairs where the definition of assaults was at its most ambiguous. When Joseph Ware knocked the hat off the head of James Jacques he found himself in court charged with an assault.[15] Indeed there are several other cases of hats being knocked off in the streets that are suggestive of youthful excess or drunken loutishness similar to the theft of the occasional unfortunate watchman's lantern or the destruction of streetlights. Dennis Connor charged Thomas Perry with assault in Barbican under similar circumstances. Perry had removed Connor's hat and put an old one on his head instead. This may have been an example of 'bonneting' (a form of indirect theft) but Connor chose to prosecute it as an assault.[16] Evidently many of these cases were trivial affairs and undoubtedly not all such incidents led to formal prosecutions or the courts would have been even busier.

Indeed London offered up a plethora of opportunities for altercations and casual violence between individuals. Londoners pushing and shoving as they tried to negotiate the dangers of the streets – animals and carts competing with hackneys and coaches, street vendors attempting to sell all manner of goods and pedestrians trying not to step in the filth and detritus that Europe's busiest urban centre generated – all possible circumstances for assault prosecutions. If the eighteenth-century's equivalent of 'road rage' was a causal factor in interpersonal violence, another important influence (that also echoes modern concerns about violence) was drink.

Male violence is frequently linked with alcohol consumption, and public houses seen as venues for male fights. In 1796 a drunken customer at *The Axe* began abusing the other customers in the coffee room (the quiet retreat in public houses), offended the landlord's wife and was thrown out on the street. Undeterred he returned and assaulted the publican.[17] In 1818 an unnamed 'fighting baronet' – who was described as being 'at least intoxicated, if not mad' – was hauled before a magistrate for picking fights with almost everyone in *The Mitre* tavern on Aldgate.[18] Further evidence of the effects of alcohol on men's propensity to challenge and fight one another can be seen in a report from the *Observer* made a few years earlier. When, rather the worse for drink, Thomas Cobham (a 'stout Hibernian') was refused more beer he declared that he was 'a gentleman' and would go and sit in the parlour until he was served. The landlord, Mr Rigg, not wanting the peace of his establishment disturbed further, threw him out. Cobham was not so easily rebuffed and after hurling verbal abuse from the street managed to get back inside. He made straight for the landlord and attacked him, kicking and punching, while his victim tried to restrain him. The fight had all the elements of a bar-room brawl as Cobham 'contrived to destroy every article of glass, china, delft, and so on in the bar, independent of which he smashed several panes of glass, a patent lamp, and other articles' before he was subdued. This case ended in a settlement between the two parties, which was the most common outcome, as we shall see later.[19]

What these particular cases illustrate is that landlords often made a strong attempt to maintain some kind of order in their premises and were prepared to deal firmly with unruly behaviour. That they did so made sound commercial and common sense. A disorderly bar was more likely to attract the unwanted attention of the authorities who periodically clamped down on gambling and prostitution and who took a dim view of pub brawls. Customers would also have been unlikely to want to frequent a place where they were constantly at risk of being witness to boorish behaviour, or to having beer thrown over them, being insulted or worse.

Violence could erupt in pubs and taverns and on the street but it could also flare up in shops, markets and other public places as the everyday frustrations of life boiled over into actual physical conflicts, however trivial. As Jonathan Holmes was strolling along the Poultry, close to the Mansion House, he was distracted by an altercation in a nearby shop. Holmes came to the assistance of the shopman who was being verbally abused by a customer, who was eventually arrested.[20] Shopkeepers were quite capable of using violence to eject abusive or violent customers from their premises. They could also resort to violence with much less legitimacy. When the formerly respectable but impoverished Mrs Devonshire complained to her baker that one of the loaves he had given her as part of her allowance from the parish was 'light' (i.e. below the required weight for a standard loaf) he struck her and threw her out of his shop, bruising her arms and neck and cutting her mouth in the process.[21] In court the baker accused her of being abusive but Mrs. Devonshire denied this and the magistrate sided with her.

As Norma Landau and Jennine Hurl-Eamon have both suggested, prosecutors sometimes used prosecution at quarter sessions to extract compensation from their assailants and this was equally a factor at summary level.[22] In 1789 Joseph Cooper turned the corner of a street and ran into Josiah Simmonds, smashing the piece of glass he was carrying. In his defence Cooper said he was trying to avoid a passing cart, and had collided with Simmonds by accident. However, it might have been seen by Simmonds as an opportunity to extract some compensation from the situation; after all he had lost a valuable piece of glass.[23] Not all incidents of violence occurred in public however, some violence took place behind closed doors and, consequently, was even less likely to reach the courts.

The nature of assaults in domestic contexts

The paucity of detail contained in the pages of the summary court minute books rarely allow us to tease out the 'struggle for the breeches' that occurred within plebeian marriages but it is sometimes possible to explore the nature of domestic violence and how it was resolved.[24] Just over half of the women who brought accusations of assault charged a man with attacking them. Many of these attacks may have been by their husbands but it is hard for us to be definite about this from the records. Marriage was not easily defined in the eighteenth century. Poorer couples living together in the urban sprawl of London may not have been concerned to get married officially with the expense that it would accrue, and secret marriages were not uncommon.[25] Within plebeian culture there was certainly some room for informal divorce and remarriage. As Anna Clark has noted, 'men often deserted their wives for other women, and it was by no means uncommon for women to desert their husbands as well.'[26] This makes it difficult to determine whether there were higher levels of prosecuted domestic violence between spouses than is apparent from the available court minutes.[27] Some of the couples that appeared in court may well have been married without sharing a common surname. Nevertheless it seems extremely likely that prosecutions of spousal violence represent the tip of the iceberg as a great deal of domestic abuse would never have reached the courts, being dealt with instead 'by friends, family and neighbours using less formal means'.[28]

Although cases of domestic violence are hard to quantify it is possible to identify 26 cases of women using the courts to prosecute their violent husbands. While small, this sample does give some indication of the way in which domestic violence was treated by the courts. The majority of cases were either discharged or settled by the justice. Only just over 30 per cent of cases were referred on to the sessions of the peace with the husbands being bailed or imprisoned in the meantime. Thus the seemingly unusual case that was highlighted at the beginning of this chapter (where a stabbing and two beatings merely resulted in the binding over of the culprit and a warning as to his future conduct) was not untypical in that respect. However, these statistics underestimate the number of domestic violence cases because they exclude warrants issued to wives which cannot be identified specifically as such in the records. Not all warrants resulted in hearings before the magistracy. The warrant represented a tool in the armoury of a battered wife and it is important to recognise that in some cases the issuing of a warrant might have been sufficient inducement to force reconciliation. Evidently many cases of domestic violence did not make it to court. What is significant therefore, is that, even within such a small sample, there were at least one or two cases of domestic violence brought before these courts each week.

Scholars have discovered that women in London and elsewhere frequently used the lower courts to publicly admonish their partners. William Hunt of Devizes brokered several agreements between husbands and wives and similar cases can be seen in the notebooks of Richard Wyatt for Surrey, Samuel Whitbread for Bedford and Henry Norris for Hackney.[29] Anna Clark, Elizabeth Foyster, Margaret Hunt and Jennie Hurl-Eamon have all shown that both plebeian and middling women in the eighteenth century were prepared to prosecute abusive husbands, despite the ambiguity of the law in this area.[30] Patriarchy allowed masters to punish their servants and fathers to correct their sons, and so it followed that husbands could beat their wives so long as they did not go too far.[31] Just how far constituted 'too far' is a moot point and Justice Buller supposedly ruled that men were allowed to beat their wives so long as they restricted their chastisement to a stick no thicker than their thumb.[32] To discover to what extent the summary courts subscribed to this view we can look at how successful victims of domestic violence were when they brought their complaints before the City magistracy for adjudication.

When Sarah Rottam's husband assaulted her 'in a violent manner' and then abandoned her to the mercy of the parish, she took him to court. The presiding justice at the Guildhall brokered a settlement that was in effect a separation and a recognition that their marriage had broken down. Her husband agreed to pay Sarah 3s.6d a week in maintenance.[33] The courts were similarly useful to Ann Hands who complained about her husband William's violent behaviour and requested a separation with an allowance of 7s a week, which she was granted.[34] In both these cases the women were able to obtain some settlement from their husbands, even if the amounts varied. Official divorce was all but impossible for plebeian women in this period, given that the costs involved amounted to more money than they were likely to earn in a decade. A separation therefore represented a significant opportunity for a new start. Whilst there are relatively few fully recorded instances of women taking their husbands before the summary courts and winning some form of financial support and separation, those that do appear suggest that plebeian women were capable of asserting themselves when confronted by male aggression. Many wives worked alongside their husbands in this period and contributed significantly to the household income, and it was not unusual for women to have independent occupations. The courts may have reflected these differences when deciding upon the levels of maintenance at separation.

It is clear that a variety of options were available to both the prosecutor and the magistrate in such cases. Mary Ray's husband was discharged by the alderman after 'a reconciliation [had] taken place' between them, perhaps prompted by the threat of court sanctions. Ann Clark encountered many more problems when she chose to use the law. Ann obtained a warrant against her abusive husband, but before she could get him to court he beat her again (quite possibly because he discovered her intention to prosecute). The night before his court appearance he threatened 'to have her life' and Ann was forced to throw herself on the court's protection. Ann swore to the assaults, the couple agreed to separate and her violent husband was discharged, but this was not the end of Ann's troubles. Several days later Ann was assaulted by a female relative of Jonathan Clark, seeking revenge for the public humiliation of the family in court.[35] Women that charged their husbands in such a public way risked future violence and this must have prevented many women from taking this route to justice. But it was not the only disincentive to prosecuting.

Having one's husband locked up or fined was not a very satisfactory outcome for poorer women as it would often undermine the family budget. However, in some cases settlements were simply impossible because the animosity had gone on for too long and the building blocks of reconciliation had long since disappeared. Catherine Moses complained that her estranged husband Mordecai and his new lover, Hannah had beaten her. The husband's defence, described as largely 'a history of recrimination' by the clerk of the court, neither convinced the Justice nor helped resolve the dispute. Because Mordecai refused to promise to behave better in the future he was, like the husband who stabbed and beat his wife in our earlier example, imprisoned until he could provide sureties.[36] What, we might ask, did Catherine gain from this action? She managed to split the couple up, albeit temporarily, which may have brought her some satisfaction, and she alerted her community to her violent husband and his treatment of her.

The public court provided an arena to host the domestic struggle that must have been a frequent occurrence in the Hanoverian City. The open nature of the court carried both advantages and disadvantages for the abused wife or partner. On the one hand, she was able to employ the magistrate as an arbiter of her dispute, do this in front of witnesses and have the outcome – the reconciliation and presumably the husband's contrition – seen and heard, giving it *gravitas* and authority. It might also act as restraint upon the aggressor in that he would perhaps not wish to risk the public opprobrium which accompanied a court appearance or arrest by a constable bearing a warrant. Thus, at summary level justice was inexpensive, swift and offered some clear benefits to the victim. However, relationships could be damaged irrevocably by such an action; men knew this and would frequently resort to the threat of desertion as a way of controlling their wives. Furthermore a determined desire to curb the excesses of their spouses' behaviour may well have left some wives without a breadwinner and reliant upon the parish or charity for assistance.[37]

Some women may have won limited financial settlements but we have no way of knowing if the men involved kept up these payments or even if the court had the power to enforce its actions. Some of these husbands shamed so publicly would have resented their wife's behaviour and have extracted revenge more violently later, or simply threatened their wives with this possibility in order to keep them quiet in future. It is therefore by no means clear that the examples we have of women using the courts against their abusive husbands is evidence that the court process was useful to them. Daniel Defoe believed that it was difficult for women to use the courts, arguing that while wives *could* swear out an article of the peace, 'obtaining these documents required "considerable charge and trouble", and often failed in their purpose'.[38] Anna Clark argues that in practice, 'the law rarely protected women and allowed private patriarchy to continue'.[39] By contrast, Jennine Hurl-Eamon suggests that women would not have used the law 'if they felt the abuse would escalate as a result.'[40]

Did the sitting justices take cases of domestic violence seriously? It would seem that while they ostensibly heard them on merit their primary purpose was to act as mediators between the combatants as they did with most other assaults. However, the evidence from the City would appear to be consistent with comparative work in revealing that abused women could and did take their husbands to court.[41] It must have taken a great deal of courage, effort and risk to do so. The best that could be achieved would be a separation with some form of financial settlement or maintenance, or perhaps a restraining order, but this was by no means a guaranteed outcome. Given that the magistracy regarded all assault as a private matter and a negotiated settlement as the preferred outcome, women were very much at the mercy of a male-dominated justice system. However, it would appear that despite these obstacles women in the City were prepared to use the law when they found themselves in abusive relationships, and this in itself may imply that at least some of them achieved outcomes that were useful to them in dealing with their partner's violence.[42]

Not all violence suffered by women was at the hands of their husbands however, as the case of Mrs Devonshire, beaten for complaining about her bread, demonstrates. Anne Bailey was assaulted in Fleet Street on a Saturday evening by 'a respectable land surveyor'. He claimed that she had struck first before causing a scene for 'some wicked purpose'.[43] Given that Fleet Street was synonymous with prostitution we might speculate that Anne had given her attacker the wrong impression or had reacted forcefully to his unwanted advances. Being on the street and dressed in the 'wrong' way could sometimes lead to violence. In 1817 a constable mistook two respectable ladies 'for strumpets', one of whom 'struck him with her umbrella' when he tried to move her on.[44]

Misunderstandings notwithstanding there are several instances of men attacking women in the streets or in lodgings and many cases where female tavern staff were attacked by customers, not infrequently for refusing to serve them when they had had too much already – once again denoting the strong casual link between alcohol and violence. Women, and particularly servant girls, were especially vulnerable to

male domination and violence. In May 1815 'a respectable tradesman' was charged by a Miss Elliot, with assaulting her. The prosecutrix
stated, that

> she had lived in the service of the prosecutor a considerable time, and
> that he had contrived to win her affections, and to effect her ruin. She
> was now likely to become a mother by him; and in consequence of
> some unpleasant words between them, he had struck her violently in
> the chest, knocked her against a wainscot, and severely bruised her
> shoulder.

This case was considered serious enough to be heard before a jury.[45]
It comes quite late in our analysis and could represent a change in
attitudes towards violence as illustrated by Lord Ellenborough's Act of
1803 that sought to punish those that offered serious harm to others,
although it might equally reflect the inability of the pair to be brought
to a satisfactory settlement by the magistrate.[46]

Plebeian women frequently found themselves in situations where
they were exposed to violence, sometimes as an indirect consequence
of their gendered role. For example, when Elizabeth Palmer became
involved in an argument with another woman about the price of eggs,
the dispute escalated and eggs were thrown, some of which landed on a
nearby stall. When Thomas Merton reacted, by angrily throwing water
over Palmer, she took him to court.[47] This dispute had originated from
an all-female quarrel and as was noted earlier approximately 27 per cent
of assault prosecutions were the result of violence between women.

Violence between women

Violence between males was often occasioned by public altercations in
alehouses, or as a result of disputes on the streets. For women the pattern is gendered but similar. Market places, shops and shared lodgings all
provided locations for battles between women. These disputes could be
petty or involve actual physical damage. Ann Bird went to law because
Mary McIntyre spat at her while Mary Clark was 'very much beat and
scratched' by her female assailant.[48] Formal weapons were less likely to
feature in assaults between women and the injuries they inflicted, such
as the scratches suffered by Mary Clark, are different (but no less upsetting) from the bruises and broken bones that occasionally resulted from
fights between men. As well as fingernails women tended to employ

any household utensils, such as pails or chamber pots, that were close to hand.[49]

Ongoing arguments were a feature of urban life; communities lived very closely together and small incidents mattered in people's lives. When Elizabeth Hemmings complained that Sarah Pipkin had thrown a chamber pot out of her window that had narrowly missed her it unveiled an ongoing feud between the two neighbours. Witnesses told the court that Pipkin had abused Hemmings outside church, and accused her of theft. Hemmings had responded by collecting her chamber pot and 'emptying a quantity of her reverence over her'.[50] Accusations of sexual infidelity, criminal behaviour or of informing (against loved ones, friends or neighbours) could all provoke violent reactions, many of which were merely verbal but could still amount to a justification to prosecute. Crowded lodgings were also regular sources of tension in this period and many assaults arose as a result.[51] Martha Phillips questioned Hannah Martin's respectability because of her choice of hair ribbons and similar incidents must have plagued relationships where money was scarce and personal possessions and self-image were placed at a premium.[52] Some cases bound for the quarter sessions started life in the summary courts. Three women were charged with threatening to murder another woman, or 'to do her some bodily harm' by throwing acid or similar things at her. Her 'gown, a valuable shawl, and other articles of dress, were burned and destroyed.' The lord mayor correctly interpreted this as a transportable felony, and remanded the prisoners for trial.[53] Such attacks were probably intended to leave a 'mark of shame' on the intended victims and assault should not be seen as simply violence: words, particularly insults and threats, could be deemed to be assaults on the reputations of the recipients, assaults every bit as damaging as blows and punches.

Men responded to insults concerning their honour or manliness and women could be equally protective of their reputations.[54] Joanna Hook used the courts to prosecute Mary Hullen and Mary Ally for striking her but she may well have been more concerned to publicly challenge the cries of 'whore' that they had levelled against her.[55] Thus, the summary court, as a public space, was a useful arena for plebeian women (and men) to obtain public apologies for attacks on their characters as well as their bodies. Women also became embroiled in tavern fights and disputes, for much the same reasons as men did. When Mary Clark refused to serve Mary Jones with more liquor she 'struck her in the breast' and when Mary Corr tried to help herself to Mary Anderson's oyster tray she was thumped for her pains.[56]

It would be wrong to dismiss all female violence as petty or trivial, although on many occasions this would have been an accurate description. Women did use violence to protect themselves and in less-legitimate circumstances. Prostitutes were quite happy to use violence to resist the attempts of the watch to arrest them or move them on – witness the case of the streetwalker who stood toe-to-toe with a watchman (discussed in Chapter 3). Sometimes the attempts of the watch to arrest women ended in street brawls as both the women and their clients resisted. Isaac Bockarah, a substitute constable, prosecuted Elizabeth Scott for assaulting him in the execution of his duty when he attempted to prevent her soliciting on the streets. Prostitutes also assaulted (and were assaulted by) their clients and other street users. The process of soliciting could vary from lewd suggestion to direct physical contact. The latter may well have led to accusations of assault from either party if accompanied with enough violence. Elizabeth Moody and Ann Steward were arrested on Saturday night at the request of a gentleman (who they claimed had assaulted *them*) who then failed to appear to prosecute them on the Monday.[57] This counter claim of assault was frequently used and must have served to make the adjudication process very problematic for the magistracy. If there was little evidence of actual bodily harm just who's word were they supposed to believe? In this latter case it is clear that the word of a gentleman was evidence enough. This sometimes prejudicial view of evidence, coupled with the discretionary nature of summary justice and the vagaries of assault itself, led to many acts of interpersonal violence and abuse being dealt with in a seemingly casual manner, as we shall see when considering the treatment of assault by the courts. Before doing so however, it is necessary to conclude our analysis of the nature of assault by looking more generally at attacks on officials.

Attacks on City officials

City constables and watchmen routinely encountered abuse and were exposed to violence in the course of their duties. Much of the work of the Watch was in moving along those who were out on the streets after dark without good reason. This naturally included a number of people who were somewhat the worse for drink. It also included those who took a dislike to the police in general or to certain officers in particular. Leman Caseby became fed up with the abuse he received every time he passed a Mrs Beal in the streets. Having been involved in prosecuting a relation of hers she had developed a habit of calling out 'there goes the informer, he'll be well paid' every time she saw him.[58] Such verbal brickbats must have been fairly common. City constables also came under attack when they tried to police the morals of the labouring classes. The aforementioned Isaac Bockarah and two colleagues, Jacob Spinoza and Edward Jolly, interrupted a card game whereupon Spinoza was seized and threatened, his assailant vowing he would 'cut his bloody head off'.[59] John Morris threatened to cut off the nose of constable McPherson when he arrested him and Isabella Carr for being disorderly.[60] When Jonathan Hilliard intervened in a disturbance at the London hospital he was assaulted by a very drunken Jonathan Peacock, who later apologised and told the court he was overwrought at the condition of his son. In 1815 the papers reported the case of a watchman who had 'been pulled by the nose', while other watchmen had their lanterns stolen (sometimes while they slept) and their boxes turned over as we saw in Chapter 3.[61] The duty of the constable was seen as an onerous one, with consequences beyond the term of office, some of which could be painful.

It would seem that most, but not all, assault prosecutions at summary level were the result of essentially minor acts of violence. There were assaults that can be viewed as little more than accidents and violence in pubs that arose as the result of an excess of alcohol and a lack of good sense. Domestic abuse and attacks upon women were depressingly common while women fought other women when everyday frustrations boiled over. Assault could mean just about anything in the late eighteenth century and this is amply demonstrated in the records of the Mansion House and Guildhall courtrooms. It is now possible to move on to see how these disputes were dealt with by the summary process.

The treatment of assault prosecutions by the City courts

Many of the prosecutors who appeared at the Middlesex Quarter Sessions hoped to gain some form of compensation for the assaults that they had suffered, and so were using the courts as *civil* rather than *criminal* courts.[62] The motive for prosecution was not, therefore, simply one of punishing violence but rather a lever to encourage (or indeed to force) the financial settlement of a dispute.[63] It also appears from related work that prosecutors were using the King's Bench court in a similar way.[64]

However, in the City relatively few cases reached the quarter sessions or King's Bench, being filtered out at the summary level, and it was here that settlement was most important in order to avoid the expense of taking the case any further. Sometimes the main point of prosecution seems to have been to simply air the grievance and obtain an apology, while

others were after a more formal settlement, perhaps with some pecu-
niary award. That settlements between parties involved some exchange
of money or material goods seems highly likely. We need only look to
the example of the Middlesex sessions where money frequently changed
hands in variable amounts, according to personal circumstances and the
nature or severity of the assault.[65] In the City while many of the cases
recorded in the minute books give little clue as to the nature of the
settlement we do have enough information to suggest that some form
of compensation and the payment of court fees was forthcoming from
defendants. Formal apologies were also frequently used to resolve disputes, and again while we should be wary of speculating it is perhaps not
unreasonable to believe that a handshake and admittance of guilt was
sufficient to allow some prosecutors to drop the case at an early stage.
As will be shown, there were a variety of ways in which reconciliations
could be brokered by the sitting magistrate.

Table 5.3 demonstrates that the vast majority of assault cases that
came before the City magistracy were dealt with without recourse to the
wider criminal justice system. Over 45 per cent of all cases were recorded
as being settled in some way or another, probably with the help of the
magistrate. A further 39 per cent were dismissed. These may have simply
been trivial (or 'frivolous') disputes or this might be another way of list-
ing cases that had been settled. A few accusations were dismissed with
an admonishment from the magistrate to one or both of the parties.

Where more serious action was required or the defendant and accused
could not be reconciled the cases were removed to the Sessions or the
defendant required to provide sureties or face imprisonment, but this

Table 5.3 Outcomes of assault cases heard before the City justice
rooms, 1784–96

Outcome	Number	Percentage
Settled and discharged	278	45.6
Dismissed	237	38.9
Reprimand and discharged	7	1.1
Fine	2	0.3
Bailed to Q/S	37	6.0
Imprisoned for want of sureties	42	6.8
Other	6	1.0
Total known	609	99.7
Outcome unknown	84	–
Total	693	–

Source: The minute books of the Guildhall and Mansion House justice rooms.[66]

seldom happened. The assault on Samuel Phillips by Charles Fisher in August 1790 was described as 'violent' and Fisher was committed to gaol to find sureties.[67] In the same month William Loveless and William Toby were committed for their assault on a local constable as he tried to carry out his duty.[68] However, less than 15 per cent of all cases required more punitive action by the court. Only 13 per cent were sent on to the Sessions and a handful punished by short spells in the Bridewell. Sureties were an important part of the justice's armoury and helped to encourage settlements in that they 'provided a financial guarantee that the defendant would fulfil the obligations stated on the recognisance, which were usually to appear at the next sessions and to keep the peace (or to be of "good behaviour") in the interim'.[69] Indeed, we can regard imprisonment for want of sureties as a punishment option in a period before imprisonment was generally used to punish violent offenders.[70] The small number of individuals (42 out of 609) that were unable to find someone to stand surety for them may have had an uncomfortable wait in prison until their case was heard at the sessions, and this may have informed prosecutors' tactics in some instances.

It would appear that female defendants in assault cases might well have been disadvantaged by the summary process. Studies from elsewhere have indicated that women received slightly harsher treatment at the quarter sessions in the punishment of assault. In Cornwall in the period 1737–1821 women found guilty were 'nearly twice as likely to be given direct prison sentences' as men.[71] Table 5.4 would suggest that

Table 5.4 Outcomes of assault cases heard before the City justice rooms by gender of the accused, 1784–96

Outcome	Male	%	Female	%	Total
Settled and discharged	194	47.7	84	41.3	278
Dismissed	160	39.4	77	37.9	237
Reprimanded and Discharged	3	0.7	4	1.9	7
Fine	0	0	2	1.0	2
Bailed to Q/S	20	4.9	17	8.3	37
Imprisoned (WOS)	26	6.4	16	7.8	42
Other	3	0.7	3	1.4	6
Total known	406	99.8	203	99.6	609
Outcome unknown	71	–	13	–	84
Total cases	477	–	216	–	693

Source: The minute books of the Guildhall and Mansion House justice rooms.[72]

this gendered difference is also in evidence at the City summary courts in the late eighteenth century.

While a similar proportion of women had the cases against them settled or dismissed a slighter higher percentage were bailed to quarter sessions or imprisoned for want of sureties. There are a couple of explanations for this. In the 609 cases of assault contained within this sample, for which the outcome is known, there are only 77 cases that require the use of the wider justice system. It may be that these cases are extraordinary. Abigail Ephraim was arrested on a warrant from King's Bench which suggests that her offence was a part of a more elongated feud.[73] Bel Peale, a prostitute who assaulted a lady's servant was unable to find sureties. She was later released when her accuser dropped the charges. George Bruce and Jonathan Thordown had gone to St. Paul's Cathedral to visit the whispering gallery but were refused entry because divine service was being heard. Undeterred they attempted to barge their way through, pushing past the two officers on duty. They were arrested, charged and bound over to find sureties for the attack, which they did. By contrast it may not have been so easy for an unmarried woman to have found someone to vouch for her (by standing surety), which may explain why proportionally more women were imprisoned.[74] It may also be the case that there was a slightly less lenient attitude towards women engendered by an anxiety about female independence in the City which would chime with recent studies elsewhere, but this conclusion is rather tentative.[75] In several instances the women that were brought in for assault were streetwalkers arrested by the watch, and they may have been treated more harshly for this related issue rather than for the violence.[76]

Leaving aside gendered differences in sentencing it is clear that less than 15 per cent of all assault prosecutions heard before the City magistrates were sent up through the wider court system. This figure may of course very slightly exaggerate the importance of the summary courts since some cases may have bypassed the City justices and been presented directly at the Sessions or King's Bench. However, it is evident that the vast majority of assault cases were settled or dismissed at summary level. While acknowledging that the minute books are hardly illuminating when it comes to assault cases it is possible to attempt to analyse the forms that these settlements took.

The nature of settlements in assault cases

In October 1789 John Goddard punched Joseph Saunders, nearly dislocating his jaw, apparently without any provocation. Both men worked at Billingsgate market and Saunders had been successful in getting work when Goddard had not. Perhaps an exchange of words led to blows. Whatever the cause Saunders took his complaint to the Mansion House and obtained a warrant for Goddard's arrest. On the following day Goddard was brought before the court and he and Saunders settled their disagreement.[77] However, there is no indication of what form that settlement took. This is the unfortunate situation with the majority of assault prosecutions that end in settlements. The violence of Goddard's attack certainly represents an assault (however loose the term), but the fact that Saunders was prepared to drop the matter perhaps suggests that it was also not uncommon and something that could be resolved without further need for troubling the wider justice system.

Table 5.5 Settlements and dismissals in assault cases before the Guildhall justice room in the 1790s where the nature of the settlement was recorded

Settlement Type	Number	Percentage
Discharged on merits (Frivolous/Equal blame)	22	23.1
At request/Consent of prosecutor/Forgiven	20	21.0
Promise of good behaviour/Asking pardon	15	15.7
Advised to make satisfaction	14	14.7
Payment of expenses	14	14.7
Prosecutor not appearing/No charge	10	10.5
Total known	95	99.7
Unknown	125	–
Total	220	–

Source: The minute books of the Guildhall justice room.[78]

Within a subset of 220 cases from the Guildhall in the 1790s there is a clear indication of the way in which assault was dealt with by the magistrates, 95 cases clearly record the rationale behind the adjudications made. While this only represents 43 per cent of settlements in the sample it is reasonable to expect that many of the cases for which we have little information would fall within the broad categories listed above.

Ten per cent of prosecutors failed to appear to press their suits, a not uncommon occurrence in property cases. Some prosecutors were concerned about the possibility of seeing the defendant sent to his or her death for relatively minor thefts, while others simply chose not to undertake the expense of a full trial. There is also the possibility that they had been unable to build an effective case or that witnesses had died or moved away. Some poorer prosecutors may have used the court system in a different way to richer victims of crime and viewed the imprisonment of offenders before trial as a sufficient sanction in some cases.[79] But does this explain the non-appearance of prosecutors in assault cases at the Guildhall in this sample? Some of those released may have spent a night or more in the compter while others would have suffered the ignominy of an arrest by a City constable, both unpleasant situations and possibly seen as punishment enough by their victims. The criminal justice system of the eighteenth century was a lengthy process, with time spent waiting for the sessions and assizes, and related expenses in the payment of witnesses and lost working time.[80] By contrast complaints before the City justices resulted in warrants that were executed within hours, and plaintiffs could usually expect to have their complaints heard within 24 or 48 hours. Here the wheels of justice turned much more quickly than at the quarter sessions or assize. Some people might have acted in the heat of the moment, but having considered the case decided to stop the process. Given that many assaults arose out of drunken brawls it is possible that they may not have looked that serious in the cold light of day when sobriety returned.

But those who did persevere with their suits often found that their complaints were simply dismissed. Nearly a quarter of assault cases in this subset were 'discharged on merits' as being unworthy of further consideration. Assaults between women were not infrequently dismissed as being frivolous, suggesting that they were either not serious or that the magistrates did not take them seriously.[81] In April 1779 Elizabeth Court was discharged when the justice ruled that her attack upon Margaret Thatcher [*sic*] was 'frivolous'.[82] Sometimes the magistrate stated that he simply did not believe the prosecutor. When Mary Whiteman accused Mary Ward of assault, Ward replied that the prosecutrix had in fact 'rushed into her house with violence' after accusing her of holding another's goods. Ward's story was upheld by witnesses and the alderman discharged her.[83] Male combatants were more likely to have their cases dismissed by the magistracy when he felt that there was little to choose between them. Thus some claims were rejected because there was 'blame on both sides' or 'equal blame' adjudged by the alderman. The charge of assault against Simon Fisher presented by John Morris was dismissed by Alderman Boydell because in his opinion it appeared to be no more than a 'drunken squabble', this despite the fact that Morris had been stabbed.[84] Here, as elsewhere, the magistrate was acting as the adjudicator and these *dismissals* should really be seen as *settlements*.

In 14.7 per cent of cases the alderman sent the parties away with the advice that they should settle their differences. Victims did not always

heed this advice however, and this could then lead to magistrates binding over the parties to appear at quarter sessions in the hope that they
might reach a settlement in the meantime. The arbitration skills possessed by the magistrate were partly dependent upon the desire of the
prosecutor (and the defendant) to reach an agreement. That most of
them did is evidenced by the relatively small number of cases that progressed to the higher courts. The sitting alderman at Guildhall ordered
the three attackers of Jonathan Humphries, a member of the patrol for
Farringdon within, to settle with him. The men had quarrelled outside
a disorderly house in the ward and had tried to wrestle away his staff
of office; they had been held in the compter overnight and Humphries
seems to have been content to let the matter drop, perhaps because some
financial recompense changed hands.[85]

A third of these cases ended in some kind of direct reconciliation
between the parties. Some cases were dropped at the request of the prosecutor because they had forgiven their attacker. This was often the case
in disputes between husbands and wives where the aim of prosecution
was in part to correct a husband's behaviour and further punishment
was rarely necessary or desired (for the reasons I outlined earlier, the loss
of a husband or a fine could actually make a bad situation worse). Men,
including constables and other City officials, could also be happy to
resolve disputes without further sanctions, especially when a defendant
had been incarcerated for a short period. William Bird, a constable, was
abused by John Brown who swore repeatedly and 'put his fist in the prosecutor's face'. However Bird was happy to let the matter rest after Brown
had been detained overnight and had apologised.[86] In some cases, the
prisoner was released after promising not to repeat the offence. This was
a less formal version of binding over. Apologies and a promise of future
good conduct may well have been the intention of many of these prosecutions. If the offence was relatively minor, which it was in many cases,
it seems likely that the aim of prosecution was a public demonstration
of remorse. This allowed the aggrieved party to show that they were in
the right in the dispute, it protected their honour and good name and
was a fast solution to a problem.

But, as Landau and Paley have suggested, sometimes an apology was
not sufficient on its own.[87] There had to be some form of financial recompense to compensate the victim. This might simply have meant the
payment of any expenses incurred in bringing the case to law. Prosecutors might ask to have their legal costs paid, the warrant or the
clerk's fees, for example. Some might have required payment for lost
time or trade. Others might have sought larger amounts if they had

suffered injury. Sarah Berry dropped her case against Mary Jenkins (for hurting her infant son) when Mary agreed to pay her expenses. Ann Thompson was similarly satisfied when she brought Sarah Hasewell in for assault.[88] Sometimes the payment did not involve money; two men called Murphy and Moor agreed to share a gallon of beer together as a reconciliation of the dispute between them which was noted as being 'customary among them'.[89] Given the frequency in which alcohol features in assault cases, we might wonder whether this was actually a very sensible way to reconcile disputes.

Overall, 85 per cent of all assault cases heard before the summary courts of the City ended in some form of settlement, with the magistrate acting as arbiter. Crucially, discretion remained firmly with the prosecutor. If the victim of violence decided not to proceed, or accepted an apology or promise of good behaviour the defendant would be released. Sometimes this apology or promise was backed by a financial settlement, which could involve anything from the payment of legal costs to significant compensation for injuries received. While the minute books are often too scanty in detail to allow us to be more forthcoming on this issue, it still seems axiomatic that the intention of the prosecutor was to receive some form of admission of guilt, backed by an apology, all of which was made in a public space and before a member of the City's elite. This appears to be what mattered to the eighteenth-century victim of petty violence in the City of London.

Concluding remarks

A great deal of the time of the City magistracy was spent in resolving assault prosecutions that arose from everyday disputes between Londoners. City dwellers were bringing more than 20 assault prosecutions a week before the magistrates, approximately 1000 annually. By contrast in 1786 the quarter sessions heard just 34 prosecutions for assault and in 1796 a slightly higher figure of 42.[90] What does this mean for our understanding of the regulation of violence in the late eighteenth-century City? Given that as many as one in seven households were involved in an assault prosecution each year this represents a staggering involvement of the City's populace in the court process. By the late nineteenth century, as Jennifer Davis has shown, London's working classes were regularly using the capital's police courts to seek resolutions in their interpersonal disputes, and there is some evidence that residents of Georgian Bath were equally comfortable with using the summary process.[91] While the lack of detailed occupational data in the minute books is problematic, it is clear that there was also a heavy plebeian usage of the City summary courts to prosecute assault. Thus we might extend Brewer and Styles' argument that the justice system was a 'multiple-use right' to include some elements of London's labouring poor.[92] Here even the very poor members of society could employ this system to resolve disputes between themselves. The direct experience of large numbers of Londoners in using the summary process for the resolution of interpersonal disputes may also have helped facilitate the 'grudging accommodation with the more egregious aspects of the criminal process'[93] that Brewer and Styles have suggested or at least have allowed a 'pragmatic acceptance of' the law's usefulness.[94]

Assault is an extremely difficult offence to quantify in any period, given the ambiguity of definition and the huge amount of incidents that passed without legal action being taken.[95] Given that so much of the day-to-day violence of the City went on without the need for any official intervention the numbers that do appear are dramatic. Many victims would have chosen not to take their disputes before the magistrates for a range of personal, economic and social reasons. Many disputes could be resolved without the need for warrants, summons or the judiciary. So what we are left with are the disputes that individuals could not (or would not) resolve amicably.

Landau has argued effectively that the motive behind assault prosecutions at the quarter sessions was primarily financial, that victims were intent upon gaining some kind of compensation for the injuries that were done to them.[96] Paley has recently used the King's Bench to draw similar conclusions.[97] Both of these studies help us to understand the nature of assault prosecutions and in particular the motivations of victims. But it is important to note that historians looking in the records of the higher courts for ways of understanding attitudes towards violence and in particular assaults are perhaps looking in the wrong place. At the quarter sessions for the City in 1796 only 22 individuals ended up with any kind of sanction being placed upon them by the court. The King's Bench court also dealt with assault cases but again the figures were small. In the period 1797–99 the average number of assault indictments to the King's Bench was 29 per year, and this is for London *and* Middlesex.[98] This is a very small number of people and while the outcome achieved by prosecutors may have been motivated by a desire for compensation and redress it is not clear that their use of the higher courts was of any real benefit to them. Most of their fellow citizens were achieving similar outcomes in the Mansion House and Guildhall with considerably less effort and time being exhausted. Only a very tiny percentage of assault prosecutions were sent on through the criminal justice system.

Finally it is important to reiterate the point that in the eighteenth century assault was treated very much as a *civil* rather than a *criminal* offence. Here the summary courts can be seen clearly as an 'arena of struggle and negotiation'.[99] The overwhelming majority of assault prosecutions were settled by negotiation, with settlements taking a variety of forms. Assault was a multi-faceted offence that engendered a multi-layered response. At the heart of this lay the conundrum that assault was both a civil and a criminal offence, at least until the mid-nineteenth century. Contemporaries viewed it as both and this had an important effect on prosecution strategies. A prosecution for assault at the summary courts could arise from an accident, from an argument that became heated or from long-term feuding, or as a result of the actions of officials policing the streets. This list is by no means exhaustive; the diversity of assault prosecutions reflects the multiplicity of petty conflicts and disputes that featured as a part of daily life in the late eighteenth-century urban environment. In the next three chapters we shall see that many of the other pressures of City life resulted in prosecutions before the magistracy.

6
Regulating the Streets

The summary courts of the City also concerned themselves with a range of regulatory actions, as well as interpersonal violence and petty theft, arising from daily life in the capital. These can be roughly divided into two types: economic and social regulatory offences and issues concerning the discipline, mobility and sexuality of the poor. Combined, these two areas probably accounted for around a third of all offences brought before the summary courts. This area of the courts' business covered disorderly behaviour, which often meant drunkenness on the City's streets, prostitution, problems with beggars and vagrants as well as traffic problems such as dangerous driving and obstruction. Much of the business of the summary courts is therefore best seen as the simple regulation of everyday life. Most of the individuals involved in these prosecutions would have been the constables, watchmen and street keepers who were the historical predecessors of modern policemen and traffic wardens.

The drivers of carts or their employers were frequently summoned to appear by constables and street keepers. Carts were licensed in the way that hackney carriages were, so that they could be controlled to some extent within the City boundaries. The toll collector at Aldgate appeared on a number of occasions not only to prosecute those refusing the toll but also to punish violations of the rules governing working vehicles. Such cases point to a desire on the behalf of the authorities to regulate street life and to impose a sense of order on the metropolis which is in line with the regulation of hackney carriages, increased street lighting and directives concerning the appearance of streets and houses.[1] The prosecution of street offences, whilst they could generate small rewards in fees for the prosecutors is therefore best seen as simple regulation. As will be seen in the discussion of bull-running in the following chapter, the City authorities were keen to keep London's streets open rather than allowing them to become blocked with vehicles or animals. Constables also brought considerable numbers of prostitutes, drunks and other disorderly individuals before the courts and charged them with a variety of offences. Much of this prosecution can be viewed as the imposition of order and authority on the inhabitants of the City by those elected to serve their communities. Similarly the actions of churchwardens and overseers who brought charges of bastardy, desertion and a variety of infringements of the poor laws, can be situated within this area of court usage. However, not all of those bringing prosecutions under the broad heading of regulatory offending were parish officers or other City officials.

Hackney coachmen appeared to prosecute those that attempted to avoid paying their fares, or who disputed the size of the fare. Other drivers, notably draymen and carters, also prosecuted those who failed to pay them. These, plus servants who were attempting to get unpaid wages or a reference from a former master, and apprentices complaining of poor treatment, make up the majority of poor prosecutors. So again significant numbers of those labelled as 'poverty vulnerable' or 'labouring poor' were using the summary process. This chapter will examine the attitude of the authorities towards a variety of actions that brought their perpetrators to the attention of the courts and ask what was the role of the summary courts in this process of regulation, and whose interests did it serve? As can be seen from Table 6.1 a variety of offences that affected the streets and communities of the City were heard before the justices.

Table 6.1   Prosecutions for regulatory offences, 1784–96

Offence	Number	Percentage
Disorderly conduct	280	31.9
Traffic violations	179	20.4
Trading violations	144	16.4
Vagrancy and begging	92	10.5
Prostitution	66	7.5
Bull-running/Animal abuse	57	6.5
Bastardy and desertion of family	52	5.9
Lottery Offences	7	0.7
Totals	877	99.8

Source: The minute books of the Guildhall and Mansion House justice rooms.[2]

This chapter will concentrate on the control of the streets, while Chapter 7 will deal with bull-running and Chapter 8 with the regulation of trade, workplace, poverty and related issues.

Table 6.2   Prosecutions for street-related regulatory offences, 1784–96

Offence	Number	Percentage
Disorderly conduct	280	48.1
Traffic violations	179	30.7
Prostitution	66	11.3
Bull-running/Animal abuse	57	9.7
Totals	582	99.8

Source: The minute books of the Guildhall and Mansion House justice rooms.[3]

As with modern local authorities and police organisations, the control of the streets was crucial to notions of good governance. The threat to civic peace, and by implication civic pride, came from a range of criminal or semi-legal activities that obstructed the thoroughfares of the City. The struggle for the control of public and commercial space was an increasingly important one to the image of a well-ordered metropolis and there were periodic clampdowns on a range of activities that were intrinsic to popular culture. Drunken and disorderly behaviour, dangerous driving, the obstruction of pavements and prostitution will be addressed in turn here.

Disorderly behaviour, drunkenness and the City streets

Table 6.2 demonstrates the high incidence of prosecutions for disorderly behaviour in the late eighteenth-century City. However, 'disorderly conduct' was a vague term that covered a multitude of actions considered inappropriate.[4] Disorderly servants, employees, apprentices and paupers could all find themselves presented before the magistrates. Other categories of disorderly offenders mask the appearance of prostitutes, suspected thieves and vagrants. In 1784 the *General Evening Post* described a gang of roughs and thieves, known as Lady Holland's Mob, as 'disorderly fellows', while disorderly houses were sometimes brothels.[5] Prostitutes were commonly labelled 'lewd and disorderly' women and suspected thieves were often termed 'loose, idle and disorderly persons'. The term was very wide ranging and could be, perhaps deliberately, loosely applied. After the Gordon riots of 1780 attitudes towards riotous disorderly behaviour may well have changed as Londoners faced up to the very real prospect of injury or death if they became embroiled in political protest and the elites increasingly saw such action as 'nothing more than a source of disorder'.[6] So the term 'disorderly', as used by the courts, newspapers and others, may have represented a general feeling of intolerance towards unruly behaviour.

Defining 'riotous' is just as problematic. 'Riotous behaviour' could involve breaking windows, being abusive in the streets or taverns or knocking doors late at night. One person arrested for 'riotous' behaviour seems to have been guilty of persecuting a Polish immigrant by continually calling him names and inciting others to join in.[7] The same types of behaviour were covered by 'disorderly conduct'; there are examples of people shouting in the streets, crying 'murder' or calling the hour, of disorderly paupers misbehaving, the insane causing disturbances and individuals who would not go quietly when moved along by the patrols. Much of this anti-social behaviour was fuelled by the consumption of alcohol and when the summary courts records concerned themselves with riotous or disorderly behaviour what they were really dealing with on many occasions was the problem of intoxication in the urban setting.

Alcohol was freely available. There were inns and taverns serving food and drinks alongside entertainment; alehouses and gin shops which catered for a less-discerning consumer, barrows and cellars where even cheaper drink could be found and consumed. London had a drinking culture that was 'interwoven with everyday life'.[8] The alehouse was an essential part of the community, acting as an informal labour exchange and as pawnbrokers and moneylenders, as well as a centre of discussion and gossip.[9] They were also home to many of London's prostitutes, especially on the long river border, their landlords well aware of the symbiotic relationship between the alcohol and the sex trade.[10]

Alehouses were also associated with gambling and crime, and this, along with the inevitable consequences of excessive alcohol consumption meant that the City's drinking establishments occupied a significant proportion of court time at Guildhall and Mansion House. Justices of the Peace (JPs) were instructed by Burn on how to deal with drunkenness, with the use of fines and the stocks and the removal of licences from landlords who failed to keep orderly houses.[11] There were clampdowns on alehouses that allowed radicals to assemble and in 1792 City of London magistrates withdrew licences from a number of establishments. There was increasing control and supervision of drinking houses, with campaigns to limit their hours of opening, raise the cost of licenses, and restrictions on almost every aspect of the business. One victualler complained that 'every house has received instructions as to where shall stand the bar, the customer, the casks, the cocks, the tap-room, nay even the very spot where the proprietor shall eat and drink'.[12]

With the loss of the American colonies and the rise of evangelism came the renewal of the campaign for the reformation of manners. The early membership of the Proclamation Society (headed by William Wilberforce) founded in 1787 included Brook Watson, a London alderman and magistrate.[13] The close-knit world of City government would inevitably have meant that the ideas of the Proclamation Society (and related movements such as the Society for Bettering the Condition of the Poor) would have been discussed at the tables of the well-to-do in London society. This echoed the previous movement for the reformation of manners that occurred in the early eighteenth century.[14] While the reformation of manners movement contained many London luminaries its judicial arm was operated by the City's magistrates. As Joanna Innes has argued; 'More than any other groups, ... magistrates set the agenda for the late eighteenth-century reformation of manners movement'.[15] The problems of disorder caused by drink and gambling were more pronounced in the capital as here drink-fuelled disorder could create disruption to trade and commerce and adversely affect external perceptions of the City. Justices were appointed 'for the conservation of the peace'; with this role in mind, and understanding that in the last quarter of the eighteenth century the focus of concern was firmly placed upon the drinking and related leisure habits of the lower orders (which is not to ignore contemporary concerns about elite immorality), we can now turn to the prosecution of drink-related offending at the summary courts.

Undoubtedly alcohol played a significant role in bringing offenders to the attention of the courts. Offenders arrested for disorderly conduct were routinely described as being 'abusive' or 'riotous' in the streets, refusing to move along when asked to by watchmen and constables or to leave public houses by landlords when they had consumed too much liquor. Charles Doute was 'very much inebriated' when he was picked up by a City constable, while Jonathan Turner was described as 'very much in liquor' when he created a disturbance in the house of Thomas Gill.[16] Others were 'very drunk', 'in liquor', 'drunk and riotous', and several of these individuals were too drunk to appear before the courts and had to be remanded until the following day. When Ann Griffith was arrested for 'making a great riot and disturbance' by a watchmen who believed she was a prostitute, the magistrate accepted that in fact she was 'but a poor woman a little overcome with liquor' who 'was now penitent'.[17] As far as the watch was concerned it probably mattered little what her offence was; their instructions were to round up the disorderly, and therefore those abroad at night without good reason to be so were likely to be arrested.

Alehouse keepers such as George Birkley were required to operate orderly houses and in protecting their licences were aware that they had to police their establishments. Birkley charged William Musgrove with drunken behaviour in his alehouse and the alderman, hearing that Musgrove had previously been the recipient of relief from the parish, sent him to Bridewell.[18] Timothy Woodhead apologised in court to the landlord of the *Devil Tavern* in Temple Bar for causing a disturbance in his establishment.[19] Again, the landlord, Joseph Smith, was mindful of the reputation of his house, which is why he prosecuted. Licensees in the City had to be freemen; a restriction not applied to those operating in the wider metropolis, and City landlords may have felt a greater need to preserve their reputations in the light of this.[20] They would also have been aware that it was the aldermen magistrates and the lord mayor that had the power to remove as well as issue the licences they depended upon.

Being imprisoned was no barrier to getting intoxicated in the eighteenth century since alcohol was freely available in London's many prisons despite attempts to restrict it.[21] Rose Queen was brought to court from Bridewell for drunkenness and was promptly sent back there with a seven-day extension to her sentence.[22] Drink was also available to those who used the workhouse. Despite their protestations that when Martha Hicks was allowed to enjoy the hospitality of the house she endeavoured to get drunk, the Churchwardens of St. Boltoph's Aldersgate were instructed to continue to relieve her by the sitting alderman.[23]

Drunk and disorderly persons were not always described as such, but frequently this can be strongly inferred from the circumstances related in court. Leaving aside disorderly prostitutes (who may often have been drunk), those arrested on the streets may have been on their way home and have drawn the attention of the watch by their rowdy behaviour. At what point did the watch decide to step in and remove these individuals from the streets? An unnamed 'young gentleman' was brought before John Wilkes in 1789, charged with 'amusing himself the preceding morning, between two and three o'clock, in breaking the Lamps in Newgate-street'.[24] For this disorderly act of drunken criminal damage he was fined and released; had he been of a more ordinary class of person he may have been treated more harshly – in part because he would have been unable to pay for the damage he had caused. There are many similar cases of damage caused to property, of windows smashed or broken, with prosecutions detailing disorderly or riotous behaviour. Most culprits were reprimanded and then released; some were fined or sent to Bridewell. Some of those that were released without official sanction had probably been persuaded to apologise to their victims and to offer them some form of compensation. The appearance of a master, parent or guardian, may have helped some escape punishment but it did not save Samuel Meardy from a spell in Bridewell. Meardy had been 'found wandering about the streets, laying upon steps, and otherwise behaving in a disorderly manner'. His father told the court that he had been unable to 'persuade his son to remain at home, or to attend to his business'. A former master told the court that Samuel had 'for a considerable time back attended very negligently to his work, and that it was impossible to keep him from getting into the streets at night, and becoming entirely careless in his dress'. Samuel's errant behaviour earned him a report in the paper as an object lesson for other young men who might be neglecting their apprenticeships.[25]

The summary courts received the majority of their defendants from the compters at Poultry and Wood Street. In delivering these gaols each day the sitting magistrates were faced with the flotsam and jetsam of the City's streets. Many of those imprisoned overnight were simply drunk and incoherent. As such they were often abusive to the watchmen and constables and this probably contributed to their arrest. Once they had sobered up and calmed down they were usually released, with a warning as to their future conduct. The social status of the accused could certainly assist in gaining a release and paupers who misbehaved or those who were seen as potential thieves were likely to be more severely punished with Bridewell being the preferred option. But some, those with funds like the young man who enjoyed breaking street lamps, might be able to buy their way out of a difficult situation. Status did not, however, render an individual immune from arrest and imprisonment as Thomas Withers discovered. Withers was out late in Bishopsgate Street with some friends, drunk and in high spirits. He was approached by a constable because he was 'knocking on doors and bawling out the hour'. Despite his insistence that he was the son of the Duke of Leeds he was arrested and was asked to spend the rest of the night in Poultry compter.[26]

The arrest of the City's drunks represents the removal of nuisances from the streets. The formal prosecution of these individuals was secondary; they were habitually reprimanded and then released having spent a night or morning sobering up in the compter. This was a common enough police practice in the nineteenth and twentieth centuries and there seems to be no reason to interpret the arrest of drunks in the late eighteenth century in any other way. Using the summary powers of magistrates to prosecute drunks was well established before the late eighteenth century. Michael Dalton exhorted his fellow justices to use their powers to lock up the 'riotous and prodigal person, that consumes all with play, or drinking' and constables and watchmen were instructed to round up offenders and bring them before the magistracy for punishment.[27]

Dangerous driving and other traffic-related offences

One of the problems the City faced was controlling the flow of traffic around its busy streets. Hackney coachmen, the key commercial conveyors of passengers in the period, had several restraints imposed upon them. They were, for example, forbidden from waiting for customers 'between *Cornhill* and *Threadneedle-street*, with the Horses towards *Cheapside*'.[28] The penalty for breaking this law was a fine. This effectively restricted them from 'parking' in the busy commercial heart of the City that included the Bank of England and the Royal Exchange. It is also suggestive of a one-way system: by insisting that all coaches faced east the authorities could hope to keep the flow of vehicles moving steadily.[29] Equally it may have been intended to restrict the number of hackney carriages waiting in the vicinity in order to minimise any obstruction to the free flow of traffic. In 1780 a marshalman who tried to arrest a coachman for 'standing with his coach for hire opposite the Bank' was surrounded by a mob and had to be rescued by a colleague and a local resident.[30] There are several other instances of prosecutions for 'standing for hire in Threadneedle street' or 'standing and plying with coach' in the minute books.[31] Evidently, as one contemporary noted, 'a quick and easy communication from place to place is of the utmost consequence to the inhabitants of a great commercial city'.[32]

It was not just hackney drivers that were prosecuted for obstructing the streets, the minute books detail many instances where constables and street keepers brought in complaints against carters, coachmen and other road users. Street keepers were employed by the wards to keep the thoroughfares free from discarded luggage and furniture.[33] William Jones was prosecuted for 'placing furniture on foot pavement in Brackley Street', and William Holloman for leaving rubbish in Goldsmith's Street near Holborn.[34] Naturally the City authorities neither could not allow unrestricted dumping of rubbish on the streets for reasons of health nor could they tolerate individuals or businesses blocking the roads that others needed to use.

As well as those that left goods on the streets watchmen, constables and street keepers were alert for carters that blocked roads or those who traded on the streets illegally. In 1821 a carman appeared before the lord mayor charged with obstructing the streets, as this report details:

> Mr. Rowe [the prosecutor] stated, that on Monday he was going down Water Lane, on his way from Fenchurch Street to the Custom House, on horseback, when he was stopped in the middle of the street by the defendant's cart, which was placed across so as to stop up all but the foot path. He desired the defendant to move his cart and allow him to pass, when the defendant said he was unloading it, and should not move to please any one until he had done. Remonstrance was unavailing, and he continued to behave both in language and manner with the most insufferable impertinence.[35]

Mr Rowe told the court that he was regularly delayed by such obstructions and complained that 'carmen in general entertained a notion that they had a right to place their carts in what position they pleased, and to keep them in it until they were unloaded' and that he had brought the prosecution in the hope that laws in place to stop this practice were more rigorously enforced.[36] Most of those that were prosecuted were either discharged with a reprimand or were fined 5s, with the fine being paid to the officer bringing the complaint. Given that they were paid for these prosecutions this reinforces an entrepreneurial view of the actions of City police agents.

Along with infringements of City bylaws the courts also dealt with actual incidents of dangerous driving, some of which resulted in injury or death. In November 1784 the *Whitehall Evening Post* carried the following report.

> On Saturday a Hackney-coachman was carried before Mr Alderman Le Mesurier for wilfully driving against a corpse carry up Fetter-lane, by which the coffin was thrown from the bearers' shoulders, and the undertaker endeavouring to keep the coach off, the wheels ran over his foot, and he was so much hurt that he was unable to attend the funeral.[37]

While this is an extraordinary case it is suggestive of the dangers of crowded City streets used for a variety of different purposes. Coaches crashed and overturned and drivers were unseated: sometimes these resulted in prosecutions for assault whilst on other occasions the authorities stepped into prosecute. Some road users, notably hackney coachmen, had particular poor reputations as is evident from this newspaper report:

> On Tuesday a hackney-coachman was whipt at the cart's – tail in a pretty severe manner, from the top of the Hay-market to the bottom, and up again, for overturning a Gentleman and Lady in a one-horse chaise, a short time since; for which he was tried at Guildhall, Westminster. It is hoped this punishment may have a proper effect on the Gentlemen of the Whip, whose insolence is often unbearable.[38]

Hackneys were licensed and regulated under rules set down in the late seventeenth century.[39] The commissioners that regulated hackney coachmen could fine transgressors and commit them to Bridewell if they were unable to pay. Licensing was not just a way of controlling individual coachmen, it also operated as a form of protectionism for the trade.[40] Regulations on working practice allowed coachmen to operate on what can be termed a level playing field, and restrictions that governed where hackneys could pick up and set down were not just of benefit to other road users but also ensured fair trade and prevented abuses. Hackney coachmen enjoyed a poor reputation for manners and for flogging their horses but we need to remember that they worked within a very competitive and demanding market. Ned Ward, the *London Spy*, described the quarrels of hackney coachmen trying to navigate a street blocked by a funeral procession.

> They attacked each other with such a volley of oaths that if a parcel of informers had stood by as witnesses to their profaneness, and would have taken the advantage, there would scarce have been one amongst 'em that would not have sworn away his coach and horses in half the time of the disorder. At last, by sundry stratagems, painful industry, and the great expense of whip-cord, they gave one another way, and then with their "hey-ups" and ill-natured cuts upon their horses, they made such a rattling over the stones that had I been in St Sepulchre's belfry upon an execution day, ... I could not have had a more ingrateful [*sic*] noise in my head than arose from their lumbering conveyances.[41]

The City authorities effectively licensed all commercial users of the streets. Drivers, or their employers, who plied a trade without displaying the evidence of their right to do so were at risk of appearing before the courts. Licensing and parking restrictions were a fairly straightforward way of raising revenue. Carmen (or Carters), the delivery drivers of their day, were licensed and the monies raised were used to fund Christ's Hospital.[42] Restrictions were placed on how carmen worked, such as when and where they entered the City. We might note that raising revenue by taxing road users has a long history in London. Commercial drivers also had to demonstrate that they were in control of their vehicles. The streets were crowded and laws were in place to minimise the opportunity for accidents. Those drivers found riding on the shafts of their wagons without 'some person on foot to guide' them were frequently brought to justice as were those riding on the dray.[43] Francis Loo was prosecuted because he was found not be in control of his vehicle and was fined 10s.[44] Accidents could be fatal: in 1756 Robert Cole was jolted from his position riding on the shafts of his cart and fell under one of the wheels. He later died, in St. Bartholomew's hospital, of his injuries.[45] Others who drove vehicles that failed to conform to laws that governed the use of the highways were also at risk of being punished by the summary courts. Jonathan Anstell was summoned by one of the City's street keepers 'for using his cart [No.14494] in this City drawn by 2 horses the wheels thereof not being 6 inches broad' the magistrate let him off, accepting that he was, on this occasion, unaware of the infringement.[46] The emphasis was on order. A clear regulation of public space was underway in the eighteenth century, reflecting the continual expansion of London, (if not the City itself where the population remained static)[47], and the growing multiplicity of demands being made upon it.[48]

Prostitution, illegitimacy and the regulation of sexual behaviour

In August 1790 Ann Green was charged (by a 'gentleman') with abusive behaviour on the streets at midnight. Ann had called him 'improper epithets' but was released after promising not to 'molest' him in future.[49] We might allow our imagination to wonder at the nature of these 'improper epithets' but the fact that Ann was on the streets at such a late hour suggests that she was one of the City's many sex workers who accosted men and made 'insolent demands of wine and treats' as they attempted to inveigle them into a nearby bawdy house or dark alley.[50] It was rare for women brought before the summary courts to be described as prostitutes. More commonly they were termed 'disorderly women' or 'loose, idle and disorderly'.[51] This was because prostitution in itself was a not an illegal activity but those making a nuisance of themselves on the streets could be arrested under the vagrancy laws.[52] Rather it was the nature of their actions that defined the offence. Women brought before the courts were accused of 'strolling' around and 'picking up men', or attempting to do so. The streets were, for prostitutes, 'a resource to be exploited'.[53] This appropriation of the pavements for soliciting brought London's sex workers into direct confrontation with the demands of civic government for order and politeness.[54] Regular orders against 'vice, prophaneness and immorality' were issued by the aldermanic court and posted up for public consumption.[55] Tony Henderson is correct when he says that 'prostitutes were charged for violating laws whose architects had had much broader, and often very different aims in mind'.[56] In the 1690s the adherents to the reformation of manners movement attempted to suppress bawdy houses and prostitution as part of their campaign to clean up society.[57] 'Night walkers' could be arrested under the statute of Winchester, which regulated the use of the streets after dark. Middlesex justices in the late seventeenth and early eighteenth century used their discretionary powers to imprison nightwalkers in the house of correction rather than simply binding them over as the act required.[58] This may reflect the activities of the reformation of manners movement and their dedication to clearing the streets. However, in the later period the attitude towards prostitution seems to be much less punitive. In the sample identified in Table 6.1 there were 66 prosecutions for prostitution.[59]

Table 6.3 Outcomes of prosecutions of prostitutes at the City courts, c.1785–96

	Discharged	Reprimanded	Imprisoned	Other	Total
Number	15	27	18	6	66
Percentage	22.7	40.9	27.2	9.0	99.8

Source: The minute books of the Guildhall and Mansion House justice rooms.[60]

Clearly imprisonment was not always used to punish prostitution in the last two decades of the eighteenth century. As the reformation of manners movement declined and its members ceased their activities the responsibility for prostitution fell back into the hands of the watch.

In London the watch seem to have taken a more relaxed attitude towards the problem. Women were still rounded up but were 'frequently expelled from the Watch house after a few hours without seeing any magistrate'.[61] There was no concerted attempt to limit street prostitution. Instead it seems to have been left in the hands of some highly motivated individuals and to the discretion of individual magistrates. So while the minute books for the 1780s and 1790s show that the courts were dealing with small numbers of disorderly women, if the minute books from 1762, 1778 and 1780 are examined it becomes clear that many more women were being brought before the justices.

Table 6.4   Outcomes of prosecutions of prostitutes at the City summary courts, 1762, 1778 and 1780

	Discharged	Reprimanded	Imprisoned	Passed	Total
Number	44	3	8	2	57
Percentage	77.1	5.2	14.0	3.5	99.8

Source: Guildhall justice room minute books.[62]

The perceived increase in prosecutions in this period can be explained by the endeavours of one particular individual constable, William Payne, who was alone responsible for the prosecution of 54 of these women.[63] Payne was a member of the revived reformation of manners movement and regularly brought in large numbers of women, sometimes as many as 13 at one time, to be charged with picking up men or disorderly behaviour. In August 1778 Payne was clearing the streets 'of common prostitutes to prevent their being at large during the time of St. Bartholomew's fair' (one of the City's more colourful annual pageants and one that attracted large crowds many of whom came for the criminal, or in the case of prostitutes, semi-legal opportunities it provided).[64] If Payne's intention was to curtail or punish such behaviour he was not always successful. The aldermen may not have shared Payne's moral outlook and certainly did not always value his words or opinions above those of other witnesses. Payne accused Jane Cox of 'wandering in Fleet Street and picking up men' and told the alderman that she had confessed to being a prostitute. Jane revealed that 'a captain of a ship had debauched her' (thereby fulfilling one contemporary view of prostitutes as the victims of powerful males, and strategically working to win the sympathy of the court as a result).[65] Joseph Thompson, another constable, told the justice that Jane had denied being a prostitute. She was discharged. Payne was thwarted, and perhaps Jane's strategy of throwing herself upon the mercy of the male-dominated court was successful.[66] It may be that Payne was calculating in his strategy; while he was aware that these women were likely to be released he could at least ensure that they received some form of punishment for what he saw as their immoral behaviour. Most streetwalkers were released without any more sanction than a simple reprimand. However, all of them had spent the previous night in a compter and those Payne arrested on Saturday night would have been incarcerated in unpleasant circumstances for two nights before they had a chance to be heard before the justice.

The discretion of the magistrate is clear in many of these judgements. The women that were sent to Bridewell were either those that had been before the justice previously or had garnered a reputation as prostitutes, or those arrested where there was clear evidence of their offence. Leticia Martin was sent to Bridewell after being found in the appropriately named Bagnio Court in 'an indecent posture' with an apprentice.[67] By contrast first-time offenders, those 'unknown' to the court, such as Ann Evans – 'a poor ignorant Welch [sic] girl' – were reprimanded and then released.[68] Previous good conduct was likely to elicit a more lenient reaction from the court system.[69] The strong correlation between poverty and prostitution might also help explain the lenient attitude of the magistracy. While not all London whores were poor, the City aldermen were capable of distinguishing need from greed on occasions. Jane Cox may have seemed more deserving of sympathy (as a victim of male lust) than Leticia Martin who had debauched an apprentice. On one occasion when Payne brought ten women to the Guildhall the aldermen released two because he thought their arrest to be 'improper' (they were 'taken together sitting quietly in a house'), while the remaining eight were discharged on the grounds that they had in 'the opinion of the alderman suffered by imprisonment' and were now 'promising to keep out of the streets'.[70] The imprisonment of streetwalkers and other disorderly and unsavoury persons by highly motivated public officials could have severe consequences in this period, given the poor conditions of London's gaols and lock-ups.[71] Sometimes the actions of the watch and patrols were merely viewed as over officious. In 1821 a constable that charged a woman with being a prostitute was roundly criticised by the justice. The magistrate was reminded of a previous occasion when 28 women had been brought before him. The women had been

> taken up for being found late in the street of a Saturday night, and kept in confinement till Monday morning, when they were brought before him, and it appeared that several of them were married

women, who had been going home with work which their husbands or themselves had executed. "The feelings of both husbands and wives on such an occasion," said the worth Alderman, "may well be supposed, though I am certain they could scarcely be more poignant than mine were, at finding that such an outrage could be committed on the peaceable inhabitants of the city of London; but I trust it will never be repeated."[72]

As a result of this 'outrage' the clerk at the Mansion House suggested that each watch house be issued with copies of the relevant acts of parliament dealing with street walking so that watchmen and constables could familiarise themselves with their duties and avoid arresting innocent pedestrians.

The behaviour of individual women could certainly affect the outcomes they received in the summary courts. In September 1821, 17 women were taken to the Guildhall and were described as being 'altogether hopeless, they being wholly destitute of money, friends, and character, and without the slightest prospect of being able to maintain themselves out of their miserable line of life'. They had been rounded up in an attempt to 'clear the city of the hordes of females that nightly infest the streets'.[73] Some were remanded so that relatives and friends could come forward to vouch for them, one or two were released after promising that they would find gainful employment, while 'five of the most abandoned and hopeless were committed to Bridewell for one month'. In 1766, 30 'disorderly women' were arrested and assembled in front of the sitting justice who sent 'ten of the most abandoned' to Bridewell.[74] It would seem likely that periodic clampdowns on prostitution (as alluded to in Figure 6.1) were characteristic of eighteenth-century London but that systematic and regular prosecutions of the trade were rare. Perhaps contemporaries realised that 'commercial sex was more an outpost of poverty than anything else'.[75] Mary Crowther was one such unfortunate woman, who turned to prostitution when she lost her position as a servant through no fault of her own.[76] This is not to suggest that communities accepted prostitution and prostitutes at all times and in all circumstances, or that individuals did not take widely different views of the trade, just that there was a mutable attitude towards prostitution that can be seen in the records of the summary courts.

Once the campaigning constable Payne had ceased his operations the levels of prosecutions for prostitution in the City fell off considerably although we do have instances where constables acted in a similar

Figure 6.1 'City scavengers cleansing the London streets of impurities', by
C. Williams (1816) © Guildhall Library

way to Payne, bringing in large numbers of women in a single swoop.
In April 1793 Richard Tilcock, a regular prosecuting constable at the
Guildhall, brought in 16 women and while one ran away the rest were
ordered to be taken to Bridewell 'in a cart.'[77] Prostitution was generally being treated alongside other disorderly behaviour, and while
outrageous and overt behaviour was punished activities that were more
discreet, and perhaps confined to certain areas, were tolerated for
the most part.[78] This is clear from this 1793 example. Two constables, Pritty and Lodge, brought in three men following a disturbance
that occurred when the officers had tried to arrest two prostitutes.
Pritty had asked the women to move along as they were acting dis-
reputably, by 'throwing pieces of apple at gentlemen and picking up
men' but they refused. When he tried to take them into custody the
men had intervened, declaring that 'these women have not picked
pockets, let them go!' abusing and threatening the constable. The
wife of a cork dealer confirmed that the women had been behaving badly but another witness denied they were prostitutes, while yet
another complained that there was an ongoing problem with such
'disorderly' women in the area. The magistrate, in the face of these conflicting reports and with the agreement of the constables, discharged
the men.[79]

By the nineteenth century the new house of correction at Giltspur Street held very few prostitutes. John Teague, the keeper of the house, told a parliamentary committee that some women were held there 'for a considerable time' but only until they could be placed in the Refuge for the Destitute or the Guardian Society. Between January 1816 and January 1817 there were only seven female inmates imprisoned for misdemeanours.[80] There is some evidence that towards the end of the Napoleonic wars more prostitutes were being routinely imprisoned by the summary courts in what was perhaps another City-wide clampdown. The clerk to the Bridewell Hospital told the same Committee that in 1814 eleven more cells were made available in Bridewell to house disorderly prostitutes. Prior to that there were just 15 cells used to house a maximum of 30 women, after the increase capacity was raised to 52. However, the former palace was rarely full. There were significant numbers of women sentenced to between seven days and one month's imprisonment with 191 admitted in 1815 and 295 in 1816.[81] Even in 1816 this suggests that relatively small numbers of prostitutes were incarcerated in the Bridewell, which supports the evidence from the 1790s that most women were simply reprimanded or discharged by the courts. However, prostitution cannot be viewed in isolation.[82] We can now turn our attention to the other instances of sexual immorality that were dealt with by the summary courts.

In December 1775 John Adams Snipes was brought before the Guildhall court on a warrant for bastardy charged with getting Arabella Todd pregnant and not supporting her. Arabella had named Snipes on oath and at the hearing he agreed to maintain the mother and child and therefore remove the need for the parish of St. Mary Magdalen to support her. At this he was released.[83] This was the most likely outcome

Table 6.5 Outcomes for offenders brought for Bastardy or desertion of families in the City summary courts, 1785–96

Outcome	Number	Percentage
Discharged	32	78.0
Bound/Bailed	5	12.1
Imprisoned WOS	3	7.3
Other	1	2.4
Total known	41	99.8
Destination unknown	11	–
Total	52	–

Source: The minute books of the Guildhall and Mansion House justice rooms.[84]

for those that appeared before the justices in this context at the end of the eighteenth century.

The outcomes shown in Table 6.5 are in line with William Hunt's actions in Wiltshire, where he seems to have settled just under half of all Bastardy actions and sent very few to gaol and also of JPs in Essex where commitments to the house of correction for Bastardy are similarly rare.[85] Innes and King have both noted the use of the house of correction as a tool for the control of the labouring poor and what we may be seeing in these records for the City is the success of that strategy.[86] When fathers were brought in the threat of Bridewell may have acted as reliable prompt to persuade them to fulfil their parental responsibilities. It has been suggested that in most of England in the period 1650–1750 the rate of illegitimacy was notably low because of self-imposed restrictions of sexual behaviour.[87] However, it may be the case that London was somewhat different. Historians who have studied demographic trends[88] and patterns alongside those looking at changing attitudes towards sexuality and sexual practice[89] have suggested that London's less-restricted society led to larger numbers of illegitimate births.[90] Perhaps the peculiar nature of London life, the opportunities for sex in a society that was seemingly so much more anonymous than the rural backgrounds and small urban centres that many of its immigrants had set out from, led to changes here earlier than for the rest of the country.[91]

It is also possible that the uniqueness of social relations in London may have led more men to desert their partners than in other areas. The opportunities to disappear into the metropolis or to move abroad or join the forces were much greater than anywhere else in Britain at this time. The temptations of the City were many and varied and the pressures on relationships would have been increased in times of dearth and with the arrival of extra mouths to feed. Thomas Jones found succour in the arms of a prostitute he met at Bartholomew fair. As a consequence he lost his job and ran away from his wife and child. The parish officers of St. Dunstan's summoned him before the alderman at Guildhall where it was discovered that despite his many letters to his wife in which he promised to return and look after her, he had attempted to sell all the furniture in their lodgings, 'even the very bed his unfortunate wife and child slept upon'. He was bound over, both to keep the peace and maintain his family while the prostitute he had taken up with was marched off to Bridewell for a month.[92] A journeyman printer was also imprisoned for failing to support his wife and children. He had driven his wife away through fear of his violence and the reporter remarked that the 'fellow seemed wholly devoid of the common feelings of humanity'.[93]

The overriding motivation for the prosecutors in bastardy and desertion cases was to save money. The court acted as a useful lever to force men to take their responsibilities seriously, using the Bridewell for those that would not indemnify the parish.

The regulation of sexual practices in the summary courts was most heavily involved in the prosecution of prostitutes and in bringing those that shirked their parental and familial responsibilities to book. However, it is worth briefly noting that the magistracy occasionally dealt with those accused of more 'morally corrupt' behaviour.

Homosexuality was illegal in the eighteenth century and the act of sodomy punishable by death.[94] There were 77 prosecutions for sodomy at Old Bailey between 1750 and 1830.[95] Of these only 23 defendants were found guilty (and sentenced to death). The reports of trials from the 1770s provided detailed accounts of the proceedings but in later ones the printer refused to publish the details on account of their obscenity. This perhaps reflected the fear of contagion which underlay contemporary rhetoric concerning homosexuality. In the records of the summary court sodomy is rare. There are a couple of cases of assault where sodomy is alleged but dismissed and a brief spate of prosecutions of young men who appear to be trying to extract money from passers by on the pretext of claiming that they had been trying to buy them for sex. In the only detailed case we have the situation seems to be quite different. William Finch-Blackley and John Wagoner were discovered together in a sheep pen at Smithfield market in the early hours of the morning by the St. Sepulchre patrol. One officer, Samuel Roberts, crept up on the pair and observed them 'hugging and squeezing one another about the waists' before they proceeded to have intercourse. At this point Roberts leapt up and sprang his rattle for assistance. Blackley tried to deny that he had been doing anything more than using the pen to relieve himself. Wagoner said they had simply met for a drink in a pub and that nothing untoward had occurred. However one of the officers of the patrol claimed that Blackley had tried to bribe him with 5s to let them go.[96] This case illustrates the discretionary role of the policing agencies in regulating behaviour within the City. Roberts could have ignored what he saw in the sheep pen, just as William Payne could have allowed those prostitutes that plied their trade discreetly to go about unmolested.

Concluding remarks

The summary courts played an important role in the regulation of certain forms of behaviour that impacted directly on the lower orders.

The control of traffic and the prosecution of prostitutes and drunks affected the rougher elements more than it did polite society. But how should we view these attempts at control? Was this a clampdown on popular culture as a part of the 'civilizing process' that Elias has described or a growing demand for order from shopkeepers and merchants who needed easy access and peaceful streets?[97] Or was it perhaps merely a pragmatic approach to regulating the streets? The detailed regulations for controlling the behaviour of hackney coachmen, carmen and street vendors when viewed alongside the arrest and prosecution of other 'nuisances' (those blocking the streets with rubbish or furniture, for example) provide a less ideological interpretation of the actions of the corporation.

The attempts to prevent prostitution were undoubtedly fragmentary and sporadic suggesting that there was either a recognition (shared to some extent by all those that have faced this issue since) that the problem was impossible to solve or that its existence was generally tolerated so long as the nuisance did not become too great. Prosecutions of prostitutes and others for immoral behaviour may also have depended to a great extent on the motivations and energies of the policing agencies.

The courts at Guildhall and Mansion House were, to a significant extent, serving to deliver the holding gaols of the City. Each morning the Poultry and Wood Street compters, as well as Bridewell and later the Giltspur, emptied their contents for the aldermen and lord mayor to sift through. The detritus of the previous night's trawling by the watch contained many that had been found drunk and disorderly; many more may have never reached the courts having been released after a few hours in the watch house or before they came to their examinations. Most were reminded to behave better in the future and were released. In this the courts served the City reasonably effectively as a well-organised system of public discipline, never too harsh but nevertheless allowing the authorities to maintain a patriarchal grasp on its population. As with the prosecution of offenders for property and petty violence the regulation of behaviour was underpinned by the use of discretion by all its participants.

7

Quelling the Smithfield Yahoos: Bullock-hunting on the Streets of London

> I prefer the Lark's note or the cry of a Cock,
> To a croaking old Watchman, crying past four O Clock;
> Or the musical Hounds in pursuit of a Fox,
> To the Smithfield Yahoos hunting down a mad Ox.
>   – *Country & Town*, Sung by Mr. Dugnum.[1]

In December 1785 *The London Chronicle* carried the following report:

> Complaint has been made to the Court of the Mayor and Aldermen of this city, that a set of idle and disorderly persons generally assemble in Smithfield-market, on Mondays and Fridays, the market days for the sale of cattle, and make a practice of following cattle; and after having separated one or more from the rest, wantonly hunt and worry them until they become wild and mischievous, whereby the lives of people are in danger[2]

Reports of 'hunting' or 'worrying' cattle are rare but not unknown in the London press in the late eighteenth century and reveal an example of the capital's popular culture that has received little attention from historians. Bull-running, a pastime that is still practised in some Spanish towns (notably Pamplona) was a traditional activity that survived in a small number of English towns into the early years of the nineteenth century. However, while in Stamford and Tutbury, bull-running was an annual event, steeped in folklore, in London 'bullock-hunting' took place weekly. Violent and disorderly folk traditions were very much a part of the calendar in England throughout the early modern period. By the late eighteenth century, however, customs such as cock-fighting, throwing at cocks and bull-baiting were coming under attack and by the middle of the nineteenth century most popular recreations associated with a vibrant and vigorous plebeian culture had been suppressed, codified or had died out.[3] What exactly did bullock-hunting in London involve? Who were the 'Smithfield yahoos' and what was their purpose? What was the role of the summary courts in the control of this practice?

Late eighteenth-century middle-class culture witnessed a growth in concern for the treatment of animals.[4] This concern with cruelty towards animals was apparent in a variety of contemporary writings. John Oswald, in advocating vegetarianism, argued that 'Animal food overpowers the faculties of the stomach, clogs the functions of the soul, and renders the mind material and gross.'[5] More pragmatically John Lawrence, the writer of a treatise on the care of horses and other livestock in 1796, campaigned for greater supervision of the meat trade and for the removal of Smithfield market from central London. Lawrence condemned the cruel treatment of calves at the meat market where animals were roughly handled by 'barbarous, unthinking, two-legged brutes'.[6]

But while concerns over cruelty to animals was one factor behind attempts to reform the meat trade and to curtail some plebeian pastimes there was another, equally important motive behind the prosecution and suppression of such activities. The industrial revolution brought with it concerns about labour discipline.[7] Some popular recreations were seen as a waste of time, energy and money. Thomas Young warned his readers that indulgence in plebeian sports such as bull-baiting, cockfighting and throwing at cocks deserved condemnation not merely for their cruelty towards animals but also because 'their evil extends to human society. They draw together idle and disorderly persons, they tend to generate in the spectators a cruel habit of mind, and universally give rise to profane swearing and drunkenness.'[8]

This viewpoint is apparent in William Hogarth's series of prints condemning the systemic and callous violence of Hanoverian society. The second print of his *Four Stages of Cruelty* series depicts a distant bullock hunt. The print described, as an anonymous contemporary tells us, 'the hunting of a Bullock through the Streets by a Rabble of Boys, and dirty Fellows, till the Creature maddens with rage, and in its Fury tosses every one that is so unhappy to come in its Way'.[9]

The most well-documented example of bull-running is that of Stamford in Lincolnshire where the annual event dated back to the fourteenth century.[10] Bull-running in Stamford, like the modern manifestation of the practice in Pamplona, was associated with a traditional festival.[11] At Martinmas (the 13th of November), a bull was released onto the town's streets by the butchers where it was then harried, chased and occasionally ridden before being turned off the bridge into the river and then slaughtered for the benefit of the locals.[12] Similar events took place in Tutbury (Shropshire), Tetbury (Gloucestershire), Wisbech (Cambridgeshire) and in Scrivelsby (Lincolnshire).[13] London bullock-hunting although it shared many of the characteristics of the Stamford bull-running, was a quite different type of pastime. Francis Place described it as a 'common amusement with boys and youths'.[14] It took place on market days at Smithfield (Mondays and Fridays) and could involve hundreds of participants.

Smithfield was a busy cattle market throughout the eighteenth and nineteenth centuries. Cattle destined for sale were driven into London from the outlying countryside and by the early years of the nineteenth century a million sheep and a quarter of a million cattle were being sold at Smithfield annually, the noise and chaos that the transportation of these beasts caused must have been considerable.[15] Amongst this maelstrom of drovers, carts, animals and the rest of London's traffic and pedestrians the youthful Place enjoyed the occasional distraction of hunting a bullock. In 1790 a small group of animals were being taken to market when a crowd of men, possibly as many as a hundred according to one witness, surrounded them and separated one of the beasts. The hunters were armed with drovers' sticks, three or four feet long with one end in the form of a knob for beating and the other sharpened to a point for goading. As soon

> as a favourable opportunity occurred, which was generally when two streets crossed, some of the bullock hunters ran up to the drovers both before and behind the cattle and flourishing their sticks made a shew of fighting' while at 'the same moment others of the bullock hunters dashed in amongst the beasts and endeavoured by noise and bellows to start the bullock which had been noticed.[16]

The first attempt to hunt the beast failed but the hunters persisted and eventually one of the crowd, John Johnson, 'got in between the beasts, and drove three of them away, by beating them with a stick he had in his hand; someone called to him, "turn out the brindled bullock"'.[17] It was common for particular beasts to be identified as suitable targets for running. Place noted that 'light long horned' cattle were considered the 'most skittish and the best runners'.[18] There were other ways to goad a bullock into running: apart from prodding with sharpened sticks hunters would place peas in the ears of cattle, or shout and 'halloo' at them, anything in fact to enrage the beasts.

While the estimations of the sizes of the crowd in the above case may be exaggerated, large groups of men and youths were congregating in and around Smithfield and other routes that drovers used, to take part in bullock-hunting. The chaos they caused was very real, as Place describes:

> From the moment a bullock started it was utterly useless to attempt to recover him. The noise and the blows soon forced him to his utmost speed which was kept up either till he was blown when he would stop and very often turn round on his pursuers ... the sport was then at its height, as there was the more danger, the beast sometimes pursuing his tormentors and they in turn pursuing him.[19]

Deaths were not unknown. In 1761 *London Magazine* reported that Common Council had been asked to act as a result of the 'many fatal accidents being frequently occasioned by the driving of horned cattle through this City and liberties, in a careless and inhumane manner'. Council agreed to recommend the lord mayor 'and the rest of the worthy magistrates' to 'assert their authority to suppress this growing evil'.[20] In 1774 a woman was killed as a result of the 'over driving of cattle' by a set of 'idle and disorderly fellows and Boys' who were making 'sport as they call it'. This time the Court of Aldermen was asked to use legislation passed earlier that year to enforce a ban on such activities. The petitioner to the court called on the authorities to arrest offenders and punish them by public whipping 'as the act directs'.[21] In 1788 a watchman 'attempting to stop a mad ox' was gored in the belly, 'in so shocking a manner, that he died on the spot'.[22] The *Argus* condemned bullock-hunting as a 'barbarous practice so disgraceful to the police of a civilized country'.[23]

Despite this bullock-hunting persisted well into the nineteenth century and was not restricted to the streets around Smithfield. In 1821 a butcher's servant in Whitechapel

> was removing a bullock ... to a slaughter house ... when the animal was rescued from him by a gang of ruffians, who, as they are wont to do on all such occasions commenced beating it in a most brutal manner. Such treatment of course tending to drive the animal wild, he proceeded in an infuriated state along the road ... chased by a motley group of desperadoes, amounting to several hundreds.[24]

Bullock-hunting in the capital was sport, a way to bring excitement and danger into everyday life, an opportunity for demonstrations of bravado. However, it was also – as the tenor of complaints in the press and elsewhere maintains – an activity that threatened the commercial and public peace of the capital (see Figure 7.1). As such, the authorities were urged to act against it. Just how concerned the magistracy were to punish bullock hunters can be assessed by looking at the prosecution of participants at the summary courts.

Within the sample of the Guildhall and Mansion House justice rooms in the last quarter of the eighteenth century, there are 57 prosecutions of bullock hunters recorded. Given that we have established that the sample used for all offences between 1784 and 1796 represents a year's business before the courts, it shows that bullock-hunting was a weekly, if not more frequent, pastime. This echoes Francis Place's recollection that in his youth bullock-hunting took place on market days, twice a week. One contemporary noted that it was an all-year-round phenomenon, but accepted that its consequences might vary. 'During the short days of winter', he noted 'they hunt till it is dark,

Figure 7.1 'Miseries of human life', by George Moutard Woodward (c.1800) ©
Guildhall Library

then frequently make a prize of the bullock. At other times of the year, he is generally recovered by his owner, after much trouble and some expence [*sic*]'.[25]

Naturally the number of prosecutions for bullock-hunting is not an accurate measure of the number of incidents of the practice. It is probable that bullock hunters usually escaped prosecution. Indeed *The Times*, in reporting a case in 1822, complained that when 'some of the respectable inhabitants of the neighbourhood' in which a bullock hunt was underway turned to the local constables to stop the 'brutal pastime' they 'were not to be seen'.[26] In 1816 Joshua King, the rector of Bethnal Green parish, told a parliamentary commission of his frustrations in trying to get both the local police and the magistracy to do something about the problem in his area. He accused Mr Merceron – a local Justice of the Peace (JP) – and his assistants of complicity in the practice declaring that: 'I cannot learn, that they took any steps to put a stop to so wanton and disgraceful an outrage; on the contrary, I have reason to believe, that the officers of my parish frequently connive at and sanction' such activities.[27] Merceron, like Place, enjoyed the sport as a youth and perhaps saw it as an acceptable part of popular culture.

By contrast in July 1788 the lord mayor awarded 40s to a constable for 'his diligence' in bringing a 'hunter' before him.[28] In October 1789 the lord mayor sent William Burbage to Bridewell for a month for 'hunting a bullock which has done a great deal of mischief'.[29] The nature of this 'mischief' is apparent in a report from the *London Chronicle* which shows just how much damage and disruption a loose beast could cause on the streets of the capital.

> a bullock having escaped from a slaughter-house in Whitechapel, ran down the Minories, followed by several hundred persons, whose attempts to stop it only tended to make it the more outrageous; in its course it upset several poor women who sat with their stalls in the streets, some of whom were much injured. The enraged animal, in running through a court in Rosemary-lane, near the Tower, came in contact with a horse drawing a cart, against which it ran with such violence as to plunge both its horns into the horse's belly, and lacerated it in such a manner as to expose its entrails: a porter, heavily laden, was killed on the spot, by being jammed between the cart and a house, in consequence of the horse's making a sudden plunge backwards, in order to disengage himself from the horns of the bullock.[30]

As we noted earlier this is not the only recorded case of bullock-hunting that led to a fatality. In October 1786 two drovers were accused of causing the death of a bystander gored to death by a 'wild and mischievous' bullock in their care.[31] The 57 cases of bullock-hunting revealed by the summary records give an indication of how the courts attempted to deal with the problem of bullock-hunting.

Table 7.1   Outcomes of hearing of persons prosecuted for bullock-hunting in the City, c.1784–96

Outcome	Number	Percentage
Fined	26	50.9
Discharged	17	33.3
Imprisoned	3	5.8
Other	3	5.8
Reprimanded	2	3.9
Total known	51	99.7
Destination unknown	6	–
Total	57	–

Source: The minute books of the Guildhall and Mansion House justice rooms.[32]

Table 7.1 shows that most individuals who were prosecuted for driving or hunting cattle were fined and then released. Albert Millingfield was convicted, on the oath of John Turner, that 'he not being a person employed to drive cattle did hunt and drive away a cow belonging to a person unknown', and was fined 20s, a not inconsiderable sum for a working man to find.[33] Those found guilty tended to be young men or boys in high spirits, taking their chances with dangerous animals and the policing bodies of the metropolis. Sometimes they got caught and were punished, on many other occasions they must have escaped arrest and any consequent penalty.

In some cases the cruelty implicit in the offender's actions was highlighted by the court. John Bambridge was fined and sent to Bridewell for 'hunting and goading a bullock in a cruel manner'.[34] In December 1789 an ox was pelted 'with stones in Moorfields', while another bullock was whistled at, worried and struck with a stick.[35] All these actions were attempts to make the bullock run, as we saw earlier. Cruelty does appear to have been a concern for the authorities who ran the City of London in the late eighteenth and early nineteenth centuries. The City's government regulated Smithfield market and the magistrates prosecuted acts of animal cruelty. In 1789 William Smith was fined 10s for admitting beating a sheep to death in Smithfield. His only defence being that it 'ran out of the pen'.[36] Joseph Bunberage's prosecution for 'wilfully and cruelly beating a heifer in Duke Street, Smithfield' in 1794 can be similarly viewed as evidence of the surveillance of the meat market.[37] The imposition of middle-class values upon the labouring class by restricting the excesses of popular culture and attitudes towards animals was typified by the creation of the Society for the Prevention of Cruelty to Animals (SPCA) in 1824. Jeremy Bentham also championed the cause of animal welfare arguing that the question society should ask was not 'Can they *reason*?' or 'Can they *talk*?' but instead, 'Can they *suffer*?'[38] The authorities may not have prosecuted every abuse of livestock but it is likely that they chose to clamp down periodically on the worst excesses of behaviour in order to encourage a new attitude towards animal husbandry.

Cruelty towards animals was not the only reason that the authorities prosecuted bullock hunters. As was noted earlier there were concerns about the existence of plebeian activities that diverted attention from work or other, higher, devotions. Place recalled that the hunting of bullocks 'used to collect the greatest of blackguards, thieves and miscreants of all kinds together'.[39] Joshua King complained 'it is most deplorable; every Sunday morning, during the time of Divine Service, several hundred persons assemble in a field adjoining the church-yard, where they fight dogs, hunt ducks, gamble' and drive bullocks 'through the most populous parts of the parish'.[40] In Stamford it was the corruption of public morality that concerned the Reverend Joseph Winks in 1829. The Reverend was a nervous witness to the annual bull-run and cowered in his lodgings as the carnival raced past his window. To him the crowd had 'cast off all appearance of decency and order, and plunge[d] into every excess of riot, without shame or restraint.'[41] Winks was appalled by the drunkenness and 'shameful' involvement of young women. To him it 'resembled more a scene of the savage of New Zealand than amongst inhabitants of a respectable town in England'.[42] Others condemned the cruelty itself but more because of its effect on the participants and witnesses than from a purely humanitarian concern for animals. The *Stamford Mercury* complained in 1819 that 'a low tone of morals can be referred to no cause more reasonable than to the continuance of an inhuman custom, the tendency of which is to deteriorate the character of the community'.[43]

In London bullock-hunting was a regular if spontaneous activity associated with Smithfield and the slaughterhouses of east London.[44] Some commentators may have opposed the practice because of the animal abuse involved but others clearly stressed that indulgence in this cruelty in some ways barbarised both the participants and the audience.

Some instances of bullock-hunting can be interpreted as attempts at theft and a handful of cases reached Old Bailey and were prosecuted as such. Richard Goodwin was charged not with hunting a bullock but with stealing one, by a drover in June 1794. The drover swore that Goodwin had separated off one of his cattle and 'halloed' it out with the help of some companions. Unfortunately for Goodwin the drover had recognised him and later that day he was arrested with the assistance of an armed patrol. The defence rested on whether Goodwin had intended to steal the bullock or was merely indulging in the 'diversion of hunting'. The drover was adamant that it was an attempt to steal, 'to apply it to his own use' as another witness declared. There was some suggestion that the drover was intent on garnering a reward for the successful prosecution of a thief, but he may also have been demonstrating that he valued his job and his master's property.[45] In swearing to the theft the drover declared was doing something that 'a thousand people' would not do, suggesting that such prosecutions were rare. Goodwin's trial was fairly brief; a butcher (someone that might have been expected to disapprove of bullock-hunting) spoke up for him as did four others. It made little difference. Goodwin was sentenced to death: he was 21.[46] Earlier in the century two butchers complained to the Court of Aldermen that their trade was regularly affected by bullock hunters as cattle were harried and chased through the City streets until they became 'unfit for provision, or else [were] murdered by the Mob to the great loss and injury of the Owner'.[47]

Whilst in a very few instances bullock-hunting was treated as theft it is perhaps more helpful to view the prosecution of bullock hunters by the London courts as part of a more general attempt to regulate the streets of the capital. The long eighteenth century was witness to a transformation of urban space.[48] Moves towards improving living conditions, the opportunities for leisure and shopping, and the movement of goods and people, placed new demands on space and necessitated greater intervention from both the state and local government. Watching and lighting schemes were developed and paving and cleansing by-laws attempted to improve both the aesthetics and economics of urban living. By the 1830s a parliamentary committee was recommending the widening of the streets of the capital as part of general process of improvement.[49] Commentators laid great emphasis on the suppression of immoral behaviour and the importance of the promotion of 'politeness' amongst the urban lower classes.[50] This general movement towards 'improvement' can be seen in the attempts to regulate everyday life in the City, a process in which the summary courts and their associated policing agents were crucial.

The City of London had established a pound, the Green Yard, where stray animals, specifically cattle and sheep, could be taken.[51] Anyone bringing cattle to the yard was entitled to a fee of 'Twelve-pence *per* Head of all such Cattle as they drove or brought hither'.[52] However, Common Council was concerned that some individuals were abusing this system and were in fact stealing animals and driving them to the Yard for the reward. In 1760 the Court of Aldermen criticised the keeper of the yard for being 'lax in taking note of the names of people bringing sheep to the Green Yard' and reduced the amount paid out to 6d.[53] That such a pound existed demonstrates the importance to local government of trying to balance the many, sometimes conflicting, uses of urban space.

The teeming streets of London represented just as much of a problem for the authorities in the eighteenth and early nineteenth centuries as they do today. The thoroughfares were crowded with all manner of users. Coaches and carts vied with each other and with hackneys and individual horse riders. Pedestrians hurried along the pavements and roads, trying to avoid each other, the traffic and the detritus of everyday London life. As they did costers and prostitutes plied for business, small boys ran about on errands, beggars demanded alms and pickpockets took advantage of careless travellers. Meanwhile those bringing in livestock for sale at the meat market also had to negotiate their herds through the throng. The activities of the young men and boys who chased and harried bulls on their way to market created unwanted further chaos on the streets. Attached to this was the very real threat of violent accidents and the underlying problem of crime and disorder. This is certainly how *The Times* saw it in 1791.

> The plan of bullock-hunting don't arise from any love of that sport, but from a deliberate plan laid by the PROPER FOLLOWERS, who are in fact the first instigators of plundering in the confusion. This is a well known fact; and as to the FINE, the Society of Thieves would pay it, were it 50l instead of twenty shillings.[54]

In 1827 the paper was still bemoaning the practice and reporting the attempts of the magistracy to prevent it. After sentencing a young man to a month's imprisonment and a 20s fine a Middlesex magistrate observed that 'the offence of bullock-hunting in that district was a very serious one, leading, as it frequently did, to the perpetration of robberies and other outrages; and in the present critical state of the neighbourhood, such an offence could not be passed over without punishment.'[55] Serious prosecutions were rare and the pages of the minute books reveal that occasionally the magistracy turned a blind eye. When Alderman Hopkins discharged three young hunters, the clerk recorded that the justice was 'avers to such repeated Complaints against Boys'.[56] As early as 1791 *The Times* commented that until 'the punishment of bullock driving is made transportation, the Smithfield gangs will continue to set the laws at defiance'.[57] A year earlier it had criticised the sitting lord mayor for his inactivity in prosecuting bullock hunters suggesting that this was a more appropriate use of his time than 'troubling himself with Politics, which are so foreign to his station'.[58]

It would seem that the authorities had a hard time preventing bullock-hunting in London, regardless of whether the will existed to do so or not. In 1787, the City paid Alexander Scott 40s for sticking up 1000 printed orders against the illegal driving of cattle but a cursory reading of later repertories suggests that it had to continually repeat this exercise.[59] However, the number of incidents seems to have declined in the late 1820s and early 1830s. In opposing an attempt at Common Council to remove Smithfield Market from its City location those speaking against the petition noted that while there may have been a case to answer some years ago, 'when vagabonds were in the habit of driving infuriated animals through the streets' [but] 'improvements in the state of the police had quite altered the matter. Whoever heard now of bullock-hunting? Nobody.'[60]

What happened to remove bullock-hunting from the columns of the newspapers and the courtrooms of the City? In Stamford a long-running campaign against the tradition orchestrated primarily by the SPCA was finally successful in 1838.[61] Horse racing on the streets of Birmingham was prohibited in the late eighteenth century in the wake of a fatal accident.[62] In the Black Country bull-baiting, a pastime enjoyed, for the most part, by the urban proletariat, was also suppressed by the urban elite.[63] In Birmingham bull-baiting 'migrated to the suburbs away from the parish constables, where it survived, with crowds more than a thousand strong, until 1840'.[64] Its prohibition was eventually enforced by the introduction of professional policing in the late 1830s. It may be the case that the creation of police magistrate courts in London in 1792 helped to reduce the number of incidents of bullock-hunting but the complaints of Joshua King and others in the early nineteenth century would suggest that not until more systematic policing arrived in

1829 did the opportunity to prevent such a popular activity become effective.

The eventual suppression of bullock-hunting in the streets of London in the early nineteenth century owed much less to contemporary concerns about cruelty towards animals and more to the needs of the developing commercial metropolis. The demands of commerce and of urban living necessitated a much tighter control of urban space in the late eighteenth and early nineteenth centuries. Thus, in the City (and outside) the magistracy and local government were increasingly under pressure to restrict and regulate those using the streets in order to accommodate the needs of as many of its residents as possible. Ultimately this left no place for raucous displays of plebeian culture and, just as such sports were proscribed elsewhere, bullock-hunting was attacked and prosecuted in the capital. This can be read as a part of the move towards improving the urban centres of Britain in the long eighteenth century. The decline of vigorous street entertainments such as bull-baiting and bullock-hunting therefore sit alongside the creation of commercial and leisure facilities, improvements in public health provision, the development of policing and, ultimately, the reorganisation of local government.[65]

That a reward was offered for prosecuting bullock hunters throws an interesting light on this practice and its policing. Were constables, officials and members of the public intervening because they wished to prevent the practice or because there was a chance of financial recompense? The answer is probably a mixture of the two. That the practice could be treated as attempted or actual theft suggests that the penalties imposed in the summary courts, a fine and possible short term imprisonment, were not deemed sufficient by some or that the chance of reward was only realisable through the higher court.

8
The Regulation of Trade and Poverty

At the heart of the role of the summary courts was the regulation of many everyday aspects of life in the capital. As we have seen the courts were involved in the regulation of public space, the streets and morality. The majority of those prosecuted before the magistracy were brought in for disorderly behaviour and drunkenness. Vagrancy and begging were also problems for a City government that prided itself on London's reputation for prosperity and culture and there were intermittent attempts to clear the streets of mendicants. Poverty also had a direct impact upon the rates paid by City dwellers and any actions that increased this burden were likely to result in prosecutions at the summary courts. Finally the City was first and foremost a place of trade. After all it was trade that underpinned the wealth and success of this geographically small area of England. The City authorities therefore had an interest in ensuring that, as far as possible, trade proceeded smoothly, without dispute, and this involved both the summary courts and the related administration of City affairs.

Vagrancy and begging

It was recognised as early as the sixteenth and seventeenth centuries that the problem of poverty was 'an integral part of the problem of law and order'.[1] London, with its huge population swelled by migrants from all over the British Isles, Europe and the rest of the world, had particular problems with poor relief, vagrancy and begging. The situation was so bad that towards the end of the eighteenth century a correspondent to *The World* complained that;

> the streets of London, to their utter disgrace, swarm with such people [common beggars], who come dressed out for the ceremony in all the hideousness and deformity which can be assumed![2]

The control and regulation of poverty was an important consideration for the City elite. Provincial Justices of the Peace (JPs) in eighteenth-century England played a crucial role in the administration of the poor laws.[3] They adjudicated on claims and counterclaims of settlement and relief; they ordered churchwardens and overseers to assist the unfortunate, as well as instructing constables to remove unsuccessful claimants to neighbouring parishes. However, these provincial magistrates were much less busy than their London counterparts were in dealing with petty criminality and interpersonal violence. In the City of London justices were necessarily less directly involved in the administration of the poor laws than their provincial counterparts.

Beggars, vagrants and vagabonds were brought before the courts by the constables having been picked up on the streets during the day or over night. Elizabeth Gurney, who died (as we saw) from malnutrition in the Poultry compter, was found begging in a doorway in Cheapside. Gurney was taken to the Guildhall to be seen by the clerk to the magistracy as it was usually his role to examine vagrants and to establish their claims to settlement and then issue them with passes to their 'home' parishes. In Gurney's case the clerk was tied up with a case in the justice room and Elizabeth was turned away. Hundreds of paupers came before the City clerks to be processed in this way: between 3 November 1787 and 20 May 1788 John Evans, clerk to the lord mayor, saw 548 vagrants and earned £81 9s for 'filling out their passes and duplicates and investigating their settlements'.[4] Some vagrants were examined before the lord mayor or the alderman who used their summary powers to send them to Bridewell for short periods of correction and imprisonment. The City did not want its streets to 'swarm with such people' and the Court of Aldermen issued regular orders to publish its rules regarding vagrancy in the daily papers.[5] Constables were ordered to round up those found on the streets and to take them to the workhouse, compters or the watch house. They could earn a reward for this but could equally be fined if they failed in this duty.[6]

As with many other aspects of the justices' work, the treatment of vagrants was highly discretionary. Some of those examined had failed to take heed of previous warnings and suffered as a result. In 1789 the secretary of the Marine Society appealed to the lord mayor for his assistance in disciplining lads who had failed to the make the best of opportunities given to them to mend their ways. He brought two of his charges into the Mansion House courtroom: John Hooper had run away from his ship and William Morris had deserted his position and stolen the clothes the society had provided. The lord mayor sent the pair to

Bridewell for a month to let them reflect on their behaviour. At the request of the Churchwardens of All-hallows-the-Less the lord mayor also punished William Murray for pawning the clothes the parish had given him and for his continuous misbehaviour.[7] These defendants were seen as ungrateful recipients of local relief and charity, they could expect little sympathy for biting the hand that fed them.

Many vagrants were temporarily locked up in Bridewell before being passed back to their place of last settlement. The underlying principle behind poor relief in this period was to make each community responsible for its own paupers. This principle was undermined however, by the tendency of individuals to move around in search of work and new opportunities. The question that troubled parish authorities was that of who was responsible for this transient population, the parish of their birth or the one to which they had moved? Oxley puts it thus: '[I]f a newcomer arrived, were they to expel him lest he become chargeable or allow him to come because there was an employment vacancy which he could fill.'[8] Naturally this was a vital consideration for London parishes whose populations were swollen by large numbers of economic migrants, who increased pressure on sparse resources. Many of these immigrants came from across the Irish Sea and so it is no surprise to find Morris Connor and Dominic Murphy in the records of the Bridewell. Connor had been sent to the gaol for begging in Bread Street ward (having previously narrowly avoided being sent back to Ireland by the magistrates of Middlesex). When Dominic Murphy was arrested for begging in the parish of St. Stephen's, Coleman Street, it was noted as being his third offence.[9]

Most of those arrested for begging or vagrancy were examined and passed with a small number being summarily imprisoned for a short period before being sent back to their last place of settlement. This was in line with stated practice at the time.[10] The intention was to get them off the streets since, in the eyes of the authorities, they represented a threat to order and were a potential source of criminality. Women were often simply removed unless they were abusive. Being removed meant they did not come before the JP but were simply taken to the boundaries of the City and released, it was only when they repeatedly had to be removed that they would be sent to Bridewell.[11] Of course, it is likely than many of those released in this way would have gravitated back inside the City boundaries at some point sooner or later. London contained a large transient population of paupers that moved around the hundreds of parishes, begging, looking for work, receiving alms and relief and being sporadically arrested, punished, removed and expelled. Elizabeth Lloyd was discharged 'with a caution against begging in future'.[12] John Richardson was sent to the Marine Society for the same offence.[13] Lloyd may have been pitied and Richardson, as a young boy, was a suitable object for service at sea in a time of European conflict and uncertainty. Clearly the penalties for vagrancy and begging were not as fixed or inflexible as they seemed, allowing the justices of the City to apply or ignore the laws as they deemed appropriate according to the nature and circumstances of the case – a cautionary reminder to historians who place too much trust in contemporary handbooks and 'advice' literature.[14]

It is possible that some paupers were using the arrest process as part of a strategy of survival, manipulating the system to their own ends. Prison offered a temporary place of refuge and there is at least some evidence to suggest that not all desperate City dwellers feared the Bridewell or City compters. Hitchcock suggests that many constables and watchmen were reluctant to arrest beggars if they felt some sympathy for their plight, sending the 'obviously ill and desperate to the workhouse door, a note in hand, rather than marching them before a justice as the law directed'.[15] The constable that arrested Elizabeth Gurney confessed that he took her to the compter because it was closer than the workhouse and he was 'not allowed to be above half an hour from the watch house'.[16] It was a decision that impacted on Elizabeth with fatal consequences. Being arrested for vagrancy or begging could lead to much needed medical care and an, albeit temporary, access to necessary resources such as food and clothing. Elizabeth found herself somewhere without even the warmth of a fire and reliant upon her fellow inmates for care and sustenance.

By the 1790s imprisonment with whipping and removal from the parish were 'mandatory punishments for male beggars'.[17] However, even this stipulation must be treated with care. It cost 5s for each male vagrant sent to be whipped and justices may have been reluctant to punish every offender regardless of their situation.[18] When the clerk to the Mansion House was examined by a parliamentary committee in 1814 he suggested that City officers were still reluctant to prosecute vagrants, saying that

> it is as much their duty to remove beggars as it is to apprehend thieves; but it is a duty I have found the officers more unwilling to attend than any of their other duties, for it is unpopular, and they always get abused when they lug these people to the prisons.[19]

While we have seen that the courts on occasion disciplined beggars, vagrants and paupers, to what extent did they also serve those in need? A small sample of cases from the 1790s reveals that several individuals brought parish officials before the aldermen to complain about non-payment of relief or other forms of subsistence, as was routinely the case in provincial England. Mary Hicks complained that the overseers of the poor of St. Boltoph's had failed to provide enough relief for her son, but the alderman dismissed the case. Her plight worsened later in the month and she again asked for assistance, arguing that her son had been ill-treated in the workhouse. She met the same cold response, the magistrate dismissing her suit as 'frivolous and vexatious'. Ann Townsend, abandoned by her husband and unable to support her son without the 2s 6d per week he had been obligated to pay her, complained that the churchwardens of St. Margaret Moses had refused to relieve her. The churchwardens of St. Stephen's Walbrook similarly evaded prosecutions brought by the wife of a militiaman and a pauper.[20] However, these examples are only representative of the minority of cases that we can identify from the minute books. Many more may well be hidden from us because most hearings would have been conducted by the clerk and the records of these examinations do not appear to have survived.

It is possible that in their attempts to get assistance from the summary courts the labouring poor of London were hamstrung by two related factors, possibly unique to the capital. First, paupers who sought relief were directed to the workhouse rather than offered out relief. This was a strategy that was easy for the parish to administer and perhaps difficult for the pauper to avoid. Most of the workhouses used by the City parishes were located outside of the City boundaries.[21] Paupers were 'farmed out' and had been since the middle of the century or earlier.[22] This practice supposedly offered value for money for the parish whilst at the same time placing the able-bodied poor in gainful employment.[23] While the City had few institutions within its boundaries into which to deposit their able-bodied paupers, the surrounding wider metropolis provided plenty of destinations for those that sought relief.

Second, this situation may have been compounded by the very nature of summary justice within the square mile. It has been suggested that the rural poor of England could pick and choose which JP they saw so as to achieve the outcome they desired. Some JPs might have been known to be sympathetic to the plight of the poor, or at least unwilling to side with employers or middling officialdom. Those seeking relief could hope to negotiate a better result for themselves by playing gentry magistrates off against middling sort parish officials.[24] However, the nature of local government in the City placed an important obstacle in the path of the pauper. City parishes were interlinked with the wards, at the head of which sat the same aldermen who presided in the City courtrooms. Conflicts between parish officials and magistrates simply do not seem to be as relevant here as they were in the countryside. The aldermen of London were, for the most part, hard-nosed business-men from the same background as the middling sorts that occupied the position of civic officialdom across the metropolis. Perhaps these courts witnessed very few poor relief claims simply because the labouring poor realised that there was little value in pressing their suits at these par-ticular institutions. On most occasions those paupers that came to the summary courts would have been processed by the clerks, and given little or no opportunity to plead their case before a magistrate. In this respect the triangulation that King has described in Essex would have been impossible in the square mile.

There is another explanation for the small numbers of paupers seek-ing relief at the summary courts in the City: the very uniqueness of London itself. London offered many more opportunities for work, petty crime and, crucially, charitable support that might keep paupers from needing to approach the magistracy. In his 1797 study, Frederick Eden listed 107 almshouses, 14 'asylums for the indigent and helpless' and 17 for the 'Sick, Lame, Diseased, and for Poor Pregnant Women' in the metropolis, many of which were to be found within the City itself.[25] The presence of numerous establishments such as these afforded the City authorities, vestries and inhabitants a range of options for dealing with the problem of poverty. Many of these may have dealt with paupers and the poor directly without the need for them to appear before the magistracy in a formal court setting.

Some City aldermen were willing to side with paupers on occasions when the claims they made seemed justifiable, and would overturn the judgements of churchwardens and overseers if that was necessary.[26] Across the metropolis the magistrates of Middlesex also interpreted the vagrancy laws quite widely in their attempts to retain 'wide discre-tionary powers' in the face of demands for more systematic carceral treatment of itinerant beggars.[27] City magistrates acted in a similar way, perhaps realising that a draconian approach was unlikely to succeed. However, paupers who tried to abuse the system or who misbehaved whilst under the care of the parish could expect to be treated firmly by the authorities. 'Refractory paupers are brought before the lord mayor, and if the cases are grave, the parties are sent to Bridewell', the parliamentary commission was told in 1834.[28] By the 1830s, when attitudes towards the provision of poor relief were hardening, able-bodied paupers who refused to work would have been unlikely to get any relief from the lord mayor.

When Patrick Kearney attempted to play off his local churchwardens against the magistracy his scheme backfired and he was forced into a workhouse outside of the City.[29] However, he did not stay there long and managed to get himself back on the streets in just over three weeks (having been reclothed by the parish) and then gained admittance to Guy's Hospital. The hospital staff described him as a 'very singular man indeed' before discharging him, the clear implication being that he was something of a nuisance. For a while the parish supported Kearney but in the spring of 1768 he was once again sent to a workhouse by the sitting alderman at Guildhall. The case of Patrick Kearney illustrates the ways in which London's poor could navigate between the various forms of authority they encountered but not always escape the attempts of those bodies to impose restrictions upon them. Hitchcock's depiction of a benign poor law system in London in this period is somewhat problematic, however his assertion that:

> The system of poor relief in eighteenth-century London was extensive, expensive and remarkably comprehensive. For the settled and parish poor, it provided a resource that could not be ignored, while for the unsettled poor and migrant beggars it represented an important component in their economy of makeshift,[30]

supports the contention that the local community of City parishes and wards operated a flexible and discretionary system of welfare provision and disciplinary control. The lives and prospects of paupers on the streets were therefore governed, to a significant extent, by the attitudes and predilections of the men that served these communities. Worthwhile or 'deserving' objects of relief – the sick, elderly, very young, and those genuinely in need – could hope to be treated with kindness and compassion. However, the 'undeserving' – the unruly, rowdy, drunk, abusive and the work-shy – were much more likely to experience the disciplinary nature of the City's poor law system. This is very much in keeping with the desire of the City authorities to maintain an ordered and well-governed environment. That this system was of little benefit to Elizabeth Gurney represents a point of caution. The vagrancy laws were not framed to benefit the poor in society and they operated as a 'catch all' for many Londoners. Doubtless many persons who were arrested and charged as 'idle and disorderly persons' could also have been labelled as vagrants and beggars, and many of the female vagrants might easily have been rounded up, by the likes of William Payne, as 'common prostitutes' in different circumstances. Even correspondents to *The Times* had occasion to remark on the abuse of the vagrancy laws by officials. One letter writer noted that even

> a man of fortune may, on the oath of any wretch, be committed to prison for near three months, without the benefit of a bail. He has indeed a remedy afterwards, but that remedy can never atone for the injury his character, health, or fortune may receive.[31]

If you were found resting or sleeping in a doorway you could be arrested for begging, for disorderly conduct or for drunkenness if you were unable to give a good account of yourself to the watchman or constable. The prosecution and punishment of begging and vagrancy needs to be understood as a part of a general determination to clean up the streets of the metropolis and to remove elements that might blight commerce or represent a threat to the pockets and persons of other road users.

City justices had considerable discretion when dealing with the poorer elements of society and this could also work in favour of the lower classes. There is evidence of the charity or generosity of the magistracy. Occasional paupers were given small amounts of money, or had the costs of their warrants or other expenses waived. The problems of poverty within the City seldom surface overtly in the minute books but the lord mayor and aldermen were clearly not inured to the situation. The same business and social links that may have prevented the poorer sorts from manipulating the system to their advantage may also have led to relief schemes and greater charity provision. Aldermen were far from being unaware of the links between poverty, unemployment and petty crime. Indeed the sitting alderman at Guildhall in February 1818 observed that increased crime was directly related to 'the harsh conduct too often displayed by parish officers to persons who applied to them for relief'.[32] In the aftermath of the French wars the lord mayor and aldermen were directly involved in a scheme to assist unemployed sailors who found themselves surplus to navy requirements in a time of peace. In January 1818 the *London Chronicle* published a report of a meeting held at the *King's Head* public house in Poultry, the purpose of which was to find 'some speedy means for relieving the numerous distressed seamen with whom the streets of London are daily crowded'. The meeting agreed that it was vital that a distinction was drawn between those genuine cases worthy of help and the idle impostors who deserved to be treated 'with the wholesome severity provided by law'.[33] The minute books, with their occasional references to monies given to paupers, would seem to reflect this attitude of distinguishing between 'deserving' and 'undeserving' cases.[34] Thus, when a subscription was raised and a boat secured to house the seamen, the *London Chronicle* was quick to complain that some of the recipients of the charity were less than grateful to their benefactors. James Mason, having been fed and clothed and set on board the *Sapphire*, repaid this charity by stealing the silverware and making off in his newly borrowed clothes.[35] One of Mason's crewmates, Thomas Walker, also ran away but afterwards, 'having pawned his clothes [he] had the impudence to return, in the hope that he would not be recognised, for another supply'.[36] We might admire the resourcefulness of the ex-tar, but we can be sure that the local authorities did not see it in that way.

This desire to keep the City streets passable and attractive for commerce and retail is evident in the way in which the summary courts, and the associated regulatory bodies, were involved in the day-to-day regulation of trade and employment in the metropolis.

The regulation of trade

On the 1 September 1790 Jasper Irons was accused by Charles Aldridge of selling him a horse 'as sound, it being glandered'.[37] This case could have been treated as fraud, and the prosecutor indeed used that term, but on this occasion the matter was resolved with Aldridge getting his money back.[38] This case is typical of the way in which prosecutors used the summary courts as a lever to obtain compensation and refunds, ensure the completion of work, and the resolution of all manner of trading disputes.

The City of London in the eighteenth century was a place of business. One might indeed argue that it was *the* place of business as it was manifestly at the commercial heart of Britain's growing empire, as well as being an international trading centre in its own right.[39] It was, as one contemporary observer put it, 'the chiefest Emporium, or Town of Trade in the World'.[40] In consequence of this there had to be a tight regulation of trade and the City's rulers were ideally suited to this role. These were men who had carved out their fortunes in trade, some from relatively humble beginnings. Sir William Plomer had worked in an oil shop in Aldgate, while John Boydell had started life in near poverty but had made his fortune in the fine art market.[41] Others had inherited their wealth but all appreciated the importance to business of rules and regulations that governed contracts of employments, payment and other aspects of business practice. The City had one of the oldest guild networks in England, and had elected Common Councils to regulate its affairs from as early as the fourteenth century.[42] Within each trade a hierarchy existed, well illustrated in Campbell's *The London Tradesman*.[43]

After disorderly behaviour and traffic offences, the regulation of trade and City markets accounted for the largest area of court business that did not involve property crime or violence. Just over 16 per cent of hearings involved disputes about working practice, pay or other contractual disputes. How did these disputes manifest themselves and what can they tell us about the nature of the summary courts and their role at the heart of City affairs? Between 25 March and 4 May 1793 there were 17 appearances by individuals in relation to disputes or violations of regulations governing trade. Of these seven related to non-payment for services. While this is a small sample it is typical of the types of dispute that feature in the minute books throughout the late eighteenth century. In these cases nearly all of those demanding payment were hackney coachmen, carters or the owners of carts. Most of the hackney drivers were successful in obtaining the outstanding fares owed to them. William Vallance, summoned for refusing to pay his fare from Cheapside to Vauxhall, was ordered to pay the fare, the fee for the summons (1s) and a penalty of 1s 6d by way of compensation for the driver's time.[44] Other coachmen had similar success, getting the fare they demanded and sometimes the expenses of the summons.[45] But the court was prepared to hear contrary evidence if it was available and drivers were not guaranteed to win their suits. William Nibb claimed that William Davis owed him 2s 6d to cover the fare and his turnpike fee. Davis was able to convince the court that Nibb had already been through the turnpike *and* had accepted 2s for his fee and so the case was dismissed.[46] The problem of fares and how much should be paid exercised the minds of eighteenth-century Londoners.[47] Hackney coachmen were amongst the most regulated of all London workers with commissioners to determine just how much they were allowed to charge for their services. The lists of fares, such as *The London Companion*, were readily available and allowed passengers to ready reckon the fare payable, and presumably to argue with the driver if they felt justified. Mark Jenner argues that this regulation of the trade represented a commodification of space in the metropolis. While I would not disagree with this view it surely also illustrates an attempt to control behaviour and limit the opportunities for dispute. The attempt to regulate Hackney coachmen, a body of individuals notorious for their insubordination and independence, was part of a gradual move to readjust the City to a changing role as a primarily *commercial* centre in the late eighteenth century.

Carters also looked to the magistracy to assist them in forcing their clients to pay them. In 1793 Osborne and company were prosecuted for refusing to pay the fee due for cartage. The magistrate awarded the plaintiff 8s in settlement of the case.[48] William Young, by contrast, produced his petty cash book to prove that he had already paid the cartage due to William Ruck and his case was dismissed.[49] On top of the evidence Young's case may have been helped by a perceived prejudice against Ruck as he had himself appeared two days earlier charged with obstructing the road around Galley Key and in the previous week had been prosecuted for an assault. He was acquitted on both occasions but perhaps the association tainted him. Carmen were reputedly 'an ill-mannered set' and so might not have found favour in court.[50] Their role was to ferry the various goods and commodities around the metropolis, sharing the streets with coachmen and other road users and forever at the mercy of thieves. However, both carters and coachmen were amongst the lowest of London's classes and the fact that the courts often operated as an arena for them to pressure their customers to pay them goes some way to helping us view the summary courts as theatres of negotiation open to a wide cross section of Londoners.

Customers and employers were equally confident of using the courts to prosecute those that left work unfinished or failed to deliver items that they had ordered. When David Maitland was summoned for refusing to pay a bill for fixing a chimney the magistrate played an important role in settling the dispute. After hearing the evidence the alderman halved the £2 10s bill and the disputants settled.[51] Brokering an agreement at this level probably saved time and money in pursing a claim to a higher court. There are other examples of servants using the courts to get references from their former employers, which clearly demonstrates that these courts were not simply a mechanism for employers to discipline and otherwise control their workers.

The City authorities also regulated the way goods were traded within the City. JPs helped to control the supply of bread and foodstuffs to ensure that outbreaks of discontent were limited, particularly in times of dearth and hardship.[52] The Court of Aldermen set the Assize of bread on a regular basis.[53] In 1795 a magistrate, called to attend a riot in Seven Dials sided with the crowd when it became clear that the baker whose property they were attacking was indeed selling his loaves at short weight.[54] A baker who was selling underweight loaves, which were weighed before the Guildhall court in April 1793, was fined 5s; the fee being paid to the constable who arrested him.[55] On other occasions loaves seized in this way were donated to the poorest felons and debtors in Newgate and other prisons within the City's administration. In 1789 three women were prosecuted for 'selling stinky and unwholesome fish', the women were reprimanded and discharged, presumably fairly quickly if they had the aforementioned fish with them![56] The City regulated the markets at Smithfield and Billingsgate where disputes over trading practice, money or goods could easily become more serious problems of disorderly conduct, and violence. Avoiding these problems was high on the agenda of the City's leaders.

Those who failed to complete work under the terms of their verbal contracts were also summoned to appear before the magistracy. In 1789 two journeymen printers were charged with 'leaving work unfinished' by their employer. No outcome was listed which suggests either insubstantial evidence and a dismissal or, and this is more likely, the court appearance was enough to persuade them to honour their previous commitment.[57] Patrick Hughes was prosecuted for 'neglecting the performance of certain work in the manufacture of leather which he had undertaken to perform, by permitting himself to be subsequently retained by another master before he had completed the same'. In short, he was accused of working for someone else whilst under contract. However, he was found innocent and discharged.[58] Servants who abandoned their masters or employment could be brought before the magistracy for punishment, and the house of correction was frequently used for such purposes.[59] Justices had the power to imprison deserting servants until they could provide surety, in effect forcing them to honour their commitments. In London restrictions were not quite as onerous as elsewhere in the country; here servants could terminate contracts with a month's notice, reflecting the capital's more fluid employment market.[60]

How far City justices were able to exercise their discretion in the face of the abusive relationships some servants undoubtedly experienced is unclear. While the numbers of poorer Londoners appearing was small it is evident that servants, coachmen and labourers recognised the City courts as an arena within which they could air their grievances. Servants 'could sue in higher courts for unpaid wages' but they were more likely to use the summary courts where legislation progressively extended the powers of magistrates to rule in these cases.[61] Catherine Thorp was certainly prepared to prosecute her former mistress, a Mrs Sharp, for refusing to give her a reference. The alderman advised Mrs Sharp to provide her with one.[62] A reference was a crucial document for an eighteenth-century worker, symbolising respectability and honesty, and any refusal to issue one could in itself be viewed as a slight on one's character. Again, as we have seen before the courts provided a public venue within which individual honour, respectability and integrity could be asserted. However, the aldermen were not always prepared to take sides with the employee. Later that month Elizabeth Leach and an unnamed fellow servant failed to get characters from Mrs Wigzell. They did, however, recover the monies owed to them.[63] Both had been dismissed and the court was in acting, as we might understand it, as an industrial tribunal, a practice common with magistrates in other areas.[64] When Phillip Levi was accused by his servant Frances Chessman of 'turning her out of his house and service at an unreasonable time of night and refusing to pay her wages', he was ordered to pay her 4s as wages and 1s for expenses (the fee due for the summons).[65] Four other women brought their mistresses before the Guildhall court for character references in this three-month period in 1796, three were successful and one had her request dismissed. This may not be a large number of complainants but it does demonstrate that members of London's poorer classes did not see the summary courts as the exclusive preserve of the elite and middling sorts. Justice in the City, at summary level at least, was available and useable by even the poorest and least influential members of society and not something that simply served the interests of a ruling mercantile class.[66]

This theme can be further developed by looking at the role the summary courts and associated agencies played in the regulation of apprenticeship. While the apprentice was in many ways at the bottom of the employment system and therefore exposed to the vagaries of their master's personality and prosperity, it is evident that they too enjoyed some limited success in seeking justice from the court system. This can be shown by looking at the role played by the City Chamberlain who acted, like his magisterial counterparts, to mediate trade disputes and to discipline recalcitrant workers. The records of the Chamberlain's Court survive seemingly intact from the 1790s well into the nineteenth century and have been sampled for the purposes of this study.[67]

Apprenticeship and the role of the Chamberlain's court

Under sixteenth-century legislation no one could 'exercise a trade in England or Wales unless he had first served seven years apprenticeship under a legal indenture which defined the mutual obligations of master and apprentice'.[68] In London apprenticeship offered a path to gaining a freedom of the City, a necessary document for those that wished to trade therein.[69] The terms of the indenture were quite specific and detailed how each side should behave.[70] The master was obliged to teach his charge his 'art' by the best means possible and to feed and clothe and provide the apprentice with shelter for a period of seven years.[71] In return the apprentice agreed to serve him. He was to study and learn, work as required and keep his Master's trade secrets. He was also expected to be obedient, as this indenture makes quite clear:

> He shall not waste the Goods of his said Master, nor lend them unlawfully to any. He shall not commit fornication, nor contract Matrimony within the said Term. He shall not play at cards, Dice, tables or any other unlawful Games whereby his said Master may have any loss. With his own Goods or others during the said Term, without licence of his said Master, he shall neither buy nor sell. He shall not haunt Taverns or Playhouses, nor absent himself from his said Master's service Day or Night unlawfully.[72]

If there was a breakdown in this relationship either the Chamberlain or the City justices could become involved, sometimes through the auspices of the summary courts but more usually these cases were dealt with by the Chamberlain in a separate court.

The relationship between the Chamberlain and the City apprentices was initiated at an early stage. All apprentices had to be enrolled at the Chamberlain's court in their first year of indenture.[73] This served a dual purpose: it formalised the role of the Chamberlain as the arbiter of relations between employer and employee, while also demonstrating that poor behaviour had potential consequences. Table 8.1 illustrates the business of the Chamberlain's court for a short period at the end of the eighteenth century and in the early decades of the nineteenth.

Table 8.1 Plaintiffs before the Chamberlain's court, 1792–99 and 1815–17

Complainant	Number	Percentage	Successful	Percentage
Master	891	73.3	812	91.1
Apprentice	324	26.6	181	55.8
Total	1215	99.9	993	

Source: Chamberlain's Court Complaint book.[74]

Masters were much more likely than apprentices to take complaints before the Chamberlain, which is unsurprising given the restrictions placed on young men and the likelihood that they would fall foul of them. Nevertheless significant numbers of apprentices were prepared to use the courtroom.[75] In the north east of England servants and apprentices brought in the most complaints, while in Bristol 'more than half' of the accusations were brought by masters.[76] In the City the large majority of appearances were by apprentices charged with indiscipline. Naturally this only represents the relatively small number of cases that reached the courtroom. In many instances the master would have used less formal, and more direct, methods of correction to discipline his charges.

Richard Howlett was prosecuted for playing dominoes with his fellow apprentice after the family was in bed, with 'great irregularity of conduct and disobedience to his master's orders'.[77] Playing at games when they should have been in bed, and a suggestion that Richard, as the elder of the two, should have been setting a better example, was what was important here. William Preston was reprimanded by the Chamberlain for being absent from his Master's service from Sunday morning 'till the Thursday following, great neglect of Duty, disobedience to his Master's orders, and not coming to business till ten or 11 o'clock in the morning'. He was warned that any repetition of this behaviour would result in 'punishments [that] would fall with double weights on him'.[78] Running away from service or staying out late at night were regular complaints that were levelled at apprentices, and formed a part of the discourse about adolescent behaviour throughout the eighteenth century.[79] The advice books that were written for apprenticeships contained instructions on good behaviour and warned against drinking, gaming and the pleasures of the flesh as distractions from the acquisition of a trade. This cannot have been easy for teenage boys who were expected to work in company with adults and in many ways act as adults, with a range of temptations placed within their reach. The greatest temptation would appear to have been female company. Marriage was not permitted for bound apprentices and London presented young men with innumerable opportunities for licit and illicit intercourse. John Boswell's indenture was cancelled after he absconded and married in secret.[80] William Shonk suffered a spell of imprisonment (probably for debt) and came out to find that his daughter had been 'taken advantage of' by his apprentice.[81] However, almost *any* behaviour could be seen as a breach of the indenture, given the wide-ranging nature of that document. Thus we find apprentices accused of a multitude of sins: a 'great neglect of duty, frequenting Public houses and disobedience to his orders'; 'being repeatedly insolent, saucy and idle and not applying himself properly to his business'; and 'staying away from his work and giving very trifling excuses for it and behaving very impertinent' are typical of complaints laid before the Chamberlain.[82]

What of the breaches alleged by apprentices themselves? Masters were obligated under the terms of the indenture to care for their charges and not to mistreat them. But given that physical chastisement was an accepted part of the relationship between master and servant the degree to which a master maltreated his apprentice was hard to judge. Here the discretion of the Chamberlain was paramount. Not all masters were as cruel as the chimney sweeps that Hanway campaigned against and cases of physical abuse brought by apprentices were 'but the most extreme examples of a general problem'.[83] Take a look at this example from the court: Charles Bettell had been apprenticed to a copperplate printer for just over a year when he complained that his Master had been 'knocking him about with a thick rope, [and had cut] a piece out of his arm with a cane'.[84] In response his master said that the lad was 'a very careless stubborn boy, always spoiling his work, so that he has been 100 pounds out of pocket since he has been with him. Mr Chamberlain severely reprimanded [the] lad and dismissed him.'[85] The Chamberlain believed the printer and perhaps felt that the lad needed to settle into his position and learn the trade, and that given this, a little discipline was not unwarranted. This was especially so since apprentice boys enjoyed a poor reputation in eighteenth-century London.[86] We need to see the treatment of apprentices in the context of the age. Physical violence was an everyday factor in working lives. Although thankfully few masters or mistresses were as cruel as the notorious Mrs Brownrigg (hanged in 1767 for beating an apprentice girl to death), masters 'who themselves worked 14 hours a day for six days a week saw nothing wrong in thus preparing children for doing so in an adult worker's life'.[87] The life of an apprentice was one of long hours, drudgery and displacement to the bottom of the pecking order. This improved as the apprentice served his term, with new boys arriving that occupied the lowest positions and did the most menial tasks and as privileges drawn from custom were earned.[88]

An apprentice that complained that his work was too hard was unlikely to receive much sympathy from the Chamberlain. Luke Hansard, a London printer, made regular appearances at the Chamberlain's Court with disorderly apprentices he wished to discipline. One lad complained that the work Hansard put him to 'cracked his fingers and made them bad'. The printer told the court that, as a result, he had given him less-painful work, cleaning his boots, but the boy had refused to do even this. The Chamberlain sent the apprentice to Bridewell for 14 days.[89] Apprentices rarely enjoyed unqualified success when they complained of poor treatment. More often both parties would be reminded of the mutuality of their relationship, and very few masters were publicly admonished in front of their charges.[90]

Some apprentices complained that they were being treated simply as manual labourers, and not educated. This was a particular concern for the sons of gentlemen. As Peter Earle notes, these future businessmen had not signed up to provide cheap labour.[91] The families of apprentices often paid considerable premiums for them to be educated into a trade that would support them in adult life.[92] In consequence masters failing to instruct their young employees could find themselves brought before the Chamberlain or the nearby lord mayor's court.[93] In an open letter to the lord mayor in 1773, the self-styled *Humanitas* complained that some employers were happier to use apprentices than to employ qualified journeymen. This, he argued, was causing poverty and forcing some craftsmen to emigrate to America in the hopes of finding work.[94] The line between cheap labour and an expert grounding in a trade was a fine one, and may well have caused many apprentices to challenge the treatment they received. The 'overstocking' of industries with apprentices, to the detriment of journeymen, was not a new development in the 1770s but it had become much more widespread 'bringing apprenticeship itself into disrepute'.[95] The lord mayor had the power to restrict the number of apprentices that a master took on (demonstrating his role in the regulation of trade); how often he exercised it is quite another matter.

The Chamberlain presided over a court of industrial disputes where the odds were stacked firmly in favour of the employer. Nearly 75 per cent of all cases here were instigated by masters and even in the minority of hearings brought at the request of apprentices the court still found for the master. Elsewhere in England apprentices may have enjoyed greater success.[96] That this study focuses on the late eighteenth and early nineteenth century may be significant. Apprenticeship was on the decline at this time and concerns about juvenile delinquency were on the increase.[97] This might well have underpinned a less conciliatory attitude towards the grievances of young men in their teens and early twenties who challenged the authority of their masters.

The Chamberlain was quite prepared to use the Bridewell as a way of disciplining troublesome or disobedient apprentices. A third of all apprentices appearing in the court were sent to Bridewell for short periods. Many more were reminded of their duties and threatened with

Bridewell while a smaller number were forgiven on the promise of behaving themselves in future. A small number of indentures were cancelled because the apprentice's persistent bad behaviour or particular transgression allowed an immediate annulment of the contract.[98] However, this and the threat of Bridewell did not always work. In April 1811 a London watchmaker brought his apprentice in for 'behaving very saucy after coming out of Bridewell'. The breakdown in the relationship had come to the notice of the court in October 1810 when the lad had complained about his master's treatment of him. Later that month the apprentice was sent to Bridewell for 14 days for 'not doing in three days what he ought to do in a day'.[99] However, this had little effect on the lad, in a show of teenage bravado he told the Chamberlain that 'he did not care, nor regard going to Bridewell'.[100] An echo perhaps of teenage rebellion and food for thought for modern legislators that have had their Anti-Social Behaviour Orders (ASBOs) turned into 'badges of honour'. Masters frequently complained about apprentices that were not working as hard or as effectively as they might wish. In February 1799 John Clark, another printer, complained that his apprentice had 'not earned 5s a week for many weeks past tho' with ease he could have earned 20s a week'.[101] Printers were 'typical of the better paid London journeymen', and their wages may have been as high as 36s a week in 1785 and 48s by 1805 so Clark was not unreasonable in his complaint.[102]

The Chamberlain was not intent on upsetting the balance of economic and social relations between master/servant; rather his role was to *reinforce* the ties that bound them together; the mutuality of responsibilities as outlined in the indenture. Thus the Chamberlain's court was an important part of the master's disciplinary armoury. The threat of the Chamberlain was dangled over the heads of young and wilful apprentices whose masters found them difficult to manage. However, while masters appear to have been given an easier time of it by the court we should not discount the potential embarrassment involved in being summoned before the Chamberlain. The mutual reprimand that was employed by the Chamberlain did not necessarily imply mutual guilt, it may simply have been a mechanism for reconciliation. The Chamberlain's court was of some use to both parties in the resolution of disputes between apprentices and masters and as such it forms an important part of our understanding of the court systems in the City of London at the end of the eighteenth century. Elsewhere most master/servant disputes were dealt with by the justices either sitting in their parlours or convened in formal petty sessions, while other, more serious, business went before the quarter sessions.[103] In London this work was separated out, at least for this form of industrial dispute, releasing the summary courts – and the magistracy – to deal with the wider regulation of the City. It also demonstrates that London apprentices, those supposedly occupying the lower levels of the employment chain, were not without agency. The records may suggest that they had limited success in challenging the terms and nature of their employment – but challenge them they did. As Rushton suggests was the case in the local courts of the north east, the Chamberlain's Court and the City justice rooms may have 'offered the illusion of security through individual redress'.[104]

Concluding remarks

The summary courts dealt with a wide variety of everyday disputes. This was vital to the smooth running of social relations in the Hanoverian capital because it enabled City residents and workers to air their grievances in a public and accessible forum. Those bringing complaints about uncompleted work and disputed fares were given the opportunity to resolve them with the assistance of the magistracy who were in turn aided by the Chamberlain and City solicitor. These courts served all levels of London society and were not exclusively arenas for the ruling elite. The courts also dealt with refractory paupers, vagrants and beggars brought in by the watch and ward constables. The summary courts seem to have been a part of a diverse selection of institutions that operated to assist, punish and deter mendicants in the late eighteenth century. It is clear that there is still much for us to understand about the treatment of poverty in this period but it would seem that, in keeping with much of their work, the role of the lord mayor and aldermen magistrates was deeply discretionary.

9
The People's Courts?

Innes and Styles recognised that our understanding of how the criminal justice system was used in the eighteenth century was incomplete without better knowledge of the actions of Justices of the Peace (JPs) and their courts of petty sessions.[1] This situation is slowly beginning to change but the summary courts remain relatively under researched.[2] This study of the City of London's summary courts therefore offers a valuable contribution to our understanding of the criminal justice system and how it was used. In answer to Innes and Styles' request it has examined the process of pre-trial examinations and considered to what extent discretion was available throughout. In doing so it has identified a number of important points for consideration.

In the period 1780–99 the London jury at the Old Bailey heard 3836 trials for all offences, an average of 192 per year (220 if 'not found' verdicts are allowed for).[3] However, in the same period the City of London's two summary courts undertook something in the region of 7000 hearings annually between them for all manner of offences, disputes and regulatory infringements. Moreover 75 per cent of these examinations resulted in decisions taken at this level without the need for the higher courts' involvement. Therefore we can argue that considerably more business went through the summary courts in the City than the Old Bailey.

The records from other summary jurisdictions in Hackney, Bedfordshire, Essex and the north east of England also suggest that local populations were used to appearing before the magistracy if not in such great numbers as in the capital.[4] Indeed the capital may well have been peculiar in this respect because of the very accessibility of the justice rooms and because of London's unique position as Britain's largest urban centre. However, the pattern of summary court usage was similar and as we uncover and analyse the records of summary courts and individual magistrates throughout the country we will discover that there was an extremely widespread use of the criminal justice system at this level which requires us to revise our understanding of the nature of that system and whom it served.

The City was home to around 14,000 dwellings in the late eighteenth century and so perhaps as many as one in two households may have come into contact with the summary courts in some capacity annually.[5] The first and fundamental conclusion of this study is therefore that in the City of London in the late eighteenth century most people experienced the law at the summary level and did so in very large numbers. The criminal justice system, in the widest sense, was not simply the distant and somewhat mysterious or quasi-religious manifestation of state power that some would have us believe.[6] It was much more mundane and ordinary than that at the summary level. The crowded justice room that Hogarth depicted wherein Tom Idle miserably pleads his innocence is a much less-ordered space than the county assize with its pomp and ceremony. It is hard to argue that those that encountered this level of the criminal justice system on a regular basis, or who read about its proceedings in the London press and discussed it in their workplaces, alehouses and lodging rooms, would have been in awe of it to any significant extent. It is much more likely that this familiarity with the law encouraged participation and interaction with it. This leads us to consider who used the law in this period.

Prosecutors came from a wide cross section of London society. As Peter King noted, previous work that has concentrated on the use of summary hearings to deal harshly with poachers in rural communities has 'unintentionally distorted our understanding of the nature of summary-court hearings'.[7] The majority of those bringing complaints before the justices were 'middling men or members of the labouring poor' and not the gentry elite.[8] More work needs to be undertaken on the social status of prosecutors in summary hearings but it would appear that the evidence from the City justice rooms broadly support these findings although there were significant differences. When property offending is the focus of investigation it is perhaps to be expected that most prosecutors were those with something to lose. Therefore, more of these individuals came from the middling and higher artisan and trading classes. However, many more poorer individuals used the courts to prosecute those that assaulted them and this is clear despite the difficulties we have in establishing social status from the brief records of examinations before the aldermen and lord mayor. When the hearings of those who brought complaints about trade and employment, and those who used the courts as a sort of industrial tribunal, are brought into the picture the numbers of poor or 'poverty vulnerable' users increased considerably. Overall it would seem that around 17–20 per cent of those using the courts as prosecutors were members of London's labouring poor. These members of London society therefore had the opportunity to use their discretion even if negotiation 'was not carried out between equals'.[9] Thus it is possible to reinforce recent work that has suggested that Hay underestimated the amount of agency the poor and vulnerable had in the criminal justice system.[10] While they may have been restricted in their use of the higher courts by preventative costs, no such bar existed at summary level. Access to the City courts was much more open. The courts were centrally located, open for business six days a week, and cost relatively little in money and lost time. Moreover the holding gaols at Poultry and Wood Street allowed for the intermediate punishment of those that offended. Londoners knew that they could get their abusers locked up in unpleasant conditions for short periods that might have seemed proportionate with the injury they themselves had suffered.

These courtrooms were indeed arenas of negotiation and struggle in which the labouring populace of London could use the law and the magistracy to improve their situation and eke advantage from difficult circumstances. Carters and coach drivers were able to force payments for unpaid fares and victims of assault found it possible to extract apologies and small amounts of compensation from their attackers. Granted, the 'room for manoeuvre may have been limited, but it was exploited to the full'.[11] It is therefore possible to suggest that this study of the use of the summary courts allows us to press the argument made by Brewer and Styles a little harder. The law was certainly not 'the absolute property of patricians' and was instead a 'limited multiple-use right' available to *all* levels of English society to some degree.[12] As has become apparent in the chapters of this study, members of the labouring poor enjoyed better success in utilising the law at summary level in certain areas (such as interpersonal violence and in pressing claims for non-payment) than they did in others. This study therefore supports King's recent conclusion that

[the] criminal law was an arena not only of terror, of exploitation, and of bloody sanction but also of struggle, of negotiation, of accommodation, and almost every group in eighteenth-century society helped to shape it, just as their behaviour was partly shaped by it.[13]

The summary courts also serviced the wider criminal justice system and were an integral part of governance and policing in the capital as described in Chapters 2 and 3. As such they served as a filter to the 'bloody code', dealing with large numbers of offenders without recourse to jury trial. This role was also carried out by men who may have had a markedly different approach to their duties than magistrates in other parts of the country. While rural JPs were essentially amateurs that could easily avoid their magisterial duty, and those in Middlesex were entrepreneurs that traded in justice, the City's aldermen justices were unpaid amateurs that were obliged to discharge their magisterial duties as a consequence of obtaining high office in local governance. Their magisterial role must also have overlapped with their other civic duties, allowing them to implement changes to the administration and control of daily life in the City.

The magistrates that presided over the City summary courts also served the London bench at the quarter sessions and assize for the City and were aware of the need to reduce pressure on the system at the higher levels. Their experience of the regular proceedings at Old Bailey, Guildhall and Mansion House must also have helped them in their adjudications at all levels of the criminal justice system. The evidence of this study points therefore to an integrated system within which the key arbitrators, the magistracy, were well informed, in touch with their community and experienced in administering the law. Newgate gaol, Bridewell and the compters provided a network of institutions that could be used to discipline the populace when necessary providing alternatives to transportation and execution. The Chamberlain's court and the other minor courts for civil adjudication also interlinked directly and indirectly with the summary courts.

This research has also highlighted some interesting aspects of the treatment of women by the summary courts. Female defendants in property cases seem to have been much less likely to be sent on up through the criminal justice system than their male counterparts. This helps us to understand why so few reached the higher courts in the period. It should also remind us that women were accused of property crimes in significant numbers in the late eighteenth century but they were being dealt with at summary level where surviving records are rare.[14] When violent crime is the focus of analysis women were affected by the courts in different ways. Female victims of domestic violence seem to have been able to employ the summary courts as part of a strategy of negotiating a better-domestic situation. Their success in doing so is very hard to measure, but in London women were perhaps more independent and more prepared to use the law to seek protection and to control male behaviour. However, if the summary courts represented a useful, if limited, environment for female victims of male violence it would seem that those women who used violence were treated more harshly than men similarly accused. Proportionally more female defendants in assault prosecutions were imprisoned for short periods because they could not find sureties. This may be simply a practical approach from the magistracy or it could represent a different attitude towards female offenders that has been identified in recent work.[15] This is an area that needs more research.

The lord mayor sat at the head of a network of policing that covered most aspects of the City's life. The City marshal and his deputy oversaw a system of watchmen and patrols that policed the streets day and night, providing a level of surveillance that was superior to that existing in most English urban areas at the time. Private watchmen supervised the docks and warehouses. Parish constables served their wards either as householders in their own right or as substitutes for those unwilling to take on this onerous responsibility. The levels of policing were consistent with, and possibly denser than, those of the first half of the nineteenth century and were clearly extensive.[16] The ability and motivations of individual watchmen and constables undoubtedly varied considerably but the evidence both from the summary records and the trial reports from Old Bailey generally support assertions that the policing of London before 1829 was not as inefficient and corrupt as contemporary writers and police historians have suggested.[17] The development of ward policing and the initiatives of individual lord mayors would also add weight to Reynolds' work on Westminster.[18] This is not to suggest that the City represented a blueprint for crime prevention or good policing but that it certainly enjoyed a better-organised system of policing than other parts of London and the country. It may well be that the ability of the City to resist pressure for police reform in the late eighteenth and early nineteenth century owed something to this perceived good governance as well as to its political power. Was the City of London well policed in the late eighteenth century? Many contemporaries believed this to be the case and the structures uncovered in this study lead us to suggest that this may well have been the case although the effectiveness of policing is an extremely difficult notion to assess.

The amount of time that City magistrates gave to regulating the use of the streets suggests that they appreciated the importance of such work. The multiple uses of the streets of the capital necessitated a system of regulation. The streets had to serve the needs of commerce, rough trade and leisure. With several markets situated within the City, drovers had to be able to bring their cattle in despite the possibilities of disruption and chaos this might cause. The transport network had to be able to operate without blocking the streets for everyone else so restrictions had to be made and enforced to stop hackneys stopping and waiting indiscriminately. Likewise carters moving the goods of wholesalers and shopkeepers (and their clients) had to be aware that illegal parking and unloading caused problems that would be tackled by warnings and fines. Both hackney coachmen and carmen had earned reputations as surly and poorly behaved individuals but they still managed to use the courts to prosecute those that tried to avoid paying them their due. The magistracy also upheld their complaints when they felt them to be fair, demonstrating that the regulation process worked in a variety of directions.

The gradual erosion of customary rights and their replacement with a more deeply regulated society is also perhaps in evidence in the way in which the authorities clamped down, periodically at least, on immorality and the more abrasive displays of popular culture. These attempts to control certain elements of plebeian life were only partly successful as we saw with the sporadic prosecution of bullock hunters. Bullock-hunting was attacked throughout the eighteenth century but persisted well into the nineteenth. From the point of view of those in authority, it had no place in a 'polite and commercial' city such as London but until the nineteenth century and the establishment of professional policing the authorities simply lacked the resources to eradicate it.

Prostitution and street gambling were also elements of plebeian behaviour that exercised the minds of contemporaries quick to bemoan the decay of London. Despite the vigorous efforts of constables such as William Payne, prostitutes were not permanently removed from London's streets nor were they likely to be while there was an ongoing demand for their services. The treatment they received from the summary courts suggests, periodic clampdowns aside, a casual tolerance of their existence if they were not too obvious in their behaviour. Prostitutes that regularly appeared before the justices were described as 'old offenders' and invariably sent to Bridewell while younger and unknown women were simply reprimanded and discharged. It appears that it was their drunken behaviour on the streets that earned the opprobrium of the magistracy and their acts of soliciting and lack of respect for authority that caused them to be arrested in the first place. Their overnight incarceration was probably considered punishment enough by the aldermen in most cases. This was also true of those brought before the courts for disorderly behaviour. As has been suggested in this study the term 'disorderly' was most often used to refer to the 'drunk and disorderly' and the use of the City compters as receptacles for the nightly trawl of the streets by the patrols presumably did little more than deal with an immediate social problem. Despite contemporary protestations about drunkenness amongst the lower orders the courts rarely took any further actions against these individuals.

It appears therefore that these courts attempted to mitigate the worst excesses of popular culture and immoral behaviour whilst recognising that severe clampdowns on the behaviour of the labouring population would result in a breakdown in social relations. The City simply did not have the means to control all aspects of life and we should not be surprised that its magistrates chose to exercise discretion in order to maintain their general authority. The aldermen and lords mayor needed the City to operate for business and leisure, to some extent it needed to serve all its residents and the wider community. At times it would have been politic to turn a blind eye or issue a warning whilst at other times the use of fines and Bridewell may have been more appropriate.

The sheer size of the wider metropolis and its difference to the rest of the country has caused some writers to suggest that social relations in the capital developed in a markedly different way to smaller provincial towns and rural areas.[19] Historians have also noted that there are differences in the urban and rural experience of crime.[20] The poverty and cramped conditions of London's lodging community may well have been conducive to the proliferation of petty squabbles and ongoing feuds, and some City residents may have been persuaded to resort to the law, especially as these courts were close by and relatively inexpensive to use.

This study of summary proceedings in the City has both added to and consolidated some of our understanding of the administration of justice in the eighteenth century. It has also enhanced our growing understanding of social relations. London was home to a diverse cross section of society in the late eighteenth, many of whom are represented both as prosecutors and defendants in the summary courts. We need more work on the City's population to support the findings here, in particular, in relation to the poor laws, how the poor could manipulate them, and how the poor and the courts could use the charitable institutions such as the Refuge for the Destitute. Elizabeth Gurney's death in the Poultry reminds us of how precarious the lives of the poor were in Hanoverian London. We also need a dedicated study of the London Bridewell as available histories are far too general and descriptive. Finally the history of crime clearly needs many more studies of summary proceedings from around the country and it is to be hoped that previously neglected or hidden justicing notebooks emerge in the coming years.

The summary courts at Guildhall and Mansion House served a wide cross section of eighteenth-century London society. Members of all classes in London were brought before the courts, even the influential on very rare occasions. More crucially the courts were available for use by all these classes even if they did not all enjoy the same levels of access and success. The amount of business they conducted compared to the higher courts demonstrates that it was here that most Londoners obtained their experience of the law. The emphasis of the courts was on the settlement of disputes. The key role of the magistrate was that of an arbiter, in the financial heart of the nation the justice of the peace was the broker of agreements between disputing City dwellers. Thus the overwhelming character of these courts was often civil rather than criminal, which suggests that we need to reflect on how we understand the criminal justice system of the eighteenth century and also how we interpret relationships within it.[21] It may be overstating the case to argue that the summary courts of the City were the 'people's courts'. But they were courts that all of the people could use; they may have been of less benefit to the poor and more useful to the propertied but we cannot dismiss them as simply a disciplinary tool of the ruling elite.

Notes

1 Introduction

1. Josiah Dornford, *Nine Letters to the Right Honorable the Lord Mayor and Aldermen of the City of London, on the State of the Prisons and Prisoners Within Their Jurisdiction* (London, 1786).
2. www.oldbaileyonline.org (hereafter OBO) t17860426-117; t17851214-65; t17840915-143.
3. D. Hay, 'Property, Authority and the Criminal Law', in D. Hay et al. (eds), *Albion's Fatal Tree: Crime and Society in Eighteenth-Century England* (London, 1975).
4. J. Brewer and J. Styles, *An Ungovernable People: The English and Their Law in the Seventeenth and Eighteenth Centuries* (London, 1980); P. King, 'Decision-Makers and Decision-Making in the English Criminal Law, 1750–1800', *Historical Journal*, 27, 1 (1984); King, *Crime, Justice and Discretion: Law and Society in South-Eastern England 1740–1820* (Oxford, 2000); J.H. Langbein, 'Albion's Fatal Flaws', *Past and Present*, 98 (1983); Thompson, *Whigs and Hunters: The Origins of the Black Act*, (London, 1975).
5. J.M. Beattie, *Crime and the Courts in England, 1660–1800* (Princeton, 1986); Hay et al., *Albion's Fatal Tree*; C. Herrup, *Participation in the Criminal Law in Seventeenth-Century England* (Cambridge, 1987); King, *Crime, Justice and Discretion*; P. Linebaugh, *The London Hanged: Crime and Civil Society in the Eighteenth Century* (London, 1991); G. Morgan and P. Rushton, *Rogues, Thieves and the Rule of Law: The Problem of Law Enforcement in North-East England, 1718–1800* (London, 1998); J.A. Sharpe, *Crime in Early Modern England 1550–1750* (London, 1999); R. Shoemaker, *Prosecution and Punishment: Petty Crime and the Law in London and Rural Middlesex c.1660–1725* (Cambridge, 1991).
6. N. Landau, *The Justices of the Peace, 1679–1760* (Berkeley, 1984); E. Moir, *The Justice of the Peace* (Harmondsworth, 1969); Sir T. Skyrme, *History of the Justices of the Peace. Volume 2: England 1689–1989* (Chichester, 1991); E. Crittall (ed.), *The Justicing Notebook of William Hunt* (Devizes, 1982); A. Cirket (ed.), *Samuel Whitbread's Notebooks, 1810–11, 1813–14* (Bedfordshire, 1971); G. Morgan and P. Rushton (eds), *The Justicing Notebook (1750–64) of Edmund Tew Rector of Boldon* (Woodbridge, 2000); R. Paley (ed.), *Justice in Eighteenth-Century Hackney: The Justicing Notebook of Henry Norris and the Hackney Petty Sessions Book* (London, 1991); E. Silverthorne (ed.), *The Deposition Book of Richard Wyatt, J.P., 1767–76* (Guildford, 1978).
7. D. Hay, 'Poaching and the Game Laws on Cannock Chase', in Hay et al. (eds), *Albion's Fatal Tree*; P.B. Munsche, *Gentlemen and Poachers. The English Games Laws 1671–1831* (Cambridge, 1981); J. Styles, 'Embezzlement, Industry and the Law in England 1500–1800', in M. Berg et al. (eds), *Manufacture in Town and Country Before the Factory* (Cambridge, 1983).

8. D. Hay, 'Master and Servant in England: Using the Law in the Eighteenth and Nineteenth Centuries', in Steinmetz, W. (ed.), *Private Law and Social Inequality in the Industrial Age* (Oxford, 2000); D. Hay, 'Patronage, Paternalism and Welfare: Masters, Workers and Magistrates in Eighteenth-Century England', *International Labor and Working Class History*, 51 (1998); King, *Crime, Justice and Discretion*.

9. P. King, 'The Summary Courts and Social Relations in Eighteenth-Century England', *Past & Present*, 183 (May, 2004); G. Morgan and P. Rushton, 'The Magistrate, the Community and the Maintenance of an Orderly Society in Eighteenth-Century England', *Historical Research*, 76, 191 (February, 2003). Two others works, D. Oberwittler, 'Crime and Authority in Eighteenth Century England. Law Enforcement on the Local Level', *Historical Social Research*, 15, 54 (1990) and S. Flynn and S. Mark, 'Petty Criminal, Publicans and Sinners: Petty Sessions Records in the Berkshire Record Office', *Journal of the Society of Archivists*, 16, 1 (1995), attempt some consideration of the summary level but are less useful to our overall understanding of the process.

10. Beattie has used the City of London records for the first half of the eighteenth century, but not beyond 1750. J. Beattie, *Policing and Punishment, 1660–1750: Urban Crime and the Limits of Terror* (Oxford, 2001).

11. Shoemaker, *Prosecution*; Paley, *Justice*; B. Smith, 'Circumventing the Jury: Petty Crime and Summary Jurisdiction in London and New York City, 1790–1855', Ph.D. thesis (Yale University, 1996). Greg Smith has also looked at the prosecution of violence the City of London in the eighteenth century. G. Smith, 'The State and the Culture of Violence in London, 1760–1840', Ph.D. thesis (University of Toronto, 1999).

12. Linebaugh, *London Hanged*.

13. T. Hitchcock, *Down and Out in Eighteenth-Century London* (London, 2004).

14. Defoe, *'The Complete English Tradesman'*, Quoted in M. Byrd, *London Transformed: Images of the City in the Eighteenth Century* (London, 1978), p. 17.

15. 'The shops stand, side by side, for entire miles. The accumulation of things is amazing; it would seem impossible that there can be purchasers for them all, until you consider what multitudes there are to buy,' wrote the American, Richard Rush. Quoted in D. Kynaston, *The City of London: A World of Its Own, 1815–1890* (London, 1994), p. 29.

16. Beattie, *Policing*; A.T. Harris, *Policing the City: Crime and Legal Authority in London, 1780–1840* (Ohio, 2004).

17. King, 'Summary Courts'; Morgan and Rushton, 'The Magistrate'; Crittall (ed.), *The Justicing Notebook of William Hunt*; Cirket (ed.), *Samuel Whitbread's Notebooks*; Morgan and Rushton (eds), *Justicing Notebook of Edmund Tew*; Paley (ed.), *Justice*; Silverthorne (ed), *Deposition Book of Richard Wyatt*.

18. King, *Crime, Justice and Discretion*, p. 117.

19. Ibid., p. 112.

20. P. Langford, *Public Life & the Propertied Englishman, 1689–1798* (Oxford, 1991), p. 401.

21. N. Landau, 'The Trading Justice's Trade', in N. Landau (ed.), *Law, Crime and English Society, 1660–1830* (Cambridge, 2002), p. 60.

22. Beattie, *Policing*, p. 108.

23. The situation in the City may have been similar to that of justices in the English boroughs but as yet we have no useful study with which to make a good comparison.

24. King, 'Summary Courts'; Morgan and Rushton, 'The Magistrate'; Crittall (ed.), *Justicing Notebook of William Hunt*; Cirket (ed.), *Samuel Whitbread's Notebooks*; Morgan and Rushton (eds), *Justicing Notebook of Edmund Tew*; Paley (ed.), *Justice*; Silverthorne (ed.), *Deposition Book of Richard Wyatt*.

25. G.T. Smith, 'State and the Culture of Violence'.

26. Although Bob Shoemaker has recently questioned the accessibility of the legal system in London in this period. R. Shoemaker, *The London Mob: Violence and Disorder in Eighteenth-Century England* (London, 2004), p. 288.

27. Beattie, *Crime*.

28. P. King, 'Punishing Assault: The Transformation of Attitudes in the English Courts', *Journal of Interdisciplinary History*, 27, 1 (Summer, 1996), p. 48; N. Landau, 'Indictment for Fun and Profit: A Prosecutor's Reward at the Eighteenth-Century Quarter Sessions', *Law and History Review* (Fall, 1999); R. Paley, 'Power, Participation and the Criminal Law: Restorative Justice Hanoverian Style' (paper given at the 16th British Legal History Conference, University of Dublin, 2–5 July 2003); Smith, 'State and the Culture of Violence'.

29. Morgan and Rushton, 'The Magistrate'; King, 'Summary Courts'.

30. King, *Crime, Justice and Discretion*, p. 86; Beattie, *Policing*, pp. 26–30.

31. Brewer and Styles, *Ungovernable People*, p. 18; King, *Crime, Justice and Discretion*.

32. Landau, *Justices of the Peace*; Shoemaker, *Prosecution*.

33. King, *Crime, Justice and Discretion*, p. 85.

34. P. King, 'Gender, Crime and Justice in Late Eighteenth and Early Nineteenth-Century England', in M. Arnott and C. Usborne (eds), *Gender and Crime in Modern Europe* (London, 1999); Beattie, *Crime*; Shoemaker, *Prosecution*. For wider work on gender and crime see, J. Beattie, 'The Criminality of Women in Eighteenth-Century England', *Journal of Social History*, 8 (1975); J. Kermode and G. Walker, *Women, Crime and the Courts in Early Modern England* (London, 1994); L. Zedner, *Women, Crime and the Courts in Victorian England* (Oxford, 1991); C. Emsley, *Crime and Society in England, 1750–1900* (London, 1996); Morgan and Rushton, *Rogues*; C. Conley, *The Unwritten Law: Criminal Justice in Victorian Kent* (Oxford, 1991); D. Palk, 'Private Crime in Public and Private Places: Pickpockets and Shoplifters in London, 1780–1823', in T. Hitchcock and H. Shore (eds), *The Streets of London from the Great Fire to the Great Stink* (London, 2003).

35. P. King, *Crime and the Law in England 1750–1840: Remaking Justice from the Margins* (Cambridge, 2006).

36. M. Foyster, *Marital Violence: An English Family History, 1660–1857* (Cambridge, 2005); M. Hunt, 'Wife-Beating, Domesticity and Women's Independence in Eighteenth-Century London', *Gender and History*, 4 (1994); A. Clark, 'Humanity or Justice? Wife-Beating and the Law in the Eighteenth and Nineteenth Centuries', in C. Smart (ed.), *Regulating Womanhood* (London, 1992); A. Clark, *The Struggle for the Breeches: Gender and the Making of the British Working Class* (London, 1995); J.M. Beattie, 'Violence and Society in Early-Modern England', in A. Doob and E. Greenspan (eds),

Perspectives in Criminal Law (Canada, 1984); Morgan and Rushton, 'The Magistrate'.

37. These are held by the London Metropolitan Archives in two series, CLA/004/02 for the Mansion House and CLA/005/01 for the Guildhall.

38. They have been sampled by several historians for information about specific areas of the law, such as violence (Smith, 'State and the Culture of Violence'), policing (Harris, *Policing the City*) and enlistment (P. King, 'War as a Judicial Resource: Press Gangs and Prosecution Rates, 1740–1830', in Landau (ed.), *Law, Crime and English Society 1660–1830* (Cambridge, 2002)). Greg Smith is also preparing a full transcript of the Guildhall court for publication by the London Record Society in 2009.

39. These are CLA/004/02/001-004, CLA/004/02/043-045 and CLA/005/01/029-30, CLA/005/01/038-39.

40. CLA/005/01/051-052 and CLA/005/01/055.

41. CLA/CHD/AP.

42. CLA/CA/01/153-208 Court of Aldermen Repertories, 1754–1800.

43. For the sessions of the peace see the series CLA/047/LJ at the LMA, for Poultry and Wood Street compters CLA/047/LJ/03/001-008 includes the calendars of prisoners in the City compters and see also CLRO 236D/8 (Wood Street compter charge book) from 1785 onwards and CLA/030/01/001-012 (Poultry Compter Charge Books) February 1782–September 1813. The Old Bailey trial records were accessed from www.oldbaileyonline.org.

44. R. Burn, *Justice of the Peace and Parish Officer* (London, 1785).

45. While the Metropolitan Police were formed in 1829 the City did not reorganise its policing agents until 1839.

2 Locating the Summary Courts

1. J. Innes, 'Managing the Metropolis: Social Problems and Their Control c1660–1830', in P. Clark and R. Gillespie (eds), *Two Capitals: London and Dublin 1500–1840* (Oxford, 2001), p. 64.

2. Aldermen also sat in the Court of Aldermen that supervised the election of all aldermen along with other City officers and civic posts. In addition the court also licensed all the brokers in the City and was authorised to spend the City's money.

3. Scot and Lot were ancient taxes, dating back to the Anglo-Saxon period. In these boroughs all male ratepayers also had the right to vote in Parliamentary elections.

4. LMA P.D.48: 16 Various Acts of Parliament 1724 Geo I CAPXVIII (1725). *An act for regulating Elections with the City of London and for preserving the Peace, good Order, and Government of the said City.*

5. See M.D. George, *London Life in the Eighteenth Century* (Middlesex 1925, 1966), p. 16.

6. The alderman for Southwark was not elected but tradition determined that when a vacancy for the seat arose it was offered to the most senior alderman.

7. Harris, *Policing the City*, pp. 73 and 84–89. Arguably the City authorities may have cast an interested eye at what was happening beyond the City walls after 1792 with the creation of police offices under the Middlesex Justices

Act. The seven police offices operated in a similar way to Bow Street and provided a service not unlike that was already available to city residents.

8. The Court of Orphans dealt with the children of deceased freemen, the Court of Pie Poudre was concerned specifically with the annual Bartholomew fair, while the Court of the Tower of London heard cases of debt and trespass.

9. *P.P.*, 1837, XXV, p. 128.

10. Premiums had become well established in the City by the mid-eighteenth century as inducements for masters to take on apprentices. See J. Lane, *Apprenticeship in England, 1600–1914* (London, 1996), p. 19.

11. *P.P.*, 1837, XXV, p. 12.

12. G. Cumberlege, *The Corporation of London* (London, 1950).

13. M. Finn, *The Character of Credit. Personal Debt in English Culture, 1740–1914*, (Cambridge, 2003), pp.197–199.

14. The Bridewell lacks a modern history but it is to be hoped that Paul Griffith's *Lost Londons: Change, Crime, and Control in the Capital City, 1550–1660* (Cambridge Social and Cultural Histories, 2008) will address this omission.

15. City JPs, like their colleagues in Middlesex and Westminster would have had to attend eight sessions. See Jennine Hurl-Eamon, *Gender and Petty Violence in London, 1680–1720* (Ohio State University Press, 2005).

16. Beattie, *Policing*, p. 134.

17. Prior to 1638 the number of aldermen who were eligible to serve as magistrates was limited. Only the recorder, the lord mayor and those aldermen who had previously served as lord mayor could act as City magistrates. The next three most senior aldermen supplemented this group in 1638 as did six more in 1692 and a further four in 1704, presumably to deal with a shortage of candidates. The situation was finally consolidated in 1741 when all aldermen were named as magistrates. In 1751 the aldermen operated on a daily rota system. At the Mansion House the lord mayor was nearly always in attendance, his periods of absence being filled by aldermen.

18. Repertory 182, 20/1/1778.

19. Repertory 188, 17/2/1784.

20. Beattie, *Policing*, p. 146.

21. In rural Essex some areas were so poorly served that an inhabitant of Foulness wishing to bring a complaint to a justice had to undertake a 28-mile round trip, with no guarantee of finding the justice at home. King, *Crime, Justice and Discretion*, pp. 113–114.

22. J. Wade, *A Treatise of the Police and Crimes of the Metropolis* (London, 1829), pp. 344–345.

23. Repertory 192, 20/5/1788.

24. CLA/004/09/002 List of Fees to be taken by Clerks in waiting at the Lord Mayors, 1753.

25. George, *London Life*, p. 166. See also L.D. Schwarz, *London in the Age of Industrialisation: Entrepreneurs, Labour Force and Living Conditions, 1700–1850* (Cambridge, 1992).

26. Marine Society, subscription lists, donations, legacies, and cash received, 1769–1772, MSY/U/1 from D.T. Andrew, *Philanthropy and Police: London Charity in the Eighteenth Century* (Princeton, 1989), p. 82.

27. See E. Crittall (ed.), *Justicing Notebook of William Hunt* entry 445 and Paley (ed.), *Justice*, entry 287.

28. Landau, 'Indictment for Fun and Profit'; Paley, 'Power, participation and the criminal law'.
29. CLA/005/01/029-30, CLA/005/01/038-39 and CLA/004/02/001-004, CLA/004/02/043-45: Figures for each court are numbers of cases heard and adjudicated. Exact dates covered by these minute books are: 10/11/1784–5/3/1785, 17/12/1784-14/2/1785, 10/11/1788-14/3/1785 and 12/12/1788–26/1/1789 a period of 48 weeks. Therefore this sample represents 24 'court weeks'.
30. For example, Outside the City boundaries.
31. Of wife, family or employment.
32. CLA/005/01/029-30, CLA/005/01/038-39 and CLA/004/02/001-004, CLA/004/02/043-45. Dates are the same as for Table 2.1.
33. The figures in Table 2.1 and 2.2 show that the Guildhall justice room heard 568 cases in the periods 17/12/1784–14/2/1785 and 12/12/1788–26/1/1789, a total of 90 working days: the court therefore dealt with on average 6.3 cases per day. The Mansion House heard 3834 cases over the two periods 10/11/1784–5/3/1785 and 10/11/1788–14/3/1789, a total of 204 working days: this court dealt with many more cases. If on average the courts heard 12 cases per day and sat six days per week then they would each be able to process 72 cases a week or 312 per month.
34. King, 'Summary Courts'; G. Morgan and P. Rushton, 'The Magistrate', and Crittall, *Justicing Notebook of William Hunt.*
35. Beattie, *Policing*, p. 104.
36. Beattie's table on page 104 does not indicate whether or not it includes warrants issued for assault or other disputes. If assault warrants were to be added to Table 2.1 the apparent emphasis on theft accusations in the 1780s would be reversed. However, if warrants *are* included in Beattie's data then the comparison stands and an argument for a change in emphasis can be supported.
37. Any person 'charged on oath with being the father of a bastard child shall be apprehended and committed to gaol until he gives security to indemnify the parish from expense.' Tate, *Parish Chest*, p. 198.
38. Burn, *Justice*, Vol. 4, p. 367.
39. Ibid., p. 368.
40. Ibid., p. 122.
41. Hogarth, *The Industrious 'Prentice Alderman of London, the Idle one Brought Before Him and Impeach'd by His Accomplice*, plate X of *Industry and Idleness* in S. Shesgreen, *Engravings by Hogarth* (Toronto, 1973).
42. Repertory 190 25/4/1786; Rhodes also supplemented his income by attending the Guildhall on Saturdays earning an extra £35 per annum. Repertory 184, 13/5/1785.
43. For a more detailed description of the operation of magistrate courts in London see, Bruce Smith, 'Circumventing the Jury', pp. 175–184.
44. Examination by magistrate underwent a change in the eighteenth century. Under sixteenth-century legislation the role of the magistrate in property offences was simply to prepare the evidence for the crown in advance of the trial. There was no obligation upon the Justice to look for evidence that could be used as a defence. However, during the century the nature of the magistrate's examination began to take on the 'some of the characteristics of a judicial hearing' as JPs regularly determined whether a case should proceed

to trial on the basis of the evidence brought before them. Beattie, *Crime*, pp. 271–274.

45. CLA/004/02/053, 7/12/1789 and 8/12/1789.
46. CLA/005/01/002, 17/12/1761.
47. CLA/005/01/007, 26/2/1779–3/4/1779.
48. CLA/005/02/007, 17/3/1779.
49. His case was heard at Old Bailey on 4th April 1779, he was acquitted. OBO t17790404-36.
50. Cheapside and the surrounding area were particularly vulnerable to fire. P. Ackroyd, *London. The Biography* (London, 2000), p. 218.
51. Burn, *Justice*; W. Blackstone, *Commentaries on the Laws of England volumes 1–4* (Oxford, 1765).
52. See King, 'Summary Courts'; Morgan and Rushton, 'The Magistrate'; *Justicing Notebook of Edmund Tew*, pp. 13–25; and Paley, *Justice*, pp. xvii–xviii.
53. It is impossible to be certain of how often the courts resorted to the press to advertise stolen property but in the early nineteenth century *The Times* has the occasional advert from the City justice rooms. For example, an advert entitled: 'Ansley, Mayor. Justice-Room, Mansion-House, 1st Oct' appears. Here a 'Cornelian Seal' is described as being found on a suspicious person. 'May be seen by applying to Mr Hobler at the Mansion House.' *The Times*, 3/10/1808.
54. Burn declares that it is reasonable to hold the prisoner in order to allow evidence or witnesses to appear but the 'time of the detainer must be no longer than is necessary for such purpose; for which it is said, that the space of three days is a reasonable time. 2 Haw.119.' Burn, *Justice*, Vol. 1, p. 537. Nevertheless, recent work has shown that suspects could be held for longer than three days, even over a week on occasions. See King, *Crime and Law*.
55. King, *Crime, Justice and Discretion*, p. 95.
56. It is possible that some cases did come directly to the higher courts when they were sitting and so bypassed the summary courts but this figure is not likely to be a high one. See Beattie, *Policing*, p. 268.
57. Shoemaker's work on misdemeanours is a notable exception. Shoemaker, *Prosecution*.
58. For example, V.A.C. Gatrell, *The Hanging Tree: Execution and the English People, 1770–1868* (Oxford, 1994) and Linebaugh, *London's Hanged*.
59. For the victim-led nature of the Hanoverian criminal justice system see Beattie, *Crime*, Hay, 'Property,' King, *Crime, Justice and Discretion*.
60. Minute books were sampled across the period for those records that provided some clear detail of offences. Information was taken from cases where some details of the hearing had been recorded. For comparison see King, 'Summary Courts'.
61. Data from CLA/004/02/014, CLA/004/02/047-048, CLA/004/02/054-055, CLA/004/02/060 and CLA/005/01/002-3, CLA/005/01/005-6, CLA/005/01/010, CLA/005/01/018, and CLA/005/01/026. 'Other category' for the majority of cases means wife or husband.
62. Data as Table 4.1.
63. King defines 'poverty vulnerable' as 'poor employees lacking significant capital resources or reserves, and vulnerable to structural underemployment and

sometimes to long periods of unemployment – in other words, they were members of the labouring poor broadly defined.' King, 'Summary Courts', Table 3, p. 140.

64. G. Rudé, *Hanoverian London, 1714–1808* (London, 1971), pp. 122–123.
65. D. Andrew, 'Aldermen and Big Bourgeoisie of London Reconsidered', *Social History*, 6, 3 (October, 1981), p. 361.
66. P.D.G. Thomas, *John Sawbridge (1732–1795)* Oxford Dictionary of National Biography (ODNB) ref:odnb/24750.
67. Ibid., p. 21 For new work on the press gang see Nicholas Rogers, *The Press Gang: Naval Impressment and Its Opponents in Georgian Britain* (Continuum, 2008).
68. King, *Crime and Law.*
69. ODNB P.D.G. Thomas, *James Townsend (bap.1737, d.1787)* ref:odnb/64140 and R.B. Sheridan, *William Beckford (bap.1709, d.1770)* ref:odnb/1903.
70. For a recent analysis of some City merchants see David Hancock's *Citizens of the World: London Merchants and the Integration of the British Atlantic Community, 1735–1785* (Cambridge, 1995).
71. N. Rogers, 'Money, Land and Lineage: The Big Bourgeoisie of Hanoverian London', *Social History*, 4, 3 (October, 1979), p. 442 and Rudé, *Hanoverian London*, p. 123.
72. T. Clayton, *John Boydell (1720–1804)* ref:odnb/3120 ODNB.
73. Rogers, 'Money, Land and Lineage', p. 443.
74. Ibid., pp. 440–441.
75. R.G. Wilson, *Harvey Christian Combe (1752–1818)* ref:odnb/50464.
76. For example Sir Richard Glyn was Bridewell president and a prominent member of the Antigallican Society; A. Turton, *Sir Richard Glyn* ref/odnb/47949 Paul le Mesurier 'was noted as a philanthropist, serving on the governing bodies of the Eastern Dispensary, the Asylum for Female Orphans, and the London Huguenot Hospital.' W.R. Meyer, *Paul Le Mesurier*: ref:odnb/16428.
77. Rudé, *Hanoverian London*, p. 122.
78. *The World*, 12/7/1790.
79. It has not been possible to determine whether it was possible for an individual to see a City Justice outside of the sitting of these courts. However, the aldermen were busy men, and while in principle it may have been possible, it is more likely that those wanting to see a magistrate were expected to attend at one of the two summary courts. In 1780 the court of aldermen acted to protect their independence and exclusive right to act as JPs in the City when a justice from Tower Hamlets encroached on their territory. Repertory 184, 8/6/1780.

3 Policing and Personnel: Constables and the Watching System

1. *London Evening Post*, 29/11/1770.
2. *General Evening Post*, 12/6/1784.
3. The Metropolitan Police was founded in 1829 while the City of London created its own separate but equivalent force in 1839.

4. Beattie, *Policing*; Harris, *Policing the City*; E.A. Reynolds, *Before the Bobbies. The Night Watch and Police Reform in Metropolitan London, 1720–1830* (London, 1998).
5. F. Dodsworth, 'The Genealogy of Police in England, c.1780–1856: Institutionalisation as a form of Insurance (A Response to O'Malley and Hutchinson)' (Paper delivered at the seventh European Social Science History Conference, Lisbon, 27/2/2008).
6. R. Paley, ' "An Imperfect, Inadequate and Wretched System"? Policing London before Peel.' *Criminal Justice History*, 10 (1989); Reynolds, *Before the Bobbies*.
7. Report from the Select Committee on the Nightly Watch and Police of the Metropolis, *P.P*, 1812, II, 2.
8. G. Howson, *Thief-taker General: The Rise and Fall of Jonathan Wild* (London, 1970), p. 26.
9. See his involvement in trials of Edward Brockett in 1772; John Davis, John Tonner and Joseph Wright in 1773; Mary, wife of, David Hart in 1775; and the trial of Thomas Baggot in 1780 OBO: t17721209-99/t17730707-79/t17731020-42/t17750531-61/tl7800628-113.
10. D. Rumbelow, *I Spy Blue: The Police and Crime in the City of London from Elizabeth I to Victoria* (London, 1971), p. 91.
11. Harris, *Policing the City*, pp. 46–49.
12. Ibid., p. 47.
13. Wade, *A Treatise of the Police*, p. 48.
14. Radzinowicz, *History of English Criminal Law and Its Administration from 1750*, 4 volumes, Volume 2 (London, 1956), p. 493.
15. *General Evening Post*, 23/1/1770.
16. C. Emsley, *The English Police: A Political and Social History* (London, 1991), p. 9.
17. Beattie, *Policing*, pp. 186–187.
18. For a full discussion of the night watch in the City prior to 1750 see Beattie, *Policing*, Chapter 4, pp.169–225.
19. Ibid., p. 194.
20. Colquhoun, *A Treatise on the Police of the Metropolis* (1795), p. 413.
21. *General Evening Post*, 3/3/1770.
22. *Morning Herald and Daily Advertiser*, 29/3/1785.
23. *Middlesex Journal or Chronicle of Liberty*, 17/4/1770.
24. Ibid., 18/9/1770.
25. *Whitehall Evening Post*, 9/9/1790.
26. CLA GJR/M4 11/12/1775.
27. *Whitehall Evening Post*, 17/5/1785.
28. *P.P.*, 1822, IV, p. 5.
29. *P.P.*, 1812, II, p. 2.
30. Harris, *Policing the City*, p. 16.
31. *London Evening Post*, 17/3/1770; *General Advertiser*, 14/2/1785; *London Chronicle*, 15/10/1785; *St. James' Chronicle or the British Evening Post*, 16/3/1790.
32. B. Smith, 'The Myth of Private Prosecution in England 1790–1850', *Yale Journal of Law & the Humanities* 29 (2006), p. 153.
33. 29 Geo. II, c.30, 1756.

34. Colquhoun, *Treatise*, p. 408.
35. OBO t17710515-8.
36. OBO t17900915-88.
37. Harris, *Policing the City*, p. 22; S. Inwood, 'Policing London's Morals. The Metropolitan Police and Popular Culture, 1829–1850', *The London Journal*, 15, 2 (1990).
38. Colquhoun calculated that the value of imports and exports from the Port of London in the year 1798 was over £60 million. Colquhoun, *Treatise*, p. 215.
39. P. D'Sena, 'Perquisites and Pilfering in the London Docks, 1700–1795' (Unpublished M.Phil Thesis, Open University, Milton Keynes, 1986), p. 34.
40. W. Blizzard, *Desultory Reflections on Police* (London, 1785) see also P. Clark, *The English Alehouse*, (London, 1983).
41. *Gazetteer and New Daily Advertiser*, 19/3/1784.
42. *English Chronicle or Universal Evening Post*, 22/5/1784.
43. See D'Sena, 'Perquisites', p. 117. William May appeared in court several times in the 1740s to give evidence at the Old Bailey against pilferers, he was also himself acquitted of receiving stolen goods OBO: t17460117-29/t17460117-11/t17460117-17/t17460409-11.
44. The creation of the Thames River Police in 1800 saw the government take responsibility for a private force that Patrick Colquhoun had introduced two years earlier. However, tensions existed between the river force and the City's extant policing networks. Where the Thames ran through the City's boundaries the lord mayor regarded its policing as the responsibility of the City authorities and not of the government, and complained if the Thames Police ventured onto City territory. C. Emsley, *Policing and Its Context, 1750–1870* (London, 1983), pp. 49–50.
45. F. Dodsworth, 'Masculinity as Governance: Police, Public Service and the Embodiment of Authority, c.1700–1850', in M. McCormack (ed.), *Public Men: Masculinity and Politics in Modern Britain* (Palgrave, 2007), p. 37.
46. Ibid, p. 41.
47. See Emsley, *English Police*; Dodsworth, 'Masculinity'; J.R. Kent, *The English Village Constable, 1580–1642: A Social and Administrative Study* (Oxford, 1986); K. Wrightson, 'Two Concepts of Order: Justices, Constables and Jurymen in Seventeenth-Century England', in Brewer and Styles (eds), *An Ungovernable People. The English and Their Law in the Seventeenth and Eighteenth Centuries* (London, 1980); J. Styles, 'Constables Considered'. Review article, *The Times Higher Education Supplement* (6 March 1987) and King, *Crime, Justice and Discretion*.
48. Beattie, *Policing*, p. 114.
49. Harris, *Policing the City*, pp. 18–19.
50. CLA/ MSS/64/6 Petition of John Dibble to be excused serving as constable.
51. CLA/048/PS/01/013.
52. J. Innes, 'William Payne of Bell Yard, Carpenter c.1718–1782: The Life and Times of a London Informing Constable' (unpublished article), p. 14.
53. For a fuller discussion of the reasons for the use of substitute constables see Harris, *Policing the City*, pp. 18–20.
54. All examples from *The Argus*, 20/1/1790.
55. Beattie, *Policing*, p. 134.
56. Kent, *English Village Constable* and Wrightson, 'Two Concepts of Order'.

57. CLA/AD/04 Cripplegate without 1784. A chaser was either a cloth worker or decorative metal beater; a packman was a term for a travelling salesman. C. Waters, *A Dictionary of Old Trades, Titles and Occupations* (Newbury, 2002), p. 66.
58. Dodsworth, 'Masculinity', p. 41.
59. Defoe, quoted in Emsley, *English Police*, p. 12.
60. Beattie, *Crime*, footnote on p. 52, see also S. Webb and B. Webb, *English Local Government from the Reformation to the Municipal Corporations Act* (London, 1906–1929), p. 19.
61. The £40 reward represented a major incentive for prosecutors and as such was the subject of much criticism throughout the late eighteenth century. The reimbursement of costs was much less contentious with the courts being allowed to give discretionary payments to individuals from 1752 onwards. In 1778 an act 'codifying existing practice' officially sanctioned the award of expenses regardless of whether the accused were found guilty or not. King, *Crime, Justice and Discretion*, p. 49.
62. *P.P.*, 1812, II, p. 493. Beattie estimates this fee as around £5 per year in the first half of the eighteenth century. See Beattie, *Policing*, Chapter 3, pp. 114–168.
63. Colquhoun, *Treatise*, p. 405.
64. Ibid.
65. Harris, *Policing the City*, p. 17.
66. See COL/WD/02/011 Box 2 Wardmotes Box 2 1771–1812, there are some omissions, presumably lost returns.
67. C.L.R.O. Wardmote Presentments 1680–1853 and C.L.R.O. 266B Box 2 Wardmote Papers 1771–1812. The number of constables, substitutes and extras are calculated by taking a mean average of each title over the 12 sampled years. Of 238 constables 132 were substitutes, 15 were 'extras' leaving just 91 men who took up their communal obligation.
68. COL/WD/02/011 Data collated for the years 1771–72, 1774, 1776–77, 1779–81, 1783, 1785, 1787, and 1789.
69. There is a suggestion that in some urban parishes in the eighteenth century that once an individual had assumed the position of constable he could not relinquish it until his successor had been found, thus incumbents could find themselves burdened for year after year. This is unlikely to have been the case in a large ward such as Cripplegate. S. Webb and B. Webb, *English Local Government*, p. 19
70. Reynolds, *Before the Bobbies*, p. 66
71. George, *London Life*, p. 168 see also L.D. Schwartz, 'The Standard of Living in the Long Run: London, 1700–1860'. *Economic History Review*, 38 (1985).
72. George, *London Life*, pp. 168–169.
73. D'Sena, 'Perquisites', p. 105.
74. I. Prothero, *Artisans and Politics in Early Nineteenth Century: John Gast and His Times* (London, 1979), p. 25.
75. Harris, *Policing the City*, p. 20.
76. Burn, *Justice* and W. Dickinson, *A Practical Exposition of the Law Relative to the Office and Duties of Justice of the Peace* (London, 1813).
77. See Shoemaker, *Prosecution*, p. 217.
78. CLA 04/02/052 12/10/1789.

79. CLA 04/02/053 14/12/1789.
80. 17 Geo II. c.5. Burn, *Justice*, Vol. 4, p. 343.
81. Burn, *Justice*, Vol. 4, p. 345; Although many escaped this situation as Hitchcock notes. Hitchcock, *Down and Out*.
82. C. Haydon, *Anti-Catholicism in Eighteenth-Century England, c.1714-1780: A Political and Social Study* (Manchester University Press, 1993), p. 204.
83. Innes, 'William Payne'.
84. The Proceedings were of course selective in what they chose to report and so any reading of 'police' activity from these records is problematic. We might also expect policing agents to act in their own interest in court and so take their evidence with some caution.
85. See Paley, 'Imperfect?'; Reynolds, *Before the Bobbies* and B. Smith, 'Myth of Private Prosecution'.
86. Data from the OBO: The 'Number' refers to the numbers of times individuals appear with the corresponding descriptors in the Old Bailey trial reports for the London Jury and give evidence (NB. Passing references to agents were *not* counted).
87. The OBSP are problematic as a source for studying policing. The ease with which researchers may now search within the trial reports for 'constables', 'patrols' and 'police' (along with all manner of other criteria) conceals the truth that this is not a complete record of business at the Old Bailey in the long eighteenth century. Trials ending in acquittals are sometimes excluded, not all prosecutions reached a trial (being rejected by the Grand jury or dismissed because the prosecutor failed to appear). Additionally policing agents are only mentioned if they appeared in court or were referred to by other witnesses.
88. Merchants and other businessmen could approach the local watch authorities to request watchmen to attend their specific properties. See Harris, *Policing the City*, p. 28.
89. CLA/004/02/052 3/10/1789.
90. *Public Advertiser*, 3/11/1785.
91. *London Evening Post*, 17/3/1770.
92. CLA/004/02/053 7/12/1789.
93. He only appears in the summary of the trial not in the full text. OBO t17860111.
94. CLA/004/02/053 15/12/1789.
95. *Gazetteer and New daily Advertiser*, 26/3/1770; *Public Advertiser*, 22/11/1785.
96. *Middlesex Journal or Chronicle of Liberty*, 18/9/1770.
97. *Lloyd's Evening Post*, 31/12/1790.
98. Peter King, 'Newspaper Reporting and Attitudes to Crime and Justice in Late Eighteenth and Early Nineteenth Century London', *Continuity and Change* 22 (Spring, 2007).
99. COL/AD/04-05 Data collated for the years 1771–72, 1774, 1776–77, 1779–80, 1781, 1783, 1785, 1787, and 1789.
100. P.J. Corfield, *The Impact of English Towns, 1700–1800* (Oxford, 1982), p. 78.
101. Beattie recorded 237 constables serving in 1663. See Beattie, *Policing*, Table 3.1, p. 116.
102. Act of Common Council 1663: C.L.R.O: Alchin MSS, E/57 as used in Beattie, *Policing*, Table 3.1, p. 116.

103. J. Smart, *A Short Account of Several Wards, Precincts, Parishes, etc. in London* (1741) as used in Beattie, *Policing*, Table 4.2, p. 195.

104. See Harris, *Policing the City*, pp. 38–52.

105. COL/CHD/AD/02/006, Military & Naval, raising men for the navy 1795. Clerk to the commissioners of taxes, lists of parishes, wards, number of houses and quotas of men.

106. Cumberlege, *Corporation*, p. 96.

107. Harris, *Policing the City*, p. 28.

108. Cumberlege, *Corporation*, p. 96.

109. In 1752 two constables were hired (at 5/- a day) to police the Old Bailey sessions, this was increased to eight in 1763. Beattie, *Policing*, p. 154.

110. Running east to west these are: Tower, Billingsgate, Bridge, Dowgate, Vintry, Queenhithe, Castle Baynard, and the two Farringdon wards.

111. East to west again: Portsoken, Bishopsgate, Broad Street, Coleman Street, Cripplegate, Aldersgate and Farringdon without.

112. Beattie, *Policing*, Table 4.2, p. 195; Rumbelow, *I Spy Blue*, p. 224; Colquhoun, *Treatise*, p. 413.

113. In 1763 for example, in response to the end of the Seven Years War and again in 1773 when concerns were raised about the usefulness of transportation. Harris, *Policing the City*, p. 27.

114. *P.P.*, 1830 (505) Return of Number of Metropolitan Police; Number of Divisions in Metropolitan Police District; General Orders issued by Secretary of State (my thanks to Dr Chris Williams for this reference).

115. Paley, 'Imperfect?', p. 115.

116. Reynolds, *Before the Bobbies*.

117. Harris, *Policing the City*, p. 8.

118. Ibid., p. 27.

119. *The World*, 25/12/1789.

120. Smith, 'Myth of Private Prosecution'.

121. Paley, 'Imperfect?', p. 123.

122. Wade, *Treatise*, p. 73.

4   Property Offending in the City of London

1. OBO t17840421-60; *Public Advertiser*, 20/4/1784.

2. See, for example, Beattie, *Policing*; King, *Crime*.

3. J. Langbein, *The Origins of the Adversarial Criminal Trial* (Oxford, 2003), pp. 46–47 and 274–275.

4. Hay, 'Property', p. 18.

5. Of 30,852 trials, 25,834 were for theft, 2131 for theft with violence, 1106 cases of deception (fraud or forgery) and 506 offences against the king (predominantly coining). Only 1365 involved non-property or violent crime. OBO.

6. Morgan and Rushton, *Rogues*, p. 49.

7. The period covers 429 days, of which 363 would have been working days.

8. Data from CLA 005/01/029-030, CLA 005/01/038-039, CLA 005/01/051-52, CLA 005/01/055 and from CLA 004/02/001-004 and CLA 004/02/043-045.

9. There are 197 property prosecutions listed in the Guildhall Minute books used for the 1793–1796 sample.
10. All London trials for the period 10/11/1784–5/3/1785, 10/11/1788–14/3/1789, 25/3/1793–4/5/1793, 23/4/1794–24/5/1794 & 15/2/1796–25/3/1796. This period represents 14 sessions.
11. In Surrey Beattie found that 11.5 per cent of indictments for capital property offences, and 17.7 per cent of non-capital property offences, were returned as 'not found'. This gives an average of 14.6 per cent for not found verdicts in Grand Jury judgements. Beattie, *Crime*, Table 8.1, p. 402.
12. The Old Bailey held eight sessions annually, therefore if we divide the 418 cases recorded by 14 we get 29.8. By multiplying this figure by eight (for the number of sessions) a figure of 238.4 is arrived at.
13. Beattie, 'Criminality of Women'; King, 'Gender, Crime and Justice'; Shoemaker, *Prosecution*.
14. Beattie, *Crime*, Table 5.3, p. 239 and Morgan and Rushton, *Rogues*, Table 3.3, p. 68.
15. In Beattie's study of prosecutors at the Old Bailey for the City in the period 1670–1750 the proportion of women accused of property offences rises significantly but it is still considerably less than men, 60.6 per cent of defendants were men while only 39.4 per cent were women. However, Beattie's work shows that this period was untypical. The period 1690–1710 saw a panic about female offenders and a rise in prosecution rates as a consequence. Beattie, *Policing*, Table 1.1, p. 17.
16. Data from CLA/004/02/014, CLA/004/02/047-048, CLA/004/02/054-055, CLA/004/02/060 and CLA/005/01/002-3, CLA/005/01/005-6, CLA/005/01/010, CLA/005/01/018 and CLA/005/01/026.
17. The theft of goods valued 5s from a shop carried a maximum penalty of death.
18. CLA/005/01/046, 8/12/1791.
19. CLA/005/01/010, 25/9/1780.
20. OBO t178012061-46.
21. CLA/004/02/047, 11/5/1789 and OBO t17890603-85.
22. CLA/004/02/047, 23/5/1789 and OBO t17890603-59.
23. Burn, *Justice*, Vol. 3, p. 63.
24. Beattie, *Policing*, pp. 24–25.
25. Data from CLA 005/01/029-030, CLA 005/01/038-039, CLA 005/01/051, CLA 005/01/053-054, CLA 004/02/001-004 and CLA 004/02/043-045.
26. CLA/005/01/004 28/12/1775.
27. Linebaugh, *London Hanged*, pp. 227–228L. Schwartz, *London*, pp. 61–65, George, *London Life*, p. 71.
28. CLA/005/01/030 24/1/1785 and OBO t17850223-39.
29. CLA/005/01/053 23/5/1794.
30. *Whitehall Evening Post*, 15/7/1784.
31. D. Palk, 'Private Crime in Public and Private Places. Pickpockets and Shoplifters in London, 1780–1823', in T. Hitchcock and H. Shore (eds), *The Streets of London from the Great Fire to the Great Stink* (London, 2003), p. 144.
32. CLA/004/02/054, 4/1/1790.
33. CLA/005/01/038, 14/1/1789.
34. *The London Chronicle*, 5–7/1/1790.

35. CLA/005/01/026 17/6/1784 and OBO t17840707-8.
36. OBO t17780218-30.
37. *English Chronicle or Universal Evening Post*, 2/10/1790.
38. P. King, 'Gleaners, Farmers and the Failure of Legal Sanctions in England, 1750–1850', *Past and Present*, 125 (1989); Sharpe, *Crime*; J. Styles, 'From an Offence Between Men to an Offence Against Property: Industrial Pilfering and the Law in the Eighteenth Century', in M. Berg, P. Hudson and M. Sonenscher (eds), *Manufacture in Town and Country Before the Factory* (London, 1983).
39. Linebaugh, *London Hanged*, p. 378.
40. According to the Oxford English Dictionary (1909 edition) pilfering 'can mean pillaging, plundering, or robbery: but often refers to stealing or thieving "in small quantities" '. To pilfer, by the same token, is to commit 'petty theft'. Reference from D'Sena, 'Perquisites', p. 43. See also, H. Phillips, *The Thames About 1750* (London, 1951).
41. Patrick Colquhoun estimated that some 90 per cent of crime went undetected or unreported. D'Sena, 'Perquisites', p. 43.
42. It may also be the case that watchmen on the quays were held accountable for goods that were stolen, as is indicated in some of the trial reports at Old Bailey. In 1785 Morris Thomas, a merchant's watchman, declared that; 'I am answerable for all sorts of goods that are lost, I have paid above a hundred pounds for deficiencies.' OBO t17851019-35.
43. Workers who did extra work or worked overtime might have been allowed to take small quantities of goods or payment in kind as a supplement to low wages. D'Sena, 'Perquisites', pp. 161–165, 142.
44. CLA/004/02/052 September 1789.
45. CLA/005/01/055 20/02/1796, 22/2/1796 and 23/2/1796.
46. CLA/005/01/055 February–March 1796.
47. Coal is both an industrial and a domestic commodity being used for a variety of purposes.
48. CLA/005/01/055 17/2/1796 OBSP t17960217-65.
49. CLA/005/01/055 19/2/1796 OBSP t17960406-52.
50. See King, *Decision Makers*. Those offenders with familial responsibilities were more likely to receive lenient treatment from the courts in this period than young single men who were considered to be more of a threat to society.
51. CLA/005/01/055 2/3/1796 OBSP T17960406-17.
52. CLA/005/01/055 15/3/1796 OBSP T17960406-81.
53. C. Walsh, 'Shop Design and the Display of Goods in Eighteenth-Century London', *Journal of Design History*, 8, 3 (1995), p. 163.
54. For a full discussion of the pre-trial process see Langbein, *Origins*, pp. 40–47.
55. Ibid., p. 44.
56. J. Beattie, 'John Fielding and the Bow Street Magistrates Court.' Unpublished paper given at the Open University 'Themes in the History of Crime, Justice and Policing in 17th and 18th Century Britain' on 18 March 2004; Langbein, *Origins*, p. 43.
57. Beattie, *Policing*, p. 111.
58. Ibid. See also, 'John Fielding', and Langbein, *Origins*, p. 274. It was said of Miles, who died in 1817, that 'there was something mysterious, or not quite

right 'about him. His son, also called Miles Augustus, went on to play a leading role in establishing professional police forces in Australia'. D. Philips, *William Augustus Miles (1796–1851): Crime, Policing and Moral Entrepreneurship in England and Australia* (History Department monograph, University of Melbourne, 2001).

59. King, *Crime, Justice and Discretion*, p. 91.
60. N. Rogers, 'Impressments and the Law in Eighteenth-Century Britain', in N. Landau (ed.), *Law, Crime*, pp. 79–80.
61. CLA/005/01/055, 23/2/1796.
62. King, *Crime, Justice and Discretion*, p. 91.
63. King, *Press gangs*, p. 111.
64. Burn, *Justice*, Vol. 4, p. 345.
65. CLA/004/02/066, 8/12/1800.
66. CLA/005/01/055, 18/2/1796.
67. CLA/005/01/052, 9/5/1794 and OBO t17940604-25.
68. Beattie noted that the City magistrates were committing offenders to the London workhouse (after its establishment in 1699) for 'idle and disorderly conduct [which] included pilfering and petty theft' who might 'have been charged with property offences if prosecutors and the authorities had chosen to do so'. Beattie, *Policing*, p. 29.
69. Ibid, p. 17.
70. Burn, *Justice*, Vol. 4 (London, 1785), p. 343.
71. Beattie, *Crime*, p. 269.
72. Data from CLA 005/01/029-030, CLA 005/01/038-039, CLA 005/01/051-52, CLA 005/01/055, CLA 004/02/001-004 and CLA 004/02/043-045.
73. CLA/004/02/047, 23/5/1789.
74. CLA/004/02/066, 2/1/1800.
75. Data from CLA 005/01/029-030, CLA 005/01/038-039, CLA 005/01/051-52, CLA 005/01/055, CLA 004/02/001-004 and CLA 004/02/043-045.
76. There were 278 prisoners in the Giltspur for felony in 1821, 2 for fraud, 65 misdemeanours, 3 runaway apprentices and a deserter, 1 receiver of stolen goods, 11 individuals for assault, 1 man for being disorderly and a couple of embezzlers. Aside from London parishes there were prisoners from Birmingham, Bristol, Essex, Hampshire, Hertfordshire, Kent, Somerset and Yorkshire, as well as several from Wales and a great number from Ireland. CLA/030/01/023.
77. CLA/005/01/045 7/9/1790.
78. *The London Chronicle*, 19/10/1821.
79. Ibid., 11/10/1821.
80. CLA/005/01/006, 4/2/1778.
81. *Whitehall Evening Post*, 26/2/1784.
82. CLA/005/01/045 27/8/1790. Unfortunately for Thomas the Society sent him back a week later and he was sent to Bridewell for a month instead. GJR/M45 7/9/1790.
83. Data from CLA 005/01/029-030, CLA 005/01/038-039, CLA 005/01/051, CLA 005/01/053-054, CLA 004/02/001-004 and CLA 004/02/043-045.
84. CLA/030/01/023.
85. See D. Palk, *Gender, Crime and Judicial Discretion 1780–1830* (London, 2006) and Beattie, 'Criminality of Women', pp. 93–94.

86. M. Feeley and D. Little, 'The Vanishing Female: The Decline of Women in the Criminal Process, 1687–1912', *Law and Society Review*, 25, 4 (1991).
87. Ibid, p. 725.
88. Beattie, 'Criminality of Women'.
89. GJR/M45 28/8/1790; OBO t17900915-60.
90. King, *Crime and Law*, pp. 142–161.
91. Beattie, *Crime*, p. 263.

5   Settling their Differences: The Prosecution of Interpersonal Violence

1. *Public Advertiser*, 16/8/1785.
2. See L. Stone, 'Interpersonal Violence in English Society, 1300–1980', *Past and Present*, 101 (1983); J.A. Sharpe, 'The History of Violence in England: Some Observations', *Past and Present*, 108 (1985); J.S. Cockburn, 'Patterns of Violence in English Society: Homicide in Kent, 1560–1985', *Past and Present*, 130 (1991) and R. Shoemaker, 'Male Honour and the Decline of Public Violence in Eighteenth-Century London', *Social History*, 26, 2 (May 2001). Homicide and manslaughter are almost always recorded because a coroner is obliged to make a report into any death and because unlawful killing is hard to conceal and engenders strong reactions in people that impels them to report it.
3. OBO. See also Beattie, *Crime*, p. 90.
4. King, 'Punishing Assault'; Landau, 'Indictment for Fun and Profit'; Smith, 'State and the Culture of Violence'.
5. King, 'Punishing Assault', p. 46.
6. Landau, 'Indictment for Fun and Profit'.
7. Burn, *Justice*, Vol. 1, p. 111.
8. GJR/M45 26/8/1790.
9. In a sample of 37 assault cases heard at the London sessions for the peace between 1793 and 1798, where the occupation of the plaintiff is known, and after City officials have been omitted, 23 (61%) were tradesmen or artisans.
10. King, 'Summary Courts', Table 3, p. 143.
11. Data from CLA/004/02/014, cl/004/02/047-048, CLA/004/02/054-055, CLA/004/02/060, CLA/005/01/002-3, CLA/005/01/005-6, CLA/005/01/010 and CLA/005/01/026.
12. A detailed search of the OBO would require a separate research project and in the period 1760–75 the database does not always list which jury heard a case, making it nearly impossible to isolate London from Middlesex cases.
13. Data from CLA/004/02/001-4, CLA/004/02/043-045, CLA/005/01/029-030, CLA/005/01/38-9, CLA/005/01/51, CLA/005/01/53 and CLA/005/01/55.
14. Foyster, *Marital Violence*, p. 23.
15. CLA/005/01/38, 18/12/1788.
16. CLA/005/01/46, 25/1/1791; see also J.E. Archer, 'Men Behaving Badly'?: Masculinity and the Uses of Violence, 1850–1900', in S. D'Cruze (ed.), *Everyday Violence in Britain, 1850–1950* (Longman, 2000), p. 48. Removing hats or wigs could be seen as insulting or aggressive behaviour in several early modern as Peter Spirenberg notes in his recent history of interpersonal violence.
17. CLA/005/01/055, 17/2/1796.

18. *London Chronicle*, 27/1/1818.
19. *The Observer*, 15/10/1815.
20. CLA/005/01/055, 16/3/1796.
21. *London Chronicle*, 20/1/1818.
22. Landau, 'Indictment for Fun and Profit', p. 518; Hurl-Eamon, *Gender and Petty Violence*.
23. CLA/005/01/053, 23/12/1789.
24. Clark, *Struggle for the Breeches*, see in particular Chapter 5.
25. T. Evans, *'Unfortunate Objects': Lone Mothers in Eighteenth-Century London* (Basingstoke, 2006), p. 3.
26. Clark, *Struggle for the Breeches*, p. 85.
27. One contemporary commentator certainly believed that marriage amongst the lower orders was of dubious benefit to them given the costs; 'the expense of being married will be so great that few of the lower class of people can afford it'. Alexander Keith quoted by J.C. Jeaffreson, *Brides and Bridals* (1872).
28. Morgan and Rushton, 'Magistrate', p. 72. See also A. Clark, 'Humanity or Justice? Wife-Beating and the Law in the Eighteenth and Nineteenth Centuries', in C. Smart (ed.), *Regulating Womanhood: Historical Essays on Marriage, Motherhood and Sexuality* (London 1992) and M. Hunt, 'Wife-Beating, Domesticity and Women's Independence in Eighteenth-Century London', *Gender & History*, 4, 1 (Spring 1994).
29. Crittal (ed.), *Justicing Notebook of William Hunt*; Cirket (ed.), *Samuel Whitbread's Notebooks*; Paley *Justice*; *Deposition Book of Richard Wyatt*.
30. Foyster, *Marital Violence*; Clark, 'Humanity or Justice?' and Hunt, 'Wife-Beating'.
31. Hunt, 'Wife-Beating', p. 19.
32. In fact 'until 1853 legal authorities equivocated as to whether wife-beating constituted legitimate correction or criminal assault'. Clark, *Struggle for the Breeches*, p. 73. In fact historians seem to be unclear whether Buller ever ruled in this way. What is clear is that very many people *believed* that men had the right to chastise their wives, so long as they did not inflict disproportionate injury on them.
33. CLA/005/01/002, 17/11/1761.
34. CLA/005/01/004, 5/12/1775.
35. CLA/005/01/053, 24/5/1794, CLA/005/01/053, 3/5/1794.
36. CLA/005/01/055, 17/2/1796.
37. See Clark, 'Humanity or Justice?', p. 194.
38. Ibid., p. 192.
39. Ibid., p. 204.
40. Hurl-Eamon, *Gender and Petty Violence*, p. 55.
41. Foyster, *Marital Violence*. This engagement with the law continued into the nineteenth century as Jennifer Davis has shown in her analysis of the use of the Police courts, J. Davis: ' "A Poor Man's System of Justice": The London Police Courts in the Second Half of the Nineteenth Century', *Historical Journal*, 27, 2 (1984).
42. This view would seem to concur with Hurl-Eamon's for Westminster in an earlier period: 'the simple fact that women prosecuted petty violence at all means that eighteenth-century law and society must have held *some* incentives for women as victims', Hurl-Eamon, *Gender and Petty Violence*, p. 5.

43. *London Chronicle*, 29/12/1818.
44. Ibid., 5/8/1820.
45. *The Observer*, 20/5/1815.
46. Smith, 'State and the Culture of Violence', p. 56.
47. CLA/005/01/055, 22/2/1796.
48. CLA/005/01/053, 23/5/1794 and CLA/005/01/039, 14/1/1788.
49. See also Hurl-Eamon, *Gender and Petty Violence*, p. 79.
50. CLA/005/01/055, 17/2/1796.
51. These neighbourly disputes were not of course restricted to the late eighteenth century as Shani D'Cruze's work has shown. S. D'Cruze, *Crimes of Outrage: Sex, Violence and Victorian Working Women* (London, 1998), see in particular, pp. 50–62.
52. CLA/005/01/053, 3/5/1794.
53. *London Chronicle*, 22/4/1817; According to Burn, 'By 6. G.c.23.S.11. Assaulting in the street or highway, with intent to spoil people's cloaths. And so spoiling them, is felony and transportation.' Burn, *Justice*, Vol. 1, p. 113.
54. T. Meldrum, 'A Women's Court in London. Defamation at the Bishop of London's Consistory Court, 1700–1745', *London Journal*, 19, 1 (1994); see also L. Gowing, 'Gender and the Language of Insult in Early Modern London', *History Workshop*, 35 (Spring, 1993); Shoemaker, *London Mob*, pp. 50–78.
55. CLA/005/01/055, 20/2/1796.
56. CLA/005/01/055, 5/3/1796; CLA/005/01/002, 17/11/1761.
57. CLA/005/01/055, 15/2/1796.
58. CLA/005/01/055, 17/2/1796.
59. CLA/004/02/054, 18/1/1790.
60. CLA/005/01/045, 25/8/1790; see also Shoemaker, *London Mob*.
61. *London Chronicle*, 4/8/1815.
62. Landau, 'Indictment for Fun and Profit'.
63. Ibid, p. 533.
64. Paley, 'Power, Participation and the Criminal Law' (forthcoming).
65. Landau, 'Indictment for Fun and Profit', pp. 518–519.
66. Data from CLA/004/02/001-004, CLA/004/02/043-045, CLA/005/01/029-030, CLA/005/01/038-039, CLA/005/01/051, CLA/005/01/053 and CLA/005/01/055. 'Other' includes two summarily imprisoned. 'Number' indicates the number of hearings before the court and 'per centage' represents the same figure expressed as a per centage of the Total.
67. CLA/005/01/045, 23/8/1790.
68. CLA/005/01/045, 25/8/1790.
69. Shoemaker, *Prosecution*, p. 107.
70. It is not clear from Burn's guidelines that justices were empowered to imprison defendants. They could facilitate a private action by the victim or they could indict perpetrators 'at the suit of the king' for which a fine was the proscribed punishment. Burn, *Justice*, Vol. 1, p. 113.
71. King, *Crime and Law*, pp. 255–278; see also King, *Crime, Justice and Discretion*, Chapter 8, pp. 259–296.
72. Data from CLA/004/02/001-004, CLA/004/02/043-045, CLA/005/01/029-030, CLA/005/01/038-039, CLA/005/01/051, CLA/005/01/053 and CLA/005/01/055.

73. See Paley, 'Power, Participation and the Criminal law' and Smith, 'State and the Culture of Violence'.
74. CLA/005/01/053, 10/5/1794.
75. King, 'Punishing Assault'.
76. Henderson, *Disorderly Women in Eighteenth-century London: Prostitution and Control in the Metropolis, 1730–1830* (London, 1999), p. 107.
77. CLA/004/02/052, 2/10/1789.
78. Data from CLA/005/01/051-052 and CLA/005/01/055. 'Number' indicates the number of cases heard while 'per centage' represents the same expressed as a per centage of the total.
79. See Beattie, *Crime*, pp. 46–47.
80. Ibid., pp. 41–48, 178–182.
81. Morgan and Rushton have suggested that magistrates 'may have regarded men's assaults against women as more serious, and were more likely to refer them to the sessions, while women's attacks on other women to be settled out of court'. Morgan and Rushton, 'The Magistrate', p. 70.
82. CLA/005/01/007 27/4/1779.
83. CLA/005/01/055, 16/2/1796.
84. GJR/M45, 6/9/1790.
85. CLA/005/01/055, 3/3/1796.
86. CLA/005/01/055, 20/2/1796.
87. Landau, 'Indictment for Fun and Profit'; Paley, 'Power, Participation and the Criminal Law'.
88. CLA/005/01/055, 18/2/1796.
89. CLA/005/01/053, 24/5/1794.
90. London Sessions of the Peace and Gaol Delivery, CLA/047/LJ/03/001-118, 21/2/1785-2/12/1799.
91. J.S. Davis, 'Prosecutions and Their Context: The Use of the Criminal Law in Later Nineteenth-Century London', in D. Hay and F. Snyder (eds), *Policing and Prosecution in Britain, 1750–1850* (Oxford, 1989); R.S. Neale, *Bath: A Social History 1680–1850* (London, 1981), pp. 87–90.
92. Brewer and Styles, *An Ungovernable People*, p. 20.
93. Ibid, p. 19.
94. King, *Crime, Justice and Discretion*, p. 365.
95. King, 'Punishing Assault', p. 46.
96. Landau, 'Indictment for Fun and Profit'.
97. Paley, 'Power, Participation and the Criminal Law'.
98. Smith, 'State and the Culture of Violence', p. 108, see Table 2.2.
99. King, *Crime, Justice and Discretion*, p. 361.

6 Regulating the Streets

1. A process that was also happening across the wider metropolis as Elaine Reynolds has demonstrated. Reynolds, *Before the Bobbies*.
2. Data from CLA 005/01/029-030, CLA 005/01/038-039, CLA 005/01/051-052, CLA 005/01/054, CLA 004/02/001-004 and CLA 004/02/043-045.
3. Data from CLA 005/01/029-030, CLA 005/01/038-039, CLA 005/01/051-052, CLA 005/01/054, CLA 004/02/001-004 and CLA 004/02/043-045.

4. Burn gave the term 'disorderly' no separate entry, including it within l discussion of vagrancy. R. Burn, *Justice*, Vol. 4, pp. 333–366.
5. Sprott, *1784* (London, 1984), p. 214; Henderson, *Disorderly Women*, p. 91.
6. Shoemaker, *London Mob*, p. 144.
7. CLA/005/01/055, 15/2/1796.
8. George, *London Life*, p. 281.
9. A. Everitt, 'The English Urban Inn, 1500–1760', in A. Everitt (ed.), *Perspectives in English Urban History* (London, 1973), pp. 91–137 and George, *London Life*, pp. 284–286; Sweet, *English Town*, p. 233.
10. Henderson, *Disorderly Women*, p. 46.
11. Burn, *Justice*, Vol. 1, pp. 41–43. First offence was a 5s fine, to be paid within one week after conviction to the churchwardens for the use of the poor, failure to pay resulted in an order of distress, and/or a period of six hours in the stocks. A second offence meant the offender would be bound by recognisance with two sureties for £10, which in effect meant until the next sessions when they were expected to appear. Alehouse keepers who were convicted were barred for three years.
12. Clark, *The English Alehouse*, pp. 257–258.
13. J. Innes, 'Politics and Morals: The Reformation of Manners Movement in Later Eighteenth-century England', in Hellmuth, Eckhart (ed.), *The Transformation of Political Culture: England and Germany in the Late Eighteenth Century* (Oxford, 1990), p. 81.
14. The first Reformation of Manners campaign was much more focused on the urban rather than the rural area, and targeted particularly at London. 'London is where the reformation of manners movement began, and where the reformers were most active.' R. Shoemaker, 'Reforming the City: The Reformation of Manners Campaign in London, 1690–1738', in Davison et al. (eds), *Stilling the Grumbling Hive: The Response to Social and Economic Problems in England, 1689–1750* (London, 1992), p. 100. See also M.J.D. Roberts, *Making English Morals: Voluntary Associations and Moral Reform in England, 1787–1886* (Cambridge, 2004).
15. Innes, 'Politics and Morals', pp. 104–105.
16. CLA/005/01/052, 30/4/1794.
17. CLA/005/01/001, 24/11/1761 – Ann was probably a prostitute as she turns up again in the following April as a defendant accused of stealing a few shillings from her client, CLA/005/01/002, 20/4/1762.
18. CLA/004/02/055, 3/2/1790 Musgrove had been 'cloathed by the parish' three months previously, 'he trembles and pretends he has the ague' but this didn't fool the court.
19. CLA/005/01/004, 30/11/1775.
20. Earle, *A City Full of People*, p. 93.
21. See Linebaugh, *London Hanged*, p. 30. In 1724 the 'Partners' established a more restrictive regime, 'refusing to allow visitors to bring beer in'. The same body failed to prevent Jack Sheppard from escaping. *The World* newspaper reported in 1789 that 'Sir Robert Taylor was the Magistrate who first started the regulation now so well adopted by the City of London – of preventing Gaolers keeping ale-houses in their prisons' (6/3/1789).
22. CLA/004/02/014, 7/11/1785.
23. CLA/005/01/005, 23/9/1777.

24. *The World* newspaper, 2/2/1789.
25. *London Chronicle*, 21/10/1815.
26. CLA/004/02/054, 4/1/1790.
27. Shoemaker, *Prosecution*, pp. 36–39 and 217.
28. CLRO P.D.10.190. An Abstract of the By-laws and Ordinances of Hackney Coaches. Dated 24/6/1717.
29. See also Mark Jenner, 'Circulation and Disorder: London Streets and Hackney Coaches, c.1640–c.1740', in T. Hitchcock and H. Shore (eds), *The Streets of London from the Great Fire to the Great Stink* (London, 2003), p. 44, for a discussion of the 'deferential choreography' of the London streets and R. Shoemaker, *The London Mob* for a wider analysis of the problems relating to street life in the capital.
30. Repertory 184, 27/4/1780.
31. CLA/005/01/053 April–May 1794 The cases of Jenks, Sadler and Whitworth who were all brought by J. Dean on that charge, found guilty but released without being fined. Similarly Chilton was also summoned by Dean and released without further penalty, as was Buston by J. Hall.
32. J. Gwynn, *London and Westminster Improved* (1766) in N.G. Brett-James (ed.), *A London Anthology* (London, 1928), p. 176.
33. Burn, *Justice*, Vol. 2, p. 425.
34. Both CLA/005/01/055, 15/2/1796 and 12/3/1796.
35. *The London Chronicle*, 14/8/1821.
36. Ibid.
37. Cited in D. Sprott, *1784* (London, 1984), pp. 273–274.
38. *The World*, 30/1/1789.
39. Jenner, 'Circulation and Disorder', p. 42.
40. Hitchcock, *Down and Out*, p. 50.
41. P. Hyland (ed.), Ned Ward, *The London Spy* (London, 1709), p. 324.
42. Rules and Ordinances for the Regulation of Carmen made by the Lord Mayor and Justices of the Peace of the City of London (London, year unknown).
43. Burn, *Justice*, Vol. 2, p. 425.
44. CLA/005/01/026, 14/6/1784.
45. *Whitehall Evening Post or London Intelligencer*, 22/5/1756.
46. CLA/005/01/004, 1/1/1776.
47. John Stevenson suggests the City parishes were 'losing population by the eighteenth century as the rich moved to more fashionable areas and the poorer craftsmen and labourers moved to the low rent areas on the periphery.' J. Stevenson, 'London, 1660–1780', in Stevenson et al. (eds), *The Rise of the New Urban Society* (Milton Keynes, 1977), p. 13.
48. M. Reed, 'The Transformation of Urban Space, 1700–1840', in P. Clark (ed.), *The Cambridge Urban History of Britain. Volume II, 1540–1840* (Cambridge, 2000), pp. 615–640.
49. CLA/005/01/045 20/8/1790.
50. D. Defoe, *Some Considerations Upon Street-Walkers* (London, 1729) quoted in Shoemaker, *London Mob*, p. 3.
51. The term 'prostitute' is not commonly used before the middle of the eighteenth century. F. Dabhoiwala, 'The Pattern of Sexual Immorality in Seventeenth and Eighteenth-Century London', in P. Griffiths and M. Jenner (eds), *Londinopolis: Essays in the Cultural and Social History of Early Modern London* (Manchester, 2000), p. 88.

52. Burn, *Justice*, Vol. 3, pp. 97–98.
53. Hitchcock, *Down and Out*, p. 52.
54. Ogborn, *Spaces of Modernity*, p. 49.
55. Repertory 179, 29/4/1774.
56. Henderson, *Disorderly Women*, p. 76.
57. Shoemaker, *Prosecution*.
58. Ibid., p. 176. See Table 7.2 in 1677, 69.5 per cent of prostitutes convicted were imprisoned, this rose to 88 per cent 1693–97, 72.5 per cent in 1712 and 89 per cent in 1721.
59. In all these cases the offenders can be identified as prostitutes by the language used in the minute books; for example, 'common prostitute', 'disorderly prostitute'.
60. Data from CLA 005/01/029-030, CLA 005/01/038-039, CLA 005/01/051, CLA 005/01/053-054, CLA 004/02/001-004 and CLA 004/02/043-045. This represents a period of 378 days of which 320 would have been working days (days when the court was in session). 'Other' includes five persons passed to their place of last settlement and one 'sent to the Hospital'.
61. Henderson, *Disorderly*, p. 90. Bawdy houses were viewed, as one contemporary magistrate described, 'as manifestly tending to corrupt the morals of young persons of both sexes; and also endangering the Public by bringing together and harboring Persons of ill Fame.' Barlow, *Justicing Manual* (London, 1756), p. 61. The Magdalen House was opened in 1758 to help repentant prostitutes, but just how effective it was is hard to judge. Dabhoiwala, 'Pattern of Sexual Immorality', p. 95 and P. Langford, *Polite and Commercial People: England 1727–1783* (Oxford, 1989), p. 144.
62. Data from CLA 005/01/03, CLA 005/01/06 and CLA 005/01/10 which cover the periods 19/4/1762–14/5/1762, 21/1/1778–16/2/1778, 28/8/1780–2/10/1780, a period of 86 days, only 74 of which were working days. Those imprisoned were sent to the Bridewell.
63. Payne was a well-known individual in Hanoverian London and was involved in anti-Catholic activities including the Gordon riots of 1780. He served as a special constable and marshalman for the City throughout the 1760s and 1770s and died soon after the riots.
64. Repertory 183, 2/12/1778.
65. CLA/005/01/006, 22/1/1778.
66. CLA/005/01/006, 22/1/1778.
67. CLA/005/01/002, 15/10/1761, Bagnio Street did indeed exist off Newgate Street; *The A-Z of Regency London ref 14Db*.
68. CLA/005/01/006, 21/1/1778.
69. King, 'Decision-Makers'.
70. CLA/005/01/010, 1/9/1780.
71. T. Hitchcock, ' "You bitches...die and be damned": Gender, Authority and the Mob in St. Martin's Roundhouse Disaster of 1742', in Hitchcock and Shore (eds), *The Streets of London*.
72. *The London Chronicle*, 16/10/1821.
73. Ibid.
74. *Whitehall Evening Post* or *London Intelligencer*, 21/10/1766.
75. Hitchcock, *Down and Out*, p. 93.
76. Refuge for the Destitute HAD/D/S/4/3, 17/06/1812.
77. CLA/005/01/051, 26/4/1793.

78. As Dabhoiwala suggests, prostitution 'was defined far more in social than in sexual terms: as the whoredom of the idle and disorderly poor, and the natural concomitant of their other vices, rather than as a distinctive form of sexual relations'. 'Pattern of Sexual Immorality', p. 100.
79. CLA/005/01/051, 9/4/1793.
80. *P.P.*, 1818 (275) VIII, p. 157 and p. 217.
81. *P.P.*, 1818 (275) VIII, pp. 145 and 227–231.
82. Dabhoiwala, *Pattern of Sexual Immorality*.
83. CLA/005/01/004, 7/12/1775.
84. Data from CLA 005/01/029-030, CLA 005/01/038-039, CLA 005/01/051-052, CLA 005/01/054 and CLA 004/02/001-004, from CLA 004/02/043-045. 'Other' was one person referred to Middlesex.
85. Shoemaker, *Prosecution*, p. 46; King, 'Summary Courts', p. 159.
86. Innes, 'Prisons for the Poor', p. 65; King, 'Summary Courts', p. 157.
87. Hitchcock, *English Sexualities*.
88. P. Laslett et al., *Bastardy and Its Comparative History: Studies in the History of Illegitimacy and Marital Nonconformism in Britain, France, Germany, Sweden, North America, Jamaica and Japan* (London, 1980); E.A. Wrigley and R.S. Schofield, 'The Growth of Population in Eighteenth-Century England: A Conundrum Resolved', *Past and Present*, 98 (1983).
89. A. Wilson, 'Illegitimacy and Its Implications in Mid-Eighteenth Century London: The Evidence of the Foundling Hospital', *Continuity and Change*, IV, 1 (1989).
90. Hitchcock, *English Sexualities, 1700–1800* (London, 1997), p. 39.
91. Evans, *'Unfortunate objects'*.
92. *London Chronicle*, 12/11/1818.
93. Ibid., 2/8/1821.
94. The offence had first been made capital in 1533 (25Hen.VIIIc.6) but was not fully applied until the reign of Elizabeth I (5Eliz.c.17). See Harvey, *Sex in Georgian England: Attitudes and Prejudices from the 1720s to the 1820s* (London, 1994), p. 122. Those receiving the death penalty were also unlikely to obtain a reprieve. Beattie, *Crime*, p. 434.
95. OBO.
96. CLA/005/01/053, 23/4/1794. They were both committed but there is no record of a trial at Old Bailey so perhaps the charges were dropped or the grand jury found no true bill against them. The rules governing sodomy trials were predicated on very strict guidelines surrounding the offence and the evidence to demonstrate it had taken place, this evidence may have been lacking here, see N.M. Goldsmith, *The Worst of Crimes. Homosexuality and the Law in Eighteenth-Century London* (Aldershot, 1998), pp. 34–37.
97. N. Elias, *State Formation & Civilization: The Civilizing Process, Volume 2* (Oxford, 1982).

7   Quelling the Smithfield Yahoos: Bullock-hunting on the Streets of London

1. *Country & Town*, Sung by Mr. Dugnum at the Theatre Royal Drury Lane (London). My thanks to Dr Matthew McCormack for this reference.

2. *London Chronicle*, 3–6/12/1785.
3. R.M. Malcolmson, *Popular Recreations in English Society 1700–1850* (Cambridge, 1973); M. Huggins, *The Victorians and Sport* (London, 2004); D. Brailsford, *British Sport: A Social History* (Cambridge, 1992); R. Holt, *Sport and the British. A Modern History* (Oxford, 1989); E. Yeo and S. Yeo (eds), *Popular Culture and Class Conflict 1590–1914: Explorations in the History of Labour and Leisure* (Harvester Press, Sussex, 1981); E. Griffin, 'Popular Culture in Industrialising England', *The Historical Journal*, 45, 3 (2002), pp. 619–635; E. Griffin, *England's Revelry: A History of Popular Sports and Pastimes 1660–1830* (Oxford, 2005); H. Cunningham, *Leisure in the Industrial Revolution, c.1780–1880* (London, 1980); D.A. Reid, 'Beasts and Brutes: Popular Blood Sports c.1780–1860', in R. Holt (ed.), *Sport and the Working Class in Modern Britain* (Manchester, 1990); B. Bushaway, *By Rite: Custom, Ceremony and Community in England 1700–1880* (London, 1982).
4. K. Thomas, *Man and the Natural World: Changing Attitudes in England, 1500–1800* (London, 1983), p. 144; Sweet, *English Town1680–1840: Government, Society and Culture* (London, 1999), p. 200; R.H. Sweet, 'Topographies of Politeness', *Transactions of the Royal Historical Society: 6th Series*, 12 (2002).
5. J. Oswald, *The Cry of Nature Or an Appeal to Mercy on Behalf of the Persecuted Animals* (1791), pp. 21–22.
6. J. Lawrence, *A Philosophical and Practical Treatise on Horses and on the Moral Duties of Man Towards the Brute Creation* (London, 1796), p. 159.
7. Malcolmson, *Popular Recreations*.
8. T. Young, *An Essay on Humanity to Animals* (Cambridge, 1798), p. 62.
9. Anon, 'A Dissertation on Mr. Hogarth's six prints lately published, viz. Gin-Lane, Beer-Street, and the Four stages of cruelty' (London, 1751), p. 37.
10. M. Smith, *The Story of Stamford* (Stamford, 1994), p. 30; Martin W. Walsh, 'November Bull-running in Stamford, Lincolnshire', *Journal of Popular Culture*, 30, 1 (1996), pp. 233–247.
11. In Pamplona the bull-running takes place during the festival of St. Fermin and has been continuous since 1591 despite concerns aired by the Catholic Church at its inception and more recently by injuries and deaths that have resulted from the release of several bulls into the crowded streets.
12. Walsh, 'Bull-running', p. 233.
13. Smith, *The Story of Stamford*, p. 30.
14. F. Place, *The Autobiography of Francis Place, 1771–1854*, M. Thale (ed.), (Cambridge, 1971), p. 68.
15. *The Times*, 24/2/1837.
16. Place, *Autobiography*, p. 69.
17. OBO t17970920-66.
18. Place, *Autobiography*, p. 69.
19. Ibid.
20. *London Magazine: Or, Gentleman's Monthly Intelligence*, Vol. XXX, 5/5/1761.
21. Repertory 1784.
22. *London Chronicle*, 24/9/1785.
23. *The Argus*, 20/1/1790.
24. *The Times*, 21/8/1823.

25. J. Middleton, Land-Surveyor, *View of the Agriculture of Middlesex; With Observations on the Means of Its Improvement, and Several Essays on Agriculture in General* (London, 1798), p. 473.
26. *The Times*, 25/9/1822.
27. *P.P.*, 1816, p. 154. Merceron, when questioned, declared that 'the fact is totally false' (p. 206).
28. *The Family Magazine or a Repository of Religious Instruction and Rational Amusement Designed to Counteract the Pernicious Tendency of Immoral BOOKS, etc, which Have Circulated of Late Years Among the Inferior Classes of People* (London, July 1788).
29. LMA CLA/004/02/052, 5/10/1789.
30. *London Chronicle*, 18/10/1820.
31. OBO t17861025-37.
32. Data from CLA 005/01/029-030, CLA 005/01/038-039, CLA 005/01/051-052, CLA 005/01/054, CLA 004/02/001-004 and CLA 004/02/043-045.
33. CLA/004/02/066, 24/11/1800.
34. CLA/004/02/052, 13/10/1789.
35. CLA/004/02/053, 22/12/1789.
36. CLA/004/02/053, 22/12/1789.
37. CLA/005/01/052, 2/5/1794.
38. Thomas, *Man and the Natural World*, p. 176.
39. Place, *Autobiography*, p. 70.
40. *P.P.*, 1816, p. 151.
41. J.F. Winks, *The Bull Running at Stamford, a Transgression of the Divine Laws* (1829), p. 16.
42. Winks, *Bull Running*, p. 15.
43. Ibid., p. 24.
44. Indeed bullock-hunting in this fashion may have been unique to London simply because of the size of the capital and the nature of its cattle markets.
45. Place noted that 'some of the butchers boys who were sent to take care of the cattle usually ran after the bullock and as far as they dared assisted to hunt him instead of taking of him' and so perhaps accusations of a neglect of duty were behind the occasional prosecutions at this level. Place, *Autobiography*, p. 70.
46. OBO tl17940604-6.
47. Repertory 187, 1/4/1783.
48. P. Borsay, *The English Urban Renaissance: Culture and Society in the Provincial Town, 1660–1760* (Oxford, 1989); P. Borsay, 'The Rise of the Promenade: The Social and Cultural Use of Space in the English Provincial Town, c.1660–1800', *British Journal of Eighteenth Century Studies*, 9 (1986), pp. 125–140; Corfield, *Impact of English Towns*; J. Innes and N. Rogers, 'Politics and Government, 1700–1840', in P. Clark (ed.), *The Cambridge Urban History of Britain, Volume II 1540–1840* (Cambridge, 2000); E.L. Jones and M.E. Falkus, 'Urban Improvemnet and the English Economy in the Seventeenth and Eighteenth Centuries', in P. Borsay (ed.), *The Eighteenth Century Town: A Reader in English Urban History, 1688–1820* (London, 1990); M. Ogborn, *Spaces of Modernity: London's Geographies, 1680–1780* (New York, 1998); S. Poole, ' "Till Our Liberties be Secure": Popular Sovereignty and Public Space in Bristol, 1780–1850', *Urban History*, 26, 1 (1999), pp. 40–54;

C. Smith, 'Urban Improvement in the Nottinghamshire Market Town, 1770–1840', *Midland History*, XXV (2000), pp. 98–114; J. Stobart, 'Shopping Streets as Social Space: Consumerism, Improvement and Leisure in an Eighteenth-Century County Town', *Urban History*, 25, 1 (1998), pp. 3–21.

49. A. Firth, 'State Form, Social Order and the Social Sciences: Urban Space and Politico-Economic Systems 1760-1850', *Journal of Historical Sociology*, 16, 1 (March 2003), p. 54.

50. Sweet, 'Topographies of Politeness', p. 369.

51. It was also used for unlicensed and unattended carts that were taken from the streets by civic officers. CLRO PD 10.163 Rules and Ordinances for the Regulation of Carmen made by the Lord Mayor and Justices of the Peace of the City of London (London year unknown).

52. Ibid.

53. Repertory, 15/11/1760.

54. *The Times*, 24/9/1791.

55. *The Times*, 30/3/1827.

56. GJR/M45 13/9/1790.

57. *The Times*, 16/9/1791.

58. *The Times*, 20/1/1790.

59. Repertory 191, 17/7/1787.

60. *The Times*, 24/2/1837.

61. In Stamford bull-running was partly suppressed after a rate of 6d in the pound was imposed in 1838 to pay for the policing of the event, as Holt notes, the SPCA 'sharply raised the cost of the sport'. Holt, *Sport and the British*, p. 35.

62. W. Hutton, *A History of Birmingham* (Birmingham, 1781) 'What singular genius introduced the horse-race into a crowded street, I am yet to learn', Hutton remarked dryly.

63. Griffin, 'Popular Culture', p. 633.

64. Reid, 'Beasts and Brutes', p. 13.

65. In 1841 the Police regulations for the City of London listed the unlawful 'pelting, driving or hunting' of cattle as an offence liable to a 40s fine, suggesting that the problem had not disappeared completely by then. E. Spettigue, *The Police Law of the City of London and Metropolitan District* (London, 1841), p. 43.

8   The Regulation of Trade and Poverty

1. G. Oxley, *Poor Relief in England and Wales, 1601–1834* (London, 1974), p. 15.

2. *The World*, 18/12/1790.

3. See King, 'Summary Courts' and Shoemaker, *Prosecution*.

4. Repertory 192, 20/5/1788; The practice had been established in 1737 and clerks were paid a shilling for each pass or examination, this was in addition to their salary of £150 per annum. Repertory 179, 29/11/1774.

5. Repertory 179, 29/11/1774.

6. By an order of 1738, constables could earn 2s for every 'rogue or vagabond' taken before the magistracy. Beattie, *Policing*, p. 154.

7. CLA/004/02/047, 28/5/1789, 1/6/1789 and 6/6/1789.

8. Oxley, *Poor Relief*, p. 19.
9. Bridewell Court Record Books (1751–61) – 21st June 1751.
10. Burn, *Justice*, Vol. IV, pp. 333–366.
11. *P.P.*, 1814–15, (473), IV, p. 252.
12. CLA/005/01/051, 1/5/1793.
13. CLA/005/01/051, 4/4/1793. The Marine Society was founded in 1756 under the influence of Jonas Hanway and Sir John Fielding with the intention of sending 'young offenders and vagrants to sea, not as convicts, but properly equipped and "cured of the various distempers that are constant companions of poverty and distress"'. George, *London Life*, p. 21. See also James S. Taylor, *Jonas Hanway, Founder of the Marine Society: Charity and Policy in Eighteenth-Century Britain* (Scolar Press, London, 1985) and Donna T. Andrew, *Philanthropy and Police: London Charity in the Eighteenth Century* (Princeton, 1989).
14. The City was criticised in 1790 for its policy of simply issuing paupers with a vagrant pass, 'though these paupers had committed no act of vagrancy, and were not in any degree, subject to the statute concerning vagrancy'. See King, *Crime and Law*, pp. 18–19.
15. Hitchcock, *Down and Out*, pp. 143, 161, 180.
16. COL/CCA/05/01.
17. Hitchcock, *Down and Out*, p. 160.
18. Webb, *English Local Government: The Old Poor Law* (1927), p. 381.
19. *P.P.*, 1814–15 (473), IV. p. 251.
20. CLA/005/01/055, 15/2/1796, CLA/005/01/052, 3/5/1794, CLA/005/01/055, 15/2/1796 and 24/2/1796.
21. S. Webb and B. Webb, *Old Poor Law*, p. 215.
22. There were 14 pauper farms situated on the borders of the City by 1800 which had grown up as an entrepreneurial reaction to the lack of indoor provision within the City E. Murphy, 'The Metropolitan Pauper Farms, 1722–1834', *London Journal*, 27, 1 (2002), pp. 3–5.
23. Murphy, 'Metropolitan Pauper Farms', pp. 2–3.
24. King, 'Summary Courts'.
25. Sir F.M. Eden, *The State of the Poor: Or an History of the Labouring Classes in England from the Conquest to the Present Period* (London 1797, 1966), Vol. 1 pp. 459–460.
26. Murphy, 'Mad Farming in the Metropolis', p. 109, Hitchcock, *Down and Out*, p. 127.
27. N. Rogers, 'Policing the Poor in Eighteenth-Century London: The Vagrancy Laws and Their Administration', *Social History*, 24 (May, 1991).
28. *P.P.*, 1834, VIII, pp. 86a and 381.
29. Hitchcock, *Down and Out*, pp. 125–131.
30. Ibid.
31. *The Times*, 4/6/1790.
32. *The London Chronicle*, 26/2/1818.
33. Ibid., 6–7/1/1818.
34. As Daunton notes it is possible to view such philanthropy as representing an consensual relationship between the middle and working classes that was aimed at the eventual creation (in the nineteenth century) of a society 'based on shared values of decency and independence, and animosity to the

undeserving poor.' Martin Daunton (ed.), *Charity, Self-Interest and Welfare in the English Past* (London, 1996), p. 11.
35. *The London Chronicle*, 27/1/1818.
36. Ibid., 13/2/1818.
37. Glander was a contagious disease of horses, causing swellings around the jaw and nasal discharges. OED.
38. LMA/005/01/045 1/9/1790.
39. Harris, *Policing the City*, pp. 6–7
40. Earle, *City Full of People: Men and Women of London 1650–1750* (London, 1994), p. 3.
41. BL 10825 CC13 'City Biography containing anecdotes and memoirs of the rise, progress, situation, & character of the Aldermen and other conspicuous personages of the Corporation and City of London.'
42. Common Councils were called in 1351 and again in 1377, see Ackroyd, *London*, p. 90.
43. R. Campbell, *The London Tradesman, Being a Compendious View of All the Trades, Professions, Arts, Both Liberal and Mechanic, now Practised in the Cities of London and Westminster* (London, 1747).
44. CLA/005/01/051, 9/4/1793.
45. As Alexander White did in December 1788, successfully claiming his fare, the summons and 1s 6d 'for the loss of time of the complainant'. CLA/005/01/038, January 1789, 29/12/1789.
46. CLA/005/01/051, 10/4/1793.
47. Jenner, 'Circulation and Disorder'.
48. CLA/005/01/051, 25/4/1793.
49. Ibid.
50. George, *London Life*, p. 161.
51. CLA/005/01/051, 16/4/1793.
52. See E.P. Thompson, 'The Moral Economy of the English Crowd in the Eighteenth Century', in E.P. Thompson (ed.), *Customs in Common* (London, 1991).
53. As is evident from the repertory for 1774–75. Repertory 179.
54. Ibid., p. 223.
55. CLA/005/01/051 23/4/1793 the courts lists the loaves by size and then how short weight they are; so No.1 is 2oz under, No.2 1oz and so on.
56. CLA/005/01/046, 23/6/1789.
57. CLA/004/02/053, 17/12/1789.
58. CLA/005/01/004, 22/12/1775.
59. Hay, 'Master and Servant', p. 229.
60. Ibid., p. 228.
61. Ibid., p. 229.
62. CLA/005/01/055, 22/2/1796.
63. CLA/005/01/055, 25/2/1796, the outstanding amount was 17s 6d.
64. See Hay, 'Patronage, Paternalism and Welfare'.
65. CLA/005/01/002, 23/11/1761.
66. As King suggested, while the summary courts 'were often used by the propertied to discipline the poor, the labouring sort were also able to mobilize these courts successfully in their disputes with employers over wages and hiring', King, *Crime, Justice and Discretion*, p. 362.

67. The Chamberlain's court files contain the names and occupations of masters, their apprentices and how long they have served. The series is held by the LMA under COL/CHD/AP.

68. Prothero, *Artisans*, p. 32.

69. Earle, *Making of the English Middle Class: Business, Society and Family Life in London, 1660–1730* (London, 1989), p. 85.

70. Hay, *Masters, Servants, and Magistrates*, pp. 6–7.

71. CLO/AP/MMSS/12/4 Indenture Certificates for an example see that of Robert Brockholes indentured to Thomas Lynall, Cloth worker (1796).

72. CLO/AP/MMSS/12/4 Indenture Certificates of Robert Brockholes 1796.

73. However, this was often deliberately neglected so as to facilitate 'an easy way out of what was otherwise a difficult contract to break'. Earle, *Making of the English Middle Class*, p. 95.

74. CLA/CHD/AP/04/02/002-003, and CLA/CHD/AP/04/02/009. The success achieved by apprentices in 181 cases must be qualified as it involved 171 cases where *both* parties were admonished to respect their duties by the Chamberlain.

75. As indeed Hay found to be the case in Cheshire in the early nineteenth century. See Hay, 'Master and Servant in England', pp. 236–237.

76. P. Rushton, 'The Matter of Variance: Adolescents and Domestic Conflict in the Pre-Industrial Economy of Northeast England', *Journal of Social History*, 25,1 (Fall, 1991), p. 92.

77. CLA/CHD/AP/04/02/007, 14/12/1809.

78. CLA/CHD/AP/04/02/004, 3/10/1799.

79. See Lane, *Apprenticeship* and Earle, *Making of the English Middle Class*. Daniel Defoe amongst others wrote on the subject of unruly apprentices, criminals such as Jack Sheppard and Dick Turpin were notable for having absconded from their masters. Indeed Sheppard, having been locked out of his master's house perfected the skills he was later to employ in housebreaking and escapology. See T. Griffith (ed.), *The Newgate Calendar* (London, 1997), p. 100.

80. CLA/CHD/AP/04/02/004, 4/9/1799.

81. CLA/CHD/AP/04/02/007, 10/12/1809.

82. CLA/CHD/AP/04/02/004 and CLA/CHD/AP/04/02/007.

83. K.H. Strange, *The Climbing Boys. A Study of Sweeps' Apprentices, 1773–1875* (London, 1982), p. 37. Hanway orchestrated a campaign to regulate the trade in chimney sweeps' apprentices and published an expose of the conditions they suffered, *The State of Chimney Sweepers' Young Apprentices*, in 1774, forming associations to further reform in 1774 and 1780. Rushton, 'Matter of Variance', p. 96.

84. CLA/CHD/AP/04/02/007, 5/7/1810.

85. Ibid.

86. Francis Place describes the drinking and whoring culture of his fellows apprentices and Sim Tappertit's gang of 'prentices in Dickens' *Barnaby Rudge* provides a similar picture of youthful excess. *Autobiography*, pp. 74–75.

87. Lane, *Apprenticeship*, p. 226. For Brownrigg's case see Griffith, *Newgate Calendar* and OBO t17670909-1.

88. Earle, *Making of the English Middle Class*, p. 102.

89. CLA/CHD/AP/04/02/007, 30/10/1811.

90. Hay found this to be the case in 1787; indeed 'no masters were punished' at this time. Hay, *Masters, Servants, and Magistrates*, p. 94.
91. Earle, *Making of the English Middle Class*, p. 86.
92. George, *London Life*, p. 165; Earle, *Making of the English Middle Class*, pp. 94 and 85.
93. Lane noted that at the Lord Mayor's court 'the facts were tried by a jury and the Recorder decided the points of law'. *Apprenticeship*, p. 235.
94. Misc.MSS/40/16.
95. Lane, *Apprenticeship*, pp. 242–247.
96. Masters elsewhere fared worse and servants better than they did in the City of London. Perhaps this reflects the close business community of the City or could be explained by differences between the treatment of adult servants and young apprentices. See Hay, *Masters*, Table 1.4, p. 45 and Table 2.1, p. 72.
97. H. Shore, *Artful Dodgers: Youth and Crime in Early Nineteenth-Century London* (London, 1999), pp. 19–22.
98. For details of how contracts could be cancelled see Lane, *Apprenticeship*.
99. CLA/CHD/AP/04/02/007, 29/4/1811.
100. CLA/CHD/AP/04/02/004, 18/2/1799.
101. Ibid.
102. George, *London Life*, p. 167.
103. King, 'Summary Courts'.
104. Rushton, 'Matter in Variance', p. 102.

9 The People's Courts?

1. J. Innes and J. Styles, 'The Crime Wave', in A. Wilson (ed.), *Rethinking Social History. English Society 1570–1920 and Its Interpretation* (Manchester, 1993).
2. King, 'Summary Courts'; Morgan and Rushton, 'The Magistrate'.
3. OBO. Although the average for the 1780s is notably higher at 218 while the figure for the 1790s is down to 166. It is suggested that 14.6 per cent of cases before the Grand Jury were returned 'not found'. See Chapter 5, Note 9. Beattie found that on average 140 persons were prosecuted for property offences by the London jury at Old Bailey in the period 1670–1750. J. Beattie, *Policing*, Table 1.1, p. 17.
4. Cirket, *Samuel Whitbread's Notebooks*; King, 'Summary Courts'; Morgan and Rushton, 'The Magistrate'; Paley, *Justice*.
5. COL/CHD/AD/02/006 lists the number of houses in the City as 13,921.
6. Hay, 'Property': the idea that the elite could use the court trial in the way that Hay implied is challenged by King who describes a much more unruly scene where the public were very much involved in the process. King, *Crime, Justice and Discretion*, pp. 252–257.
7. King, 'Summary Courts', p. 154.
8. Ibid.
9. Brewer and Styles, *An Ungovernable People*, pp. 17–18.
10. Hay, 'Property'; King, *Crime, Justice and Discretion*.
11. Brewer and Styles, *An Ungovernable People*, p. 20.
12. Ibid.

13. King, *Crime, Justice and Discretion*, p. 373.
14. Feeley and Little, 'Vanishing female'.
15. King, *Crime and the Law*.
16. Beattie, *Policing*.
17. Paley, 'Imperfect?' and Reynolds, *Before the Bobbies*.
18. Reynolds, *Before the Bobbies*.
19. Wrigley, E.A., *A Simple Model of London's Importance 1650–1750* in P. Abrams and Wrigley, *Towns in Societies: Essays in Economic History and Historical Sociology* (Cambridge, 1978), p. 222.
20. Beattie, *Crime* and King, *Crime, Justice and Discretion*.
21. Christopher Brooks noted that the eighteenth century saw the growth in the number of poorer defendants using the law to purpose cases of low-level debt. The massive use of the summary courts in the City of London to resolve civil disputes echoes Brooks' work on the courts of request. C.W. Brooks, 'Interpersonal Conflict and Social Tension: Civil Litigation in England, 1640–1830', in Beier, Cannadine and Rosenheim (eds), *The First Modern Society* (Cambridge, 1989), p. 372.

Bibliography

Archival sources

London Metropolitan Archives*

The Guildhall and Mansion House Courtrooms

CLA/005/01/001-055, Guildhall Justice Room Minute Books Series, 1752–1796.

CLA/004/02/001-066, Mansion House Justice Room Minute Books Series, 1784–1821.

CLA/004/03/001, Information Book, 15/11/1792–16/3/1793.

CLA/004/03/006, Summonses Book, 9/7/1798–7/11/1798.

CLA/004/03/007-010, Recognizances Books, 12/11/1800–17/10/1803.

CLA/004/03/017, Letter Book, 16/11/1808–18/3/1810.

CLA/004/09/002, List of Fees to be taken by Clerks in waiting at the Lord Mayors, 1753.

CLA/004/09/007, Mansion House, Prisoners by whom committed and discharged, 5/6/1785–15/2/1787.

CLA/004/09/014, Daily Rota agreed for the attendance of Justice at Guildhall (no date).

Constables and Wardmotes

COL/WD/02/001, Miscellaneous returns of aldermen, common councilmen, constables etc. 1683–1711.

COL/WD/02/011, Wardmotes, 18th century.

COL/WD/02/028, Wardmote inquest 1721–1851.

COL/AD/04-05, Ward Presentments Series.

CLA/015/AD/02/032, Contains warrants for payments to constables and others for apprehending those driving cattle without a license.

CLA/048/PS/01/013, Relates to constables.

CLA/MMSS 181, Constables returns 1812.

CLA/MMSS 391, Extracts from the court of aldermen – appeals against serving as constable or inquest man.

CLA/MMSS 226, Various relating to constables – refusals to serve etc.

---

* The Corporation of London Archives moved to amalgamate with the LMA in the summer of 2004. Where possible I have provided the new LMA finding reference but for the few sources that this has proved impossible the original CLRO reference has been adhered to.

City Gaols

CLRO 236D/8, Wood Street compter charge book from 1785 onwards.
CLA/030/01/001-012, Poultry Compter Charge Books, February 1782–September 1813.
CLA/030/01/023, Giltspur Compter commitment book, 1811–1823.

The London Sessions

CLA/047/LJ/03/001-008, Sessions of the Peace Files (includes calendar of prisoners in Wood Street & Poultry Street Compters).
CLA/047/LJ/04/149, Sessions Minute Book (Fair) December 1784–January 1785.
CLA/047/LJ/06/001, Sessions of the Peace Minute Books February 1785–February 1791.
CLA/047/LJ/01/1115-23, London Sessions of the Peace and Gaol Delivery, 13/1/1784–12/1/1785.
CLA/047/LJ/03/001-118, London Sessions of the Peace Files, 21/2/1785–2/12/1799 (Series runs from 1785–1927).
CLA/047/LJ/05/001, Sessions of Gaol Delivery and Oyer & Terminer minute book (fair) February 1785–February 1789.

The Chamberlain's Court/Apprentices

CLA/CHD/AP/04/02/002-009, Chamberlain's Court Complaint books.
COL/CHD/AP/01/004, Inrolment of Apprentices' Indentures Book.
CLRO Misc.MSS/40/16, 'Humanitas' letter.

Other Sources from the LMA

COL/CHD/AD/02/006, Military & Naval, raising men for the navy 1795. Clerk to the commissioners of taxes, lists of parishes, wards, number of houses and quotas of men.
CLA/004/03/011, Water Bailiffs Charges 1807–1809.
CLA/CA/01/153-208, Court of Aldermen Repertories, 1754–1800.
CLA/015/AD/02, Under the statute, 'An Act to Prevent the Mischief's that Arise from the Driving of Cattle within the Cities of London and Westminster and Liberties thereof, and Bills of Mortality' Geo III (21st year).
CLRO PD.48.16 1724 Geo. I CAPXVIII (1725), An act for the regulating Elections within the City of London and for preserving the Peace, good Order, and Government of the said City.
COL/SJ/06/028, An Abstract of the By-laws and Ordinances of Hackney Coaches. Dated from 24th June 1717.
COL/SP/05/084, Rules and Ordinances for the Regulation of Carmen (no date).

Guildhall Library Records

Ms 33131/1 & 2 – Prison Committee Minute books 1775–1802 (2 volumes).
Ms 33132 1-12 – Prison Sub-committee books 1792–1854 (12 volumes).
Ms 33137/2 – Prisoner's admission and discharge book for 1773.
Ms 33138 – Prisoner's Committal books 1809–1916 (9 volumes).

Ms 33140/1-14 – Weekly returns of prisoners in custody 1817–1830.
Bridewell Court Record Books (1751–1761) – 21st June 1751.
MS33051 – Bridewell Case Book.
MS33045 1842 'Respecting the power of the Lord Mayor and Aldermen as magistrates of the City to commit offenders to Bridewell.'

The National Archives

KB10/44, Court of King's Bench, Crown Side, Indictments 1785–1786.
KB29/444, Court of King's Bench, Crown Side. Controlment Rolls.

Parliamentary Papers

Report of the Select Committee on the State of the Nightly watch of the Metropolis, 1812 (127) II. 95.
Report of the Select Committee on the State of the Police of the Metropolis, 1816 (510) V. 1.
First Report of the Select Committee on the State of the Police of the Metropolis, and the Execution of the Law for Licensees and Victuallers, 1817 (233) VII. 1.
Second Report of the Select Committee on the State of the Police of the Metropolis, and the Execution of the Law for Licensees and Victuallers, 1817 (484) VII. 321.
Report of the Select Committee on the State of the Police of the Metropolis, 1822 (440) IV. 1.
Report of the Select Committee on the Causes of Increase in Number of Commitments and Convictions in London and Middlesex, and the State of the Police in the Metropolis, 1828 (533) VI. 1.
Report of the Select Committee on the State of Newgate Gaol, and Poultry, Giltspur-street, Ludgate and Borough Compters, 1813–14 (157) IV. 249.
Report of the Select Committee on the State of Gaols in London, 1813–14 (152) IV. 249.
Report of the Select Committee on the Prisons within the City of London and Borough of Southwark, 1818 (275) VIII. 297.
Return of Stipendiary Magistrates Metropolitan Police Offices, 1812 (55) X. 273.
Bill to Facilitate Summary Proceedings before Justices of the Peace, 1821 (625) III. 11.
Return of Number of Persons Charged with Criminal Offences in London and Middlesex, 1806–10. 1812 (21) X. 215.
Return of Number of Persons Committed for Trial at the Sessions for London and Middlesex, 1810–12. 1813–14 (336) XIII. 195.
Bill to Amend the Laws Relating to Vagrancy, 1821 (564) II. 1105.
Report of the Select Committee on the State of Mendicity in the Metropolis, 1814–15 (473) III. 231.
Report from His Majesty's Commissioners for Inquiring into the Administration and Practical Operation of the Poor Laws. Appendix A. Part III. 1834 (44) XXIX. 111.

Second Report of the Commissioners appointed to enquire into the Municipal Corporation in England and Wales (London and Southwark), 1837 (239) XXV. 1.
Population from the 1801 census 1831 (1) XVIII.

Web Resources

Oxford Dictionary of National Biography www.oxforddnb.com.
Old Bailey Proceedings Online www.oldbaileyonline.org.
The Times digital archive http://www.gale.com/Times/.
17th and 18th Century Newspapers: The Burney Collection Online www.bl.uk/eresources.

Printed Primary Sources before 1900

Anon., 'City Biography containing anecdotes and memoirs of the rise, progress, situation, & character of the Aldermen and other conspicuous personages of the Corporation and City of London' (1800) BL 10825.
Anon., *Country & Town*, Sung by Mr. Dugnum at the Theatre Royal Drury Lane ([London], n.d.). BL G.249, f. 55.
Anon., 'A Dissertation on Mr. Hogarth's six prints lately publish'd, viz. Gin-Lane, Beer-Street, and the Four stages of cruelty' (London, 1751).
Barlow, T. *Justicing Manual* (1765).
Blackstone, W. *Commentaries on the Laws of England volumes 1–4* (Oxford, 1765; London, 1979).
Blizzard, W. *Desultory Reflections on Police* (1785).
Burn, R. *Justice of the Peace and Parish Officer* (London, 1785).
Campbell, R. *The London Tradesman, Being a Compendious View of All the Trades, Professions, Arts, Both Liberal and Mechanic, now practiced in the Cities of London and Westminster. Calculated for the Information of Parents, and Instruction of YOUTH in Their Choice of Business* (London: T. Gardner, 1747).
Cirket, A.F. *Samuel Whitbread's Notebooks, 1810–11, 1813–14* Bedfordshire Historical Record Society, 50 (Ampthill, 1971).
Colquhoun, P. *A Treatise on the Police of the Metropolis* (1795).
Copeland, A.J. *Bridewell Royal Hospital Past and Present* (1888).
Crittall, E. (ed.), *The Justicing Notebook of William Hunt, 1744–1749* (Devizes, 1982).
Deveil, Sir T. *Observations on the Practice of a Justice of the Peace: Intended for Such Gentlemen as Design to Act for Middlesex or Westminster* (London, 1747).
—— *Memoirs of the Life and Times of Sir Thomas Deveil, Knight, One of His Majesty's Justices of the Peace for the Counties of Middlesex, Essex, Surry and Hertfordshire the City and Liberty of Westminster, the Tower of London, and the Liberties thereof* (London, 1748).
Dickinson, W. *A Practical Exposition of the Law Relative to the Office and Duties of Justice of the Peace* (1813).
Dornford, J. *Nine Letters to the Right Honorable the Lord Mayor and Aldermen of the City of London, on the State of the Prisons and Prisoners Within Their Jurisdiction: Shewing the Necessity of a Reform of them: Urging the Great Advantage of Solitary*

Confinement, and the Treating of Prisoners with Humanity: with Observations on the Building of the New Compters, and Some Extracts of Mr. Howard's Proposed Improvements: To Which Is Added an Account of the Deaths of Rob. May, Eliz. Gurney & T. Trimer, who 'died for want in the poultry compter' (London, 1786).

Fielding, H. *An Enquiry Into the Causes of the Late Increase of Robbers, & with Some Proposals for Remedying this Growing Evil* (London, 1751).

Fielding, Sir J. *An Account of the Origin and Effects of a Police Set on Foot by His Grace the Duke of Newcastle in the Year 1753, upon a Plan Presented to His Grace by the Late Henry Fielding, esq. To Which Is Added a Plan For Preserving Those Deserted Girls in this Town, who Become Prostitutes from Necessity.* (London, 1780) BL103.L16).

—— *Extracts from Such of the Penal Laws as Particularly Relate to the Peace and Good Order of this Metropolis* (1762).

Hutton, W. *A History of Birmingham* (Birmingham, 1781).

Jeaffreson, J.C. *Brides and Bridals* (1872).

Lamoine, G. (ed.), *Charges to the Grand Jury, 1689–1803.* Camden Fourth Series, 43 (London, 1992).

Lawrence, J. *A Philosophical and Practical Treatise on Horses and on the Moral Duties of Man towards the Brute Creation* (London, 1796).

Middleton, J. *Land-Surveyor, View of the Agriculture of Middlesex; with Observations on the Means of Its Improvement, and Several Essays on Agriculture in General* (London, 1798).

Morgan, G. and Rushton, P. (eds.), *The Justicing Notebook (1750–64) of Edmund Tew, Rector of Bolton* (Woodbridge, 2000).

Oswald, J. *The Cry of Nature or an Appeal to Mercy on Behalf of the Persecuted Animals* (1791).

Paley, R. (ed.), *Justice in Eighteenth-century Hackney: The Justicing Notebook of Henry Norris and the Hackney Petty Sessions Book* (London Record Society, 1991).

Stone, J. *The Practice of the Petty Sessions* (London, 1838).

Trimmer. *The Family Magazine or a Repository of Religious Instruction and Rational Amusement Designed to Counteract the Pernicious Tendency of Immoral Books, etc, which Have Circulated of Late Years among the Inferior Classes of People* (London, July 1788).

Thale, M. (ed.), *The Autobiography of Francis Place 1771–1854* (Cambridge, 1972).

Waithman, R. *Maxims of Robert Lord Waithman Some While Chief Magistrate of London* (London, 1824).

Wade, J. *A Treatise on the Police and Crimes of the Metropolis* (1829).

Welch. C. *Modern History of the City of London* (London, 1896).

Willcock, J.W. *The Office of Constable* (London, 1827) BL516.k.25.

Winks, J.F. *The Bull Running at Stamford, a Transgression of the Divine Laws* (London, 1829).

The Deposition Book of Richard Wyatt, JP, 1767–1776 (Surrey Record Office).

Young, T. *An Essay on Humanity to Animals* (Cambridge, 1798).

Published Secondary Sources Post 1900

Abrams, Phillips & Wrigley. *Towns in Societies: Essays in Economic History and Historical Sociology* (Cambridge, 1978).

Ackroyd, P. *London: The Biography* (London, 2003).

Andrew, D.T. 'Aldermen and Big Bourgeoisie of London Reconsidered', *Social History*, 6, 3 (October, 1981), pp. 359–364.

—— *Philanthropy and Police: London Charity in the Eighteenth Century* (Princeton, 1989).

Anon. *The Corporation of London: Its Origin, Constitution, Powers and Duties* (Oxford, 1950).

Archer, J.E. 'Men Behaving badly'?: Masculinity and the Uses of Violence, 1850–1900', in D'Cruze, S. (ed.), *Everyday Violence in Britain, 1850–1950* (Longman, 2000).

Arkel, T. 'Illuminations and Distortions: Gregory King's Scheme Calculated for the Year 1688 and the Social Structure of Later Stuart England', *Economic History Review*, LIX, 1 (2006), pp. 32–69.

Arnot, L and Usborne, C. (eds.), *Gender and Crime in Modern Europe* (London, 1999).

Ashton, R. 'Popular Entertainment and Social Control in Later Elizabethan and Early Stuart London', *The London Journal*, 9, 1 (Summer, 1983), pp. 3–19.

Beattie, J.M. 'The Criminality of Women in Eighteenth-Century England', *Journal of Social History*, 8 (1975), pp. 80–116.

—— 'Violence and Society in Early-Modern England', in Doob, A. and Greenspan, E. (eds.), *Perspectives in Criminal Law* (Canada, 1984).

—— *Crime and the Courts in England, 1660–1800* (Princeton, 1986).

—— 'Crime and Inequality in Eighteenth-Century London', in Hagan, J. and Peterson, R. (eds.), *Crime and Inequality* (Stanford, 1994).

—— *Policing and Punishment in London, 1660–1750: Urban Crime and the Limits of Terror* (Oxford, 2001).

Beaven, E. *The Aldermen of the City of London* (London, 1908).

Beier, A.L. and Finlay, R. (eds.), *London 1500–1700: The Making of the Metropolis* (London, 1986).

Bertelsen, L. 'Committed by Justice Fielding: Judicial and Journalistic Representation in the Bow Street Magistrate's Office January 3–November 24, 1752', *Eighteenth-Century Studies*, 30, 4 (1997), pp. 337–363.

Borsay, P. *The English Urban Renaissance: Culture and Society in the Provincial Town, 1660–1770* (Oxford, 1989).

—— (ed.), *The Eighteenth Century Town: A Reader in English Urban History 1688–1820* (London, 1990).

Brewer, J. and Styles, J. *An Ungovernable People: The English and Their Law in the Seventeenth and Eighteenth Centuries* (London, 1980).

Broad, J. 'Parish Economies of Welfare 1650–1834', *The Historical Journal*, 42, 4 (December, 1999), pp. 985–1006.

Brooks, C.W. 'Interpersonal Conflict and Social Tension: Civil Litigation in England, 1640–1830', in Beier, Cannadine and Rosenheim (eds.), *The First Modern Society* (Cambridge, 1989).

—— *Lawyers: Litigation and English Society Since 1450* (London, 1998).

Byrne, R. *Prisons and Punishments of London* (London, 1989).

Cardwell, M.J. *Arts and Arms: Literature, Politics and Patriotism during the Seven Years War* (Manchester, 2004).

Carter, P. 'An "Effeminate" or "Efficient" Nation? Masculinity and Eighteenth-Century Social Documentary', *Textual Practice*, 11, 3 (Winter, 1997), pp. 429–443.

Chalklin, C.W. 'The Reconstruction of London's Prisons, 1770–1799: An Aspect of the Growth of Georgian London', *The London Journal*, 9, 1 (Summer, 1983), pp. 21–34.

Clark, A. *Women's Silence, Men's Violence: Sexual Assault in England, 1770–1845* (London, 1987).

—— 'Humanity or Justice? Wife Beating and the Law in the Eighteenth and Nineteenth Centuries', in Smart, C. (ed.), *Regulating Womanhood: Historical Essays on Marriage, Motherhood and Sexuality* (London, 1992).

—— *The Struggle for the Breeches: Gender and the Making of the British Working Class* (London, 1995).

Clark, P. *The English Alehouse: A Social History* (London, 1983).

—— (ed.), *The Cambridge Urban History of Britain: Volume II, 1540–1840* (Cambridge, 2000).

Cockburn, J.S. 'Patterns of Violence in English Society: Homicide in Kent, 1560–1985', *Past and Present*, 130 (1991), pp. 70–106.

—— and T.A. Green (eds.), *Twelve Good Men and True: The Criminal Trial Jury in England 1200–1800* (Princeton, 1988).

Conley, C. *The Unwritten Rule: Criminal Justice in Victorian Kent*, (Oxford, 1991).

Corfield, P.J. *The Impact of English Towns, 1700–1800* (Oxford, 1982).

Critchley, T.A. *A History of Police in England and Wales* (London, 1978).

Cumberlege, G. *The Corporation of London* (London, 1950).

Dabhoiwala, F. 'The Pattern of Sexual Immorality in Seventeenth- and Eighteenth-Century London', in Griffiths, P. and Jenner, M. (eds.), *Londinopolis: Essays in the Cultural and Social History of Early Modern London* (Manchester, 2000).

—— 'Summary Justice in Early Modern London', *English Historical Review*, CXXI, 492, (2006), pp. 796–822.

Davidoff, L. *Family Fortunes: Men and Women of the English Middle Class, 1780–1850* (London, 1987).

Davis, J S. 'Prosecutions and Their Context: The Use of the Criminal Law in Later Nineteenth-Century London', in Hay, D. and Snyder, F. (eds.), *Policing and Prosecution in Britain, 1750* (Oxford, 1989).

—— '"A Poor Man's System of Justice": The London Police Courts in the Second Half of the Nineteenth Century', *The Historical Journal*, 27, 2 (1984) pp. 309–335.

Davison, L. (ed.), *Stilling the Grumbling Hive the Response to Social and Economic Problems in England, 1689–1750* (Stroud, 1992).

De Krey, G.S. *A Fractured Society: The Politics of London in the First Age of Party 1688–1715* (Oxford, 1985).

Devereaux, S. and Griffiths, P. (eds.), *Penal Practice and Culture, 1500–1900: Punishing the English* (Basingstoke, 2004).

Dobson, C.R. *Masters and Journeymen: A Prehistory of Industrial Relations 1717–1800* (London, 1980).

Dodsworth, F. 'Masculinity as Governance: Police, Public Service and the Embodiment of Authority, c.1700–1850', in M. McCormack (ed.), *Public Men: Masculinity and Politics in Modern Britain* (Palgrave, 2007).

—— 'The Genealogy of Police in England, c.1780–1856: Institutionalisation as a Form of Insurance (A Response to O'Malley and Hutchinson)' (Paper delivered at the seventh European Social Science History Conference, Lisbon, 27/2/2008).

D'Sena, P. 'Perquisites and Casual Labour on the London Wharfside in the Eighteenth Century', *The London Journal*, 14, 2 (1989), pp. 130–147.

Earle, P. 'The Female Labour Market in London in the Late Seventeenth and Early Nineteenth Centuries', *Economic History Review*, XLII, 3 (1989), pp. 328–353.

—— *The Making of the English Middle Class. Business, Society and Family Life in London, 1660–1730* (London, 1989).

—— *A City Full of People. Men and Women of London 1650–1750* (London, 1994).

Eisner, M. 'Modernization, Self-Control and Lethal Violence: The Long-Term Dynamics of European Homicide Rates in Theoretical Perspective', *British Journal of Criminology*, 41, 4 (Autumn, 2001), pp. 618–638.

Elias, N. *State Formation & Civilization: The Civilizing Process*, Volume 2 (Oxford, 1982).

Emsley, C. *Policing and Its Context 1750–1870* (London, 1983).

—— *Crime and Society in England, 1750–1900*, 2nd edition (London, 1996).

—— *The English Police: A Political and Social History* (London, 1996).

Evans, E.J. *The Forging of the Modern State 1783–1870* (London, 1983).

Evans, T. '"Unfortunate objects": London's Unmarried Mothers in the Eighteenth Century', *Gender & History*, 17, 1 (April, 2005), pp. 127–153.

—— *'Unfortunate Objects': Lone Mothers in Eighteenth-Century London* (Basingstoke, 2006).

Everitt, A. 'The English Urban Inn, 1500–1760', in Everitt, A. (ed.), *Perspectives in English Urban History* (London, 1973).

Feeley, M. and Little, D. 'The Vanishing Female: The Decline of Women in the Criminal Process, 1687–1912', *Law and Society Review*, 25, 4 (1991), pp. 719–757.

Finn, M. *The Character of Credit: Personal Debt in English Culture, 1740–1914* (Cambridge, 2003).

Fletcher, A.J. *Gender, Sex and Subordination in England, 1500–1800* (London, 1995).

Flynn, S. and Mark, S. 'Petty Criminal, Publicans and Sinners: Petty Sessions Records in the Berkshire Record Office', *Journal of the Society of Archivists*, 16, 1 (1995), pp. 41–53.

Foucault, M. *Discipline and Punish: The Birth of the Prison* (London, 1977).

Foyster, E. *Manhood in Early Modern England: Honour, Sex and Marriage* (London, 1999).

—— *Marital Violence: An English Family History, 1660–1857* (Cambridge, 2005).

Friedrichs, C.R. *The Early Modern City 1450–1750* (London, 1995).

Gadd, I. (ed.), *Guilds, Society and Economy in London, 1450–1800* (London, 2002).

Gatrell, V.A.C. *The Hanging Tree: Execution and the English People 1770–1868* (Oxford, 1994).

George, M.D. *London Life in the Eighteenth Century* (London, 1925).

Godfrey, B. and Lawrence, P. *Crime and Justice 1750–1950* (Cullompton, 2005).

——, Farrall, S. and Karstedt, S. 'Explaining Gendered Sentencing Patterns for Violent Men and Women in the Late Victorian and Edwardian Period', *The British Journal of Criminology*, 45, 5 (2005), pp. 696–720.

Goldsmith, N.M. *The Worst of Crimes: Homosexuality and the Law in Eighteenth-Century London* (Aldershot, 1998).

Gowing, L. *Domestic Dangers: Women, Words and Sex in Early Modern London*, (Oxford, 1996).

Green, D.R. *From Artisans to Paupers: Economic Change and Poverty in London, 1790–1870* (Aldershot, 1995).

Griffin, E. *England's Revelry: A History of Popular Sports and Pastimes 1660–1830* (Oxford, 2005).

Griffith, T. (ed.), *The Newgate Calendar* (London, 1997).

Griffiths, P., Fox, A. and Hindle, S. (eds.), *The Experience of Authority in Early Modern England* (Basingstoke, 1996).

—— and Jenner, M. (eds.), *Londinopolis: Essays in the Cultural and Social History of Early Modern London* (Manchester, 2000).

Hancock, D. *Citizens of the World: London Merchants and the Integration of the British Atlantic Community, 1735–1785* (Cambridge, 1995).

Harding, V. 'Controlling a Complex Metropolis, 1650–1750: Politics, Parishes and Powers', *London Journal*, 25, 1 (2001), pp. 29–37.

Harris, A.T. 'Policing and Public Order in the City of London, 1784–1815', *The London Journal*, 28, 2 (2003), pp. 1–20.

—— *Policing the City: Crime and Legal Authority in London, 1780–1840* (Ohio, 2004).

Harvey, A.D. *Sex in Georgian England: Attitudes and Prejudices from the 1720s to the 1820s* (London, 1994).

Harvey, K. 'Gender, Space and Modernity in Eighteenth-Century England: A Place Called Sex', *History Workshop Journal*, 51 (2001), pp. 158–179.

Hay, D. 'War, Dearth and Theft in the Eighteenth Century: The Record of the English Courts', *Past and Present*, 95 (1982), pp. 117–160.

—— 'Patronage, Paternalism and Welfare: Masters, Workers and Magistrates in Eighteenth-Century England', *International Labor and Working Class History*, 51 (1998), pp. 27–48.

—— 'The State and the Market in 1800: Lord Kenyon and Mr. Waddington', *Past and Present*, 162 (February, 1999), pp. 101–162.

—— 'Master and Servant in England: Using the Law in the Eighteenth and Nineteenth Centuries', in Steinmetz, W. (ed.), *Private Law and Social Inequality in the Industrial Age* (Oxford, 2000).

—— *Masters, Servants, and Magistrates in Britain and the Empire, 1562–1955* (North Carolina, 2004).

—— and Snyder, F. *Policing and Prosecution in Britain, 1750–1850* (Oxford, 1989).

—— and Rogers, N. *Eighteenth-Century English Society: Shuttles and Swords* (Oxford, 1997).

Hay, D., Linebaugh, P. and Thompson, E.P. *Albion's Fatal Tree: Crime and Society in Eighteenth-Century England* (London, 1975).

Henderson, A. *Disorderly Women in Eighteenth-Century London. Prostitution and Control in the Metropolis, 1730–1830* (London, 1999).

Hill, B. *Women, Work, and Sexual Politics in Eighteenth-Century England* (Oxford, 1989).

—— *Servants: English Domestics in the Eighteenth Century* (Oxford, 1996).

Hitchcock, T. *English Sexualities, 1700–1800* (London, 1997).

—— 'Unlawfully Begotten on Her Body', in Hitchcock et al. (eds.), *Chronicling Poverty: The Voices and Strategies of the English Poor, 1640–1840* (London, 1997).

—— *Down and Out in Eighteenth-Century London* (London, 2004).

—— "You bitches... die and be damned" Gender, Authority and the Mob in St. Martin's Roundhouse Disaster of 1742', in Hitchcock and Shore (eds.), *The Streets of London* (London, 2003).

—— and Black, J. (eds.), *Chelsea Settlement and Bastardy Examinations 1733–1766* (London Record Society, 1999).

—— and Cohen, M. *English Masculinities, 1660–1800* (London, 1999).

—— Shore, H. (eds.), *The Streets of London from the Great Fire to the Great Stink* (London, 2003).

Hitchcock, T., King, P. and Sharpe, P.O. *Chronicling Poverty: The Voices and Strategies of the English Poor, 1640–1840* (London, 1997).

Howson, G. *Thief-Taker General: The Rise and Fall of Jonathan Wild* (London, 1970).

Hunt, M. 'Wife-Beating, Domesticity and Women's Independence in Eighteenth-Century London', *Gender & History*, 4, 1 (Spring, 1994), pp. 10–33.

Hurl, J. ' "She Being Bigg with Child Is Likely to Miscarry": Pregnant Victims Prosecuting Assault in Westminster, 1685–1720', *The London Journal*, 24, 2 (1999).

Hurl-Eamon, J. 'Policing Male Heterosexuality: The Reformation of Manners Societies' Campaign against the Brothels in Westminster, 1690–1720', *Journal of Social History*, 37, 4 (2004), pp. 1017–1035.

—— *Gender and Petty Violence in London, 1680–1720* (Ohio State University Press, 2005).

Innes, J. 'Managing the Metropolis: Social Problems and Their Control c.1660–1830', in Clark, P. and Gillespie, R. (eds.), *Two Capitals: London and Dublin 1500–1840* (Oxford, 2001), pp. 18–33.

—— 'Prisons for the Poor. English Bridewells, 1555–1800', in Hay, D. and Synder, F. (eds.), *Labour, Law and Crime: An Historical Perspective* (London, 1987).

—— 'Politics and Morals: The Reformation of Manners Movement in Later Eighteenth-Century England', in Hellmuth, E. (ed.), *The Transformation of Political Culture: England and Germany in the Late Eighteenth Century* (Oxford, 1990).

Inwood, S. 'Policing London's Morals: The Metropolitan Police and Popular Culture, 1829–1850', *The London Journal*, 15, 2 (1990), pp. 129–146.

—— *A History of London* (London, 1998).

Jenner, M. 'Circulation and Disorder: London Streets and Hackney Coaches, c.1640–c.1740', in Hitchcock, T. and Shore, H. (eds.), *The Streets of London from the Great Fire to the Great Stink* (London, 2003).

Kellett, J.R. 'The Breakdown of Guild and Corporative Control over the Handicraft and Retail Trade in London', *Economic History Review*, 10, 3 (1958), pp. 381–394.

Kent, D.A. 'Ubiquitous but Invisible: Female Domestic Servants in Mid-Eighteenth Century London', *History Workshop Journal* (1989), pp. 111–128.

Kent, J.R. *The English Village Constable, 1580–1642: A Social and Administrative Study* (Oxford, 1986).

Kermode, J. and Walker, G. *Women, Crime & the Courts in Early Modern England* (London, 1994).

King, P. 'Decision-Makers and Decision-Making in the English Criminal Law, 1750–1800', *The Historical Journal*, 27, 1 (1984), pp. 25–58.

—— 'Gleaners, Farmers and the Failure of Legal Sanctions in England, 1750–1850', *Past and Present*, 125 (1989), pp. 116–150.

—— 'Female Offenders, Work and Life-Cycle Change in Late Eighteenth-Century London', *Continuity and Change*, 11, 1 (1996), pp. 61–90.

—— 'Punishing Assault: The Transformation of Attitudes in the English Courts', *Journal of Interdisciplinary History*, 27, 1 (Summer, 1996), pp. 43–74.

—— 'The Rise of Juvenile Delinquency in England 1780–1840: Changing Patterns of Perception and Prosecution', *Past and Present*, 160 (August, 1998), pp. 116–166.

—— 'Gender, Crime and Justice in Late Eighteenth and Early Nineteenth-Century England', in M. Arnott and C. Usborne (eds.), Gender *and Crime in Modern Europe* (London, 1999).

—— 'Locating Histories of Crime: A Bibliographical Study', *British Journal of Criminology*, 39, 1 (1999).

—— *Crime, Justice and Discretion in England, 1740–1820* (Oxford, 2000).

—— 'War as a Judicial Resource: Press Gangs and Prosecution Rates, 1740–1830', in Landau, N. (ed.), *Law, Crime and English Society 1660–1830* (Cambridge, 2002).

—— 'The Summary Courts and Social Relations in Eighteenth-Century England', *Past & Present*, 183 (May, 2004), pp. 125–172.

—— *Crime and the Law in the Age of Reform 1750–1850: Remaking Justice from the Margins* (Cambridge, 2006).

—— and Noel, J. 'The Origins of "The Problem of Juvenile Delinquency". The Growth of Juvenile Prosecutions in London in the Late Eighteenth and Early Nineteenth Centuries', *Criminal Justice History*, 14 (1993), pp. 17–44.

King, S. *Poverty and Welfare in England 1700–1850: A Regional Perspective*, (Manchester, 2000).

Kynaston, D. *The City of London: Volume 1: A World of Its Own, 1815–1890*, (London, 1994).

Landau, N. *The Justices of the Peace, 1679–1760* (University of California Press, 1984).

—— 'The Eighteenth-Century Context of the Laws of Settlement', *Continuity and Change*, 6, 3 (1991), pp. 417–439.

—— 'Appearance at the Quarter Sessions of Eighteenth-Century Middlesex', *The London Journal*, 23, 2 (1998), pp. 30–52.

—— 'Indictment for Fun and Profit: A Prosecutor's Reward at the Eighteenth-Century Quarter Sessions', *Law and History Review* (Fall, 1999), pp. 507–536.

—— (ed.), *Law, Crime and English Society 1660–1830* (Cambridge, 2002).

—— 'Summary Conviction and the Development of the Penal Law', *Law and History Review*, 23, 1 (2005), pp. 173–189.

Lane, J. *Apprenticeship in England, 1600–1914* (London, 1996).

Lane, P. 'Work on the Margins: Poor Women and the Informal Economy of Eighteenth and Early Nineteenth Century Leicestershire', *Midland History*, 22 (1997), pp. 85–99.

Langbein, J.H. 'Albion's Fatal Flaws', *Past and Present*, 98 (1983), pp. 96–120.

—— 'Shaping the Eighteenth-Century Criminal Trial: A View from the Ryder Sources', *University of Chicago Law Review*, 50 (1983).

—— *The Origins of the Adversary Criminal Trial* (Oxford, 2003).

Langford, P. *A Polite and Commercial People. England 1727–1783* (Oxford, 1989).

—— *Public Life & the Propertied Englishman, 1689–1798* (Oxford, 1991).

Laslett, P., Oosterveen, K. and Smith, Richard M. *Bastardy and Its Comparative History: Studies in the History of Illegitimacy and Marital Nonconformism in Britain, France, Germany, Sweden, North America, Jamaica and Japan* (London, 1980).

Lindert, P.H. and Williamson, J.G. 'Revising England's Social Tables 1688–1812', *Explorations in Economic History*, 19 (1982), pp. 385–408.

Linebaugh, P. '(Marxist) Social History and (Conservative) Legal History: A Reply to Professor Langbein', *New York University Law Review* (May, 1985), pp. 212–243.

—— *The London Hanged. Crime and Civil Society in the Eighteenth Century* (London, 1991).

Macfarlane, A. *Marriage and Love in England: Modes of Reproduction, 1300–1840* (Oxford, 1986).

Magarey, S. 'The Invention of Juvenile Delinquency in Early Nineteenth-Century England', *Labour History*, 34 (1978), pp. 11–27.

Malcolmson, R.W. *Popular Recreations in English Society, 1700–1850* (Cambridge, 1973).

—— *Life and Labour in England 1700–1780* (London, 1981).

Margary, H. *The A to Z of Regency London* (London, 1985).

Marshall, D. *Dr. Johnson's London* (New York, 1968).

Mathias, P. *The First Industrial Nation: An Economic History of Britain 1700–1914* (London, 1969, 1997).

Meldrum, T. 'A Women's Court in London: Defamation at the Bishop of London's Consistory Court, 1700–1745', *The London Journal*, 19, 1 (1994), pp. 1–20.

Michie, R.C. 'London and the Process of Economic Growth Since 1750', *The London Journal*, 22, 1 (1997), pp. 63–90.

Moir, E. *The Justice of the Peace* (Harmondsworth, 1969).

Morgan, G. and Rushton, P. *Rogues, Thieves and the Rule of Law. The Problem of Law Enforcement in North-East England, 1718–1800* (London, 1998).

—— 'The Magistrate, the Community and the Maintenance of an Orderly Society in Eighteenth-Century England', *Historical* Research, 76, 191 (February, 2003), pp. 54–77.

Muldrew, C. *The Economy of Obligation: The Culture of Credit and Social Relations in Early Modern England* (London, 1998).

Mullan, J. and Reid, C. *Eighteenth-Century Popular Culture: A Selection* (Oxford, 2000).

Murphy, E. 'The Metropolitan Pauper Farms, 1722–1834', *The London Journal*, 27, 1 (2002), pp. 1–18.

Murphy, E. 'Mad Farming in the Metropolis. Part 2: The Administration of the Old Poor Law of Insanity in the City and East London 1800–1834', *History of Psychiatry*, 12 (2001), pp. 405–430.

Neale, R.S. *Bath: A Social History 1680–1850* (London, 1981).

Neocleous, M. 'Social Police and the Mechanisms of Prevention: Patrick Colquhoun and the Condition of Poverty', *British Journal of Criminology*, 40 (2000), pp. 710–726.

Nicholls, E. *Crime Within the Square Mile: The History of Crime in the City of London* (London, 1935).

Norton, R. *Mother Clap's Molly House: The Gay Subculture in England, 1700–1830* (London, 1992).

Oberwittler, D. 'Crime and Authority in Eighteenth Century England: Law Enforcement on the Local Level', *Historical Social Research*, 15, 54 (1990), pp. 3–34.

O'Donoghue, E. *Bridewell Hospital: From the Death of Elizabeth to Modern Times*, vol. 2 (London, 1929).

Ogborn, M. *Spaces of Modernity: London's Geographies, 1680–1780* (New York, 1998).

Oxley, G. *Poor Relief in England and Wales, 1601–1834* (London, 1974).

Paley, R. 'Thief-Takers in the Age of the McDaniel Gang, c.1745–1754', in Hay, D. and Snyder, F. (eds.), *Policing and Prosecution in Britain, 1750–1850* (Oxford, 1989).

—— '"An Imperfect, Inadequate and Wretched System"? Policing London Before Peel', *Criminal Justice History*, 10 (1989), pp. 95–130.

Palk, D. 'Private Crime in Public and Private Places: Pickpockets and Shoplifters in London, 1780–1823', in Hitchcock, T. and Shore, H. (eds.), *The Streets of London from the Great Fire to the Great Stink* (London, 2003).

Parker, S. *Informal Marriage, Cohabitation and the Law, 1750–1989* (Basingstoke, 1990).

Perkin, H. *The Origins of Modern English Society, 1780–1880* (London, 1969).

Philips, D. *William Augustus Miles (1796–1851): Crime, Policing and Moral Entrepreneurship in England and Australia* (University of Melbourne, 2001).

Phillips, H. *The Thames about 1750* (London, 1951).

Porter, R. *English Society in the Eighteenth Century* (London, 1982).

—— *London: A Social History* (London, 1994).

—— and Mulvey, M. (eds.), *Pleasure in the Eighteenth Century* (Basingstoke, 1996).

Poynter, J.R. *Society and Pauperism: English Ideas on Poor Relief, 1795–1834* (London, 1969).

Prothero, I. *Artisans and politics in Early Nineteenth Century London: John Gast and His Times* (London, 1979).

Quinault, R. 'From National to World Metropolis: Governing London, 1750–1850', *The London Journal*, 25, 1 (2001), pp. 38–46.

Radzinowicz, L. *History of English Criminal Law and Its Administration from 1750*, in four volumes (London, 1956).

Raven, J. 'The Abolition of the English State Lotteries', *The Historical Journal*, 34, 2 (1991), pp. 371–389.

Rawlings, P. *Drunks, Whores and Idle Apprentices: Criminal Biographies of the Eighteenth Century* (London, 1992).

Reay, B. *Popular Cultures in England 1550–1750* (London, 1998).

Reed, M. 'The Transformation of Urban Space, 1700–1840', in Clark, P. (ed.), *The Cambridge Urban History of Britain. Volume II, 1540–1840* (Cambridge, 2000).

Reith, C. *The Police Idea* (Oxford, 1938).

Reynolds, E.A. 'St. Marylebone: Local Police Reform in London, 1755–1829', *The Historian*, 51, 3 (1989), pp. 446–466.

—— *Before the Bobbies: Night Watch and Police Reform in Metropolitan London, 1720–1830* (London, 1998).

Roberts, M.J.D. *Making English Morals: Voluntary Associations and Moral Reform in England, 1786-1886* (Cambridge, 2004).

Rodger, N.A.M. *The Command of the Sea: A Naval History of Britain, 1649–1815* (London, 2004).

Rogers, N. 'Money, Land and Lineage: The Big Bourgeoisie of Hanoverian London', *Social History*, 4, 3 (October, 1979), pp. 437–454.

—— 'Policing the Poor in Eighteenth-Century London: The Vagrancy Laws and their Administration', *Histoire Sociale*, 24, 47 (May, 1991), pp. 127–147.

—— *Crowds, Culture and Politics in Georgian Britain* (Oxford, 1998).

—— 'Impressments and the Law in Eighteenth-Century Britain', in Landau, N. (ed.), *Law, Crime and English Society 1660–1830* (Cambridge, 2002).

—— *The Press Gang: Naval Impressment and Its Opponents in Georgian Britain* (Continuum, 2008).

Rose, M.E. *The English Poor Law, 1780–1930* (Newton Abbot, 1971).

Rudé, G. *Paris and London in the Eighteenth Century: Studies in Popular Protest* (London, 1970).

—— *Hanoverian London: 1714–1808* (London, 1971).

Rumbelow, D. *I Spy Blue: The Police and Crime in the City of London from Elizabeth to Victoria* (London, 1971).

Rushton, P. 'The Matter in Variance: Adolescents and Domestic Conflict in the Pre-Industrial Economy of Northeast England, 1600–1800', *Journal of Social History*, 25, 1 (Fall, 1991), pp. 89–107.

Schwarz, L.D. 'The Standard of Living in the Long Run: London, 1700–1860', *Economic History Review*, 38 (1985), pp. 24–41.

—— *London in the Age of Industrialisation: Entrepreneurs, Labour Force and Living Conditions, 1700–1850* (Cambridge, 1992).

—— 'London, 1700–1850', *The London Journal*, 20, 2 (1995), pp. 46–53.

Sharpe, J.A. 'The History of Violence in England: Some Observations', *Past and Present*, 108 (1985), pp. 206–215.

Sharpe, J. A. *Crime in Early Modern England 1550–1750* (London, 1999).

Sheppard, F. *London 1808–1870: The Infernal Wen* (London, 1971).

Shesgreen, S. (ed.), *Engravings by Hogarth* (New York, 1973).

Shoemaker, R. *Prosecution and Punishment: Petty Crime and the Law in London and Rural Middlesex, c.1660–1725* (Cambridge, 1991).

Shoemaker, R. 'Reforming the City: The Reformation of Manners Campaign in London, 1690–1738', in Davison, L. et al. (eds.), *Stilling the Grumbling Hive: The Response to Social and Economic Problems in England, 1689–1750* (Stroud, 1992).

—— 'The Decline of Public Insult in London 1660–1800', *Past and Present*, 169 (2000), pp. 97–131.

—— 'Male Honour and the Decline of Public Violence in Eighteenth-Century London', *Social History*, 26, 2 (May, 2001), pp. 190–208.

—— *The London Mob: Violence and Disorder in Eighteenth-Century England* (London, 2004).

Shore, H. 'Cross Coves, Buzzers and General sorts of Prigs: Juvenile Crime and the Criminal "Underworld" in the Early Nineteenth Century', *British Journal of Criminology*, 39, 1 (1999), pp. 10–24.

—— *Artful Dodgers: Youth and Crime in Nineteenth-Century London* (London, 1999).

Skyrme, Sir T. *History of the Justices of the Peace. Volume 2. England 1689–1989.* (Chichester, 1991).

Smart, C. (ed.), *Regulating Womanhood: Historical Essays on Marriage, Motherhood and Sexuality* (London, 1992).

Smith, B. 'Did the Presumption of Innocence Exist in Summary Proceedings?', *Law and History Review*, 23, 1 (2005), pp. 191–199.

—— 'The Myth of Private Prosecution in England, 1750–1850', in M.D. Dubber and L. Farmer (eds.), *Modern Histories of Crime and Punishment* (Stanford, 2007).

Smith, S. 'The Ideal and Reality: Apprentice-Master Relationships in Seventeenth Century London', *History of Education Quarterly* (Winter, 1981), pp. 449–459.

Smith, K.H. (ed.), *Warwickshire Apprentices and Their Masters, 1710–1760* (Oxford, 1975).

Sprott, D. *1784* (London, 1984).

Steinberg, M. 'The Dialogue of Struggle: The Contest over Ideological Boundaries in the Case of the London Silk Weavers in the Early Eighteenth Century', *Social Science History*, 18, 4 (Winter, 1994), pp. 505–541.

Stevenson, J. 'London, 1660–1780', in Stevenson. J. et al. (eds.), *The Rise of the New Urban Society*, Open University Block IV (Milton Keynes, 1977).

—— *Popular Disturbances in England, 1700–1832* (London, 1992).

Stirk, N. 'Arresting Ambiguity: The Shifting Geographies of a London Debtors' Sanctuary in the Eighteenth Century', *Social History*, 25, 3 (October, 2000), pp. 316–329.

Stone, L. 'Interpersonal Violence in English Society, 1300–1980', *Past and Present*, 101 (1983), pp. 22–33.

Stone, L. *The Family, Sex and Marriage in England, 1500–1800* (London, 1990).

Storch, R. '"The Plague of Blue Locusts". Police Reform and Popular Resistance in Northern England 1840–1857', *International Review of Social History*, 20 (1975), pp. 61–90.

—— 'The Policeman as Domestic Missionary: Urban Discipline and Popular Culture in Northern England, 1850–1880', *Journal of Social History*, 9 (1976), pp. 481–509.

Strange, K.H. *The Climbing Boys: A Study of Sweeps' Apprentices, 1773–1875* (London, 1982).

Styles, J. 'From an Offence between Men to an Offence against Property: Industrial Pilfering and the Law in the Eighteenth Century', in M. Berg, P. Hudson and M. Sonenscher (eds.), *Manufacture in Town and Country Before the Factory* (London, 1983).

—— 'Constables Considered'. Review article. *The Times Higher Education Supplement* (6 March 1987).

Summerston, J. *Georgian London* (London, 1945).

Sweet, R. *The English Town 1680–1840: Government, Society and Culture* (London, 1999).

Tate, W.E. *The Parish Chest* (Cambridge 1946, 1969, 3rd Edition).

Taylor, D. *The New Police in Nineteenth Century England: Crime, Conflict and Control* (Manchester, 1997).

—— *Crime, Policing and Punishment in England, 1750–1914* (London, 1998).

Thomas, K. *Man and the Natural World. Changing Attitudes in England, 1500–1800* (London, 1983)

Thompson, E.P. *Whigs and Hunters. The Origins of the Black Act* (London, 1975).

Thompson, E.P. *Customs in Common* (London, 1991).

Tobias, J.J. *Crime and the Police in England, 1700–1900* (Dublin, 1979).

Uglow, J. *Hogarth. A Life and a World* (London, 1997).

Voth, H.-J. *Time and Work in England 1750–1830* (Oxford, 2000).

Walsh, C. 'Shop Design and the Display of Goods in Eighteenth-Century London', *Journal of Design History*, 8, 3 (1995), pp. 157–176.

—— *A Dictionary of Old Trades, Titles and Occupations* (Newbury, 2002).

Watson, J.S. *The Reign of George III 1760–1815* (Oxford, 1960).

Wiener, M. 'The Victorian Criminalization of Men', in Spierenburg, P. (ed.), *Men and Violence: Gender, Honor, and Rituals in Modern Europe and America* (Ohio, 1998).

—— *Men of Blood: Violence, Manliness and Criminal Justice in Victorian England* (Cambridge, 2004).

Wilson, A. 'Illegitimacy and Its Implications in Mid-Eighteenth Century London: The Evidence of the Foundling Hospital', *Continuity and Change*, 4, 1 (1989), pp. 103–164.

—— (ed.), *Rethinking Social History: English Society 1570–1920 and Its Interpretation* (Manchester, 1993).

Wood, J.C. *Violence and Crime in Nineteenth-century England: The Shadow of Our Refinement* (London, 2004).

Wrightson, K. 'Two Concepts of Order: Justices, Constables and Jurymen in Seventeenth-century England', in J. Brewer and J. Styles (eds.), *An Ungovernable People: The English and Their Law in the Seventeenth and Eighteenth Centuries* (London, 1980).

Wrigley, E.A. and Schofield, R.S. 'The Growth of Population in Eighteenth-Century England: A Conundrum Resolved', *Past and Present*, 98 (1983), pp. 121–150.

Yeo, E. and Yeo, S. *Popular Culture and Class Conflict 1590–1914: Explorations in the History of Labour and Leisure* (Brighton, 1981).

Zedner, L. 'Women, Crime, and Penal Responses: A Historical Account', in M. Tenry (ed.), *Crime and Justice*, Vol. 14 (1991).

Unpublished Secondary Sources

Beattie, J.M. *John Fielding and the Bow Street Magistrates Court* (unpublished paper 2004).

Gray, D. '"Lewd Women" and "Canny Wenches": Bedfordshire Women before the Courts, 1807–1828', B.A. (hons) History dissertation (University College Northampton, 1999).

PhD/MPhil Thesis Consulted

Balch-Lindsay, V.G. 'An Orderly Metropolis: The Evolution of Criminal Justice in London, 1750–1830', Ph.D. thesis (Texas Tech University, 1998).

Brown, S.E. *Politics*, 'Commerce and Social Policy in the City of London, 1782–1802', Ph.D. thesis (Balliol College, Oxford, 1992).

Davis, J.S. 'Law Breaking and Law Enforcement: A Criminal Class in Mid-Victorian London', Ph.D. thesis (Boston College, 1989).

D'Sena, P. 'Perquisites and Pilfering in the London Docks', MPhil thesis (Open University, 1986).

Linebaugh, P. 'Tyburn: A Study of Crime and the Labouring Poor in London During the First Half of the Eighteenth Century', Ph.D. thesis (Warwick University, 1975).

Shoemaker, R. 'Crime, Courts and Community: The Prosecution of Misdemeanors in Middlesex County, 1663–1723', Ph.D. thesis (Stanford University, 1986).

Smith, B. 'Circumventing the Jury: Petty Crime and Summary Jurisdiction in London and New York City, 1790–1855', Ph.D. thesis (Yale University, 1996).

Smith, G. 'The State and the Culture of Violence in London, 1760–1840', Ph.D. thesis (University of Toronto, 1999).

Index